Ham
slices of a life

Ham

slices of a life

Essay & Stories

SAM HARRIS

GALLERY BOOKS

New York   London   Toronto   Sydney   New Delhi

Gallery Books
A Division of Simon & Schuster, Inc.
1230 Avenue of the Americas
New York, NY 10020

First Gallery Books hardcover edition January 2014

GALLERY BOOKS and colophon are registered trademarks
of Simon & Schuster, Inc.

For information about special discounts for bulk purchases,
please contact Simon & Schuster Special Sales at 1-866-506-1949
or business@simonandschuster.com.

The Simon & Schuster Speakers Bureau can bring authors
to your live event. For more information or to book an event
contact the Simon & Schuster Speakers Bureau at 1-866-248-3049
or visit our website at www.simonspeakers.com.

Designed by Esther Paradelo

Manufactured in the United States of America

10   9   8   7   6   5   4   3   2   1

Library of Congress Cataloging-in-Publication Data is available.

ISBN 978-1-4767-3341-8
ISBN 978-1-4767-3345-6 (ebook)

For my father, Bill
And my mother, Carolyn

Contents

1. Unwrapped

When I was nineteen years old, while helping my aunt Betty reorganize her kitchen cabinets, I discovered a beaten and worn plastic *Mary Poppins* cup and saucer marooned in the back corner of an ignored shelf. They were issued in 1964, the year of the movie's release. My aunt told me they'd been intended for me when I was little, but my father had returned them to her because I was "too obsessed with Mary Poppins and singing and dancing."

In the next room, my dad, uncle, brother, and all four boy cousins could be heard yelling in that guttural, grunting Cro-Magnon caterwauling exclusively reserved for watching football games on television and killing wild pigs on a hunt. I marched into the living room and presented the cup and saucer with outstretched arms.

"Do you remember these?" I said, my confrontational passion unbefitting some battered old plastic children's dishes.

They all stared at me, confused, as if I'd just asked for an honest opinion about the chances of a fashion comeback for the ascot.

"Uh, no, son," said my father. "Ask your mother."

The Cowboys scored another touchdown and the room erupted as they hug-slapped and adjusted their crotches. My father loved the Cowboys and could recount the great plays of the last twenty years. But he had no memory of banning the *Mary Poppins* treasures.

Cue home movie: Christmas 1964.

I am three years old. My mother is operating the camera. It is in grainy, Super 8 color, and there is no sound. A toy army tank and various toy guns are strewn about and a mini-rifle is propped against the wall. Plastic grenades litter the floor. GI Joe lies in a coffinlike cellophane-covered box. It is a battlefield of unwrapped but unattended boy toys around the base of our silver aluminum Christmas tree, which is bobbed with shiny red and green Woolworth balls, reflecting the muted shades of an electric color wheel. I open a new wool coat, charcoal with a spattering of white, knee length, with large lapels and giant black buttons. Now *this* is a present!

I eagerly put it on and model it full-tilt. I am overtaken with euphoria and begin to dance. The camera pans to capture the delight of each of my three grandparents, until it lands on my father, whose young, handsome face steams with displeasure and perhaps a touch of anger. His posture reflects a just released sigh of defeat. The camera pans back to me, still dancing. I look to my father and take in his reaction. For a split second I lose my timing.

Then I take a big breath, turn back at the camera, smile, and . . . just dance harder.

2. Holy Shit

Word was that God could heal anyone. The wounded, the in-firm, even lepers. I figured I should be a breeze.

At the age of ten, I decided to explore religion more closely.

For quite some time I'd been drawn to Judaism; however, in my little town of Sand Springs, Oklahoma, Jew's, having killed Christ, were ne'er to be seen. At first, my attraction emerged from the discovery that everyone I considered really funny and talented turned out to be Jewish. Woody Allen, Neil Simon, and Barbra Streisand were obvious testaments to racial and religious superiority.

But my affinity reached an entirely new level when I was eight years old and Teresa Fisher's father gave me his paperback copy of *The Rise and Fall of the Third Reich*. Its pages were soon soiled and warped with my tears and I dog-eared those that pertained to Auschwitz so I could go back and cry again in less time. I'd found a tribe, and related and attached myself to the Jewish plight of oppression, adopting it as my own.

I'd heard that Jews were the chosen people. I already knew I was oppressed and I thought I was funny and talented, but what I wanted more than anything was to be chosen.

I declined pork, celebrated Rosh Hashanah, and attempted to grow *payos,* however, my parents drew the line when I asked them to take me to the only temple in Tulsa, which was more than fifteen miles from Sand Springs, so it might as well have been in a shtetl somewhere between Minsk and Pinsk.

Southern Baptism was more accessible. In fact, it was unavoidable. Not only in churches but in schools, in pamphlets, in newspapers, on billboards and in local shops, where signs were emblazoned with messages like JESUS SAVES! ROUND STEAK ONLY 59¢ A POUND!

I became entranced by our preacher at Broadway Baptist Church. The very name, "Broadway Baptist," had an air of show business, and Brother Bill was the star. He was a fire-and-brimstone man, short in stature, with a face that turned so bright red with the glory of God that you thought his full white-haired head would explode. Brother Bill had suffered a number of heart attacks, five or six, I think, and part of the thrill of watching him stomp about, throwing the Bible onto the pulpit and pressing his hands up to God Almighty, was the on-the-edge-of-your-pew chance that he just might have another heart attack and drop dead on the spot.

I decided to be baptized. I'd seen a few of the ceremonial dunkings and they were spine tingling. People cried. And the younger the soul rescued from Satan, the more stirring, not to mention the added plus of no distracting plastic bubble bonnets for bouffant protection.

There was a traditional convention for baptism: at the end of every sermon, the congregation sang "Just As I Am," and, should Jesus touch your soul, you would be spiritually propelled down the aisle to offer it.

Just as I am, poor, wretched, blind;
Sight, riches, healing of the mind,

Yea, all I need in thee to find,
Oh Lamb of God, I come! I come!

It was a little grim, but who could resist? For some, the revelation was tantamount to being zapped with an electroshock weapon, causing the zealots to twitch and fling their arms, fall to their knees, cry and rock and sway, and, if you were lucky, speak in tongues. Your baptism was scheduled and consummated, after which your life was forever changed and you were then allowed to say hateful things about everybody and how they would suffer eternal hellfire on judgment day, but you wouldn't because you were saved by our Lord Jesus Christ, who loved children and animals but hated communists and homosexuals.

My parents made me wait through the summer following my tenth birthday to make sure I was truly dedicated to Jesus and that this was not another of my whims, like the time I went for the title of World's Longest Time-Stepper. So I attended church—religiously—singing and praying and crying and giving my soul to the everlasting Savior. My Sunday school class was taught by a man whose fingernails were so black and filthy from his work at the oil refinery that I couldn't concentrate. If cleanliness was next to godliness, he was surely going to hell. I begged to be transferred to a clean-nailed instructor. If I was preparing to give my soul to Jesus, distractions like these were out of the question. My baptism was scheduled for September.

On the morning of my redemption, the heavy, humid air clung to my skin like paste. My parents and I arrived at the church, an oddly architectural juxtaposition of redbrick with antebellum framing and Tuscan columns, and I beamed at the congregants milling at the entrance, fanning themselves with Sunday Morning Bulletins. My father remained outside to smoke and my mother and I hurried to a Bible study room to pray. I thanked God that I was the only soul scheduled to be saved that morning, as I didn't want to follow anyone with the same routine, or worse, be anybody's warm-up act.

I changed into a white flowing gown and waited in the vestibule outside the sanctuary until I heard the organ broadcast my entrance. Slowly, I walked down the aisle barefoot, angelic and pure, my heart overflowing with Jesus. The lavender-haired ladies were stuffed into pews, spruced in competitively decorated hats, netted and speckled with silk daisies and violets and fake baby's breath. They gazed at me as if I were the little Jesus himself, dabbing their dewy eyes with white cotton hankies and oohing and aahing as I took my time—*step, touch . . . step, touch*—while the choir sang "Shall We Gather at the River?" in a celestial, spotless blend. Above the altar, golden velvet curtains squeakily parted to reveal a shallow pool in which Brother Bill stood, gowned and yoked for the occasion. The music swelled as I took his hand and stepped into the cool water.

A gust of chlorine stung my eyes to tears. Perfect.

I solemnly looked out to my audience and the preacher asked me if I was ready. "Yes!" I cried, in my most southern accent, pronouncing both syllables equally. "Yay-ess!"

White people don't applaud in church, but I knew I had 'em.

Then Brother Bill gently held my head and clasped my nose and dunked me into the holy water in the name of the Father. The Son. The Holy Ghost. My blond hair glistened and my eyes were full. I was cleansed of all the sins of my ten years.

I never went back.

I figured I had done the big eleven o'clock number and what was going to top that? Besides, Bible stories in Sunday school were getting more confusing—a strange mix of "God Is Love" and "Fear of God"—an old man with a beard who seemed superemotional and sort of unpredictable. Kind of like my dad between televised baseball games or my mom on diet pills.

Also He seemed a little needy.

God: "Abraham, if you love me you'll kill your son. Go on, kill him! Who do you love more? . . . Just kidding! I was just testing you!"

My parents had never once asked me to kill my little brother, even in fun.

God: "Okay, humankind, maybe I overreacted. You guys just really pissed me off, so I flooded the world and killed pretty much everybody. Sorry. Here's a rainbow."

The closest thing in my life to flooding had been when my parents commanded I take unwanted swimming lessons when I was five, prying my little white-knuckled grip from a chain-link fence and forcibly dragging me into the community pool.

I always did better with positive encouragement than fear of plagues and eternal fire, but maybe that was just me. I wanted a God who was more huggy than punishy. More happy-go-lucky. The kind of guy you could talk to about stuff, but who didn't decide whether to let your football team win the championship. Or cure someone of cancer. My questions went unanswered and even asking them was considered blasphemy. I was told by more than a few kids and my new, clean-nailed Sunday school teacher that if I didn't keep quiet I was going to Hell.

I thought that seemed extreme.

That's when I decided there couldn't be such a thing as Hell. If I had second thoughts, they were deep-sixed by the realization that if *any* of these religions, or even denominations, was right—and it was the *only* way and its believers were the *only* ones permitted through the Pearly Gates—Hell had to be terribly overcrowded, and Heaven had to be a colossal bore. All those people who thought alike and looked alike and dressed alike and ate alike. It would be like never venturing beyond Sand Springs. For eternity.

I needed a different kind of church and a different kind of Heaven. And I found it at Tulsa Little Theatre.

I was cast in their production of William Inge's *The Dark at the Top of the Stairs,* a straight play set in 1920s Oklahoma. It was my first semiprofessional role, where the actors actually played their own ages. I was Sonny Flood, a misfit child who was regularly beaten up by the town bullies for being a sissy, choosing to escape through movies and his scrapbook of the stars. Hmm . . .

My mother ran lines with me. Not just mine. The entire play, including scenes I wasn't in. She said it was for a sense of story line, but I think she really just wanted to read all the parts. She longed for the theater, and my doing a play trumped the times we sat cross-legged and face-to-face on the green-flecked shag carpeting while she read poetry. Kahlil Gibran's *The Prophet* was recited cover to cover, but Edna St. Vincent Millay's "Renascence" was her favorite. It said everything she couldn't about the need to break free, death and resurrection, and the quest for spiritual awakening. Though the words were beyond my understanding, her reading made it accessible. She was as committed to my performance in *Dark* as I was, but she refutes the story that during rehearsals she was asked to leave the theater by the director because her notes on my performance conflicted with his.

My next role at Tulsa Little Theatre was as one of the newsboys in *Gypsy*—my favorite musical. We were only in the first act, along with Baby June and young Louise, but we had to stick around for the curtain call. *Gypsy* is a long show. So, to kill time during Act Two, all of us would climb the narrow stairwell up two flights to the costume room, where they kept the monkey and the little lamb, both of whom were also idle in the second act. We would throw on layers of various costumes: Dickensian sacque jackets, World War I khaki breeches and canvas-wrap leggings, feathered Elizabethan hats, a crown of thorns from *The Glory of Easter* pageant, multiple gloves—and play strip poker. We were all ten to thirteen years old—I was the youngest—but we considered ourselves veterans and we were, after all, in a show about stripping.

Five card, Seven card, Hold 'em, Stud! We shared cigarettes pinched from adult actors' dressing room stations and enjoyed an occasional nip of something stolen from Baby June's parents' liquor cabinet.

"I'll raise you."

"I call."

"My jacks beat your tens."

"Strip!"

The girls always chickened out when it got down to our regular layer of clothing. Baby June was a tease and little Louise a bore. But strangely, the boys usually stayed. One night, long about time for the showstopping finale, "Rose's Turn," the game had siphoned down to me and two kids named Daniel and Jason.

As the three of us betted in (and for) our Fruit of the Looms, I couldn't help but notice that Jason, who was thirteen years old, was getting a conspicuous erection. There is a big difference between a ten-year-old penis and a thirteen-year-old penis. Growth spurts and pubic hair and hormones and all sorts of other things are kicking in. I was entranced, and determined to win so that Jason would lose and have to drop his skivvies.

I had three eights. Daniel folded. It was me and Mr. Boner.

I forged poise but the excitement was overwhelming. The monkey could sense the tension and began screeching and throwing monkey shit out of his cage.

Jason asked for two cards.

I called.

The room stood still and a rivulet of sweat inched down my cheek from beneath my crown of thorns.

He had a measly pair of prophetic queens. "Strip!" I said, and waited breathlessly to see if he would remove his clinging briefs or quit the game. He casually pulled them off, exposing a *huge* penis, thirteen years old or otherwise (though I have not seen it since and do not know whether to attach the "your childhood house is always smaller when you go back home" theory to this experience). He then proceeded to masturbate in front of me and Daniel. We were agape with jaw-dropping wonder. The backstage speakers were blaring:

Everything's coming up Rose!
Everything's coming up roses!
Everything's coming up roses this time for me!
For me! For me! For me! For me! . . .

On the timpani roll before the last note, Jason worked harder and faster, finally erupting at the same time that Mama Rose hit the final "For meeeeeeee!!!"

On the musical cutoff, Jason lay spent, pearly goop pooling in his belly button and glistening on his chest, as the audience cheered and applauded from downstairs. I nearly joined them. Show business was fabulous. It was joyous and adventurous and accepting. Heaven and Hell were on earth. Right here.

I swiftly dressed in my newsboy costume, replaced the thistly crown with an apple cap, and dashed down the stairs in time for my bow.

3. Promises

Everyone makes mistakes: Leon Lett and the '93 Super Bowl. Richard Nixon and Watergate. The architect who built the Tower of Pisa. Since I wasn't a big sports fan, hadn't met Nixon, and hadn't traveled to Pisa, the closest thing in my life to a mistake of that magnitude was the marriage of my dear friend Liza to the Man Whose Name Shall Go Unmentioned. I refer to him in that manner because I promised Liza that I would never again utter his first name unless it were in reference to Beckham, Bowie, the Michelangelo statue, or "The Star of . . ."

Saying his name is not taboo in the same way that mentioning "the Scottish Play" by title is for theater people, who would then have to leave the building, spit, curse, and knock to be let back in. I swore to my friend that if I verbalized his name, I would light myself on fire and commit hari-kari.

She knows it was a mistake. Everybody knows it was a mistake. The wedding itself was well documented by a hundred publications. But beyond the facts and the scuttlebutt, this event should be acknowledged as one of the greatest shows on earth. I was a witness and a player. I even sang. "Bridge over Troubled Water." A peculiar choice for a wedding, but it was requested. And prophetic. If only they'd chosen "Can You Feel the Love Tonight," things might have turned out differently.

Well, not really.

I was there the day she met him. I was musically supervising her segment on the *Michael Jackson: 30th Anniversary Celebration* television special at Madison Square Garden, which was being produced by the Man Whose Name Shall Go Unmentioned. I don't know what put me off first—the fact that he wore sunglasses indoors and at night or his boastful claims of having "the largest Shirley Temple paraphernalia collection in the world"—a feat for which I suspected there was little competition. Bottom line, the guy creeped me out and I told her so. But as the romance budded, my friend begged me to give him a chance.

On Thanksgiving Day, Liza called to tell me he had proposed the previous evening.

"Schmooli, I really want you to try to get close to him. I know he's kind of quirky, but I need for you to accept him and try to love him."

Liza had suffered from brain encephalitis earlier in the year and I reminded her as such. "You're still recovering. Is it possible that . . . you're not yet in your right mind? Literally."

"Oh, who is, Schmool? All I know is he really seems to get me. And he's funny."

"Funny?" I asked. "Or . . . *funny*?"

"He's our kind of funny."

I wasn't sure that answered my question.

"Please call him now and congratulate him," she pleaded. "It means everything to me."

I did as I was asked and told him that I was "so, so happy"

for them, mustering cheer in my voice against the dead eyes he couldn't see.

I had to admit that he did dote on her and had big plans. The kind of plans I knew she loved. So against every instinct in my body, I had no choice but to hope I was wrong about him. She seemed happy and that's all I wanted for her. What any friend wants for a friend.

A mere seven months after their collision, the who's who of New York and old Hollywood showbiz were invited to assemble at the Marble Collegiate Church, at Fifth Avenue and Twenty-Ninth Street in Manhattan, for the nuptials. This was, no doubt, the first time the church entrance had been set up with such tight security, and the most eclectic guest list *ever* ambled through airport metal detectors and opened their pocketbooks for inspection. The enormous number of titanium hip replacements set off the detectors, which slowed the line considerably. Janet Leigh, Anthony Hopkins, Joan Collins, Kirk Douglas, Carol Channing, and Robert Goulet were there. In odd juxtaposition, so were Snoop Dogg, Donny Osmond, Martha Stewart, and Gloria Gaynor. In the same room. At the same time. I knew for a fact that Liza didn't know most of these people or had met them only in passing.

But then, she really only knew the groom in passing.

She should have kept walking.

I knew she had personally invited Lauren Bacall, Liz Smith, Mia Farrow, Cynthia McFadden, Mickey Rooney, Billy Stritch, and Gina Lollobrigida, but most of the others were acquaintances of the groom's, PR invitations, or celebrities who had begged to be on the list. Like signing up to witness the launching of the Hindenburg.

I forget sometimes that my friend Liza is, you know—*Liza!* Truth was that she would have been happy getting married in a private house with ten close friends, but the groom's knack and desperate need for the spotlight had turned this into an epic extravaganza.

I ran to a back room and found Liza, who seemed nervous. "Let's sneak out of here and go to the movies," I said. "No one will notice."

She laughed and then suddenly said, "What's playing?" An odd doubt crept over her enormous brown eyes.

"Are you okay?"

"Yes . . . I don't know. That thing you said about recovering from brain encephalitis?"

"Yes?"

"I've recovered," she said, dryly.

"Oh, honey."

"But I'm here and this is happening and I'm gonna make it be okay."

I kissed her on the cheek and ran out to join my partner, Danny, nestling into our reserved third-row pew. Jane Russell soon squeezed in beside me. Then we had to squeeze over even more so Donald Trump could fit in. And he has wide hips.

The church was stunning. The entire wall behind the altar was blanketed in white orchids, probably to cover a giant bleeding Jesus, which would have been a downer. We waited. We chatted. Danny and I looked around the room to see whom we'd missed. I stood and waved to much more famous friends who were seated farther back, to show them I was among the chosen.

We continued to wait. For about an hour.

Then the news arrived, whispered from person to person, pew to pew, like the telephone game: Elizabeth Taylor had forgotten her shoes and had arrived at the church in hotel house slippers. No one in her entourage of seventy-two had noticed:

terry cloth—*The Plaza*, so we had to wait while some gay lackey schlepped up thirty blocks to retrieve her shoes. Finally Elizabeth was shoed, everyone was ready, and the music began.

Then a familiar voice shouted, "Wait for me!" The music stopped as Diana Ross flitted down the aisle, her hair over three feet in diameter, tickling aisle-seated guests as she flounced her way to the second row to take a seat.

The music resumed. The enormous wedding party entered from the downstage left and right wings, I mean *aisles*, and made their way to the platformed stage, I mean *altar*. Elizabeth Taylor was the co-matron of honor and was helped to her seat by the other co-, Marissa Berenson. The groom was escorted by Michael Jackson and his brother, Tito or Tootie or Toyota, I couldn't know or keep up.

The music abruptly stopped again—and then started up, louder, as everyone turned to the back of the church for the star's, I mean *bride's*, entrance. Traditionally, when a bride walks down the aisle at her wedding, the guests rise in her honor. When Liza entered at the back of the house, I mean *church*, the entire who's who audience, I mean *congregation*, jumped to their feet and yelped and applauded like it was Carnegie Hall. They cheered, "Liza! Liza!" I was certain the orchestra was going to launch into "And the World Goes 'Round." It was mayhem. Cindy Adams stood on top of Mickey Rooney and still couldn't see.

Liza was escorted by her longtime music director/drummer/father figure Bill "Pappy" Lavorgna, who was perhaps the only real "family" in the wedding party. She'd made a lot of entrances in her career, but as she glided down the aisle in a fitted white Bob Mackie gown, this was Liza at her most dazzling.

Naturally, like at any wedding, all the attention should be paid to the bride and groom, so I tried, I tried, I tried tried tried not to stare at Michael, but I just couldn't not. He was wearing a rigorously tailored black suit, festooned with velvet and sequined piping and a darling Peter Pan collar centered with a diamond brooch. His hair was flat-ironed into a flirty Marlo Thomas flip. His face couldn't have been whiter if he'd been an Irishman locked in a windowless basement his entire life.

I'd met Michael on several previous occasions since the mid-eighties and he'd become less and less human each time—not only in appearance but in manner. His very person. The man was on his own planet: Michael Planet. His eyes, darkly lined in black, remained closed throughout the service and his head bobbed and wobbled from side to side to the rhythm of a music no one else could hear. Occasionally, he would titter to himself at an internal joke, showing his teeth, just a shade less white than his face, and raise his shoulders like a five-year-old girl who'd just said the word "penis" for the first time.

On the other side of the altar sat Elizabeth Taylor. She was wearing an ensemble that made me think she'd looked in her closet that morning and said, "What shall I wear? . . . Everything!" But she was still Liz Taylor and somehow it worked on her, down to the veiled black tulled and feathered hat, set slightly askew on her head.

Or was she tilting to one side?

I'd also met Elizabeth on many occasions since the eighties and I truly adored and admired her as an actor, humanitarian, and one of the great purveyors of nasty, nasty dirty jokes. But she was clearly exhausted from the trauma of the shoe ordeal, and when the priest requested we lower our heads in prayer, she did. And she never came back up.

She. Never. Came. Back. Up.

She remained slumped, ever leaning to the left, threatening to topple onto the floor at any moment. Even unconscious, she created a sense of mystic tension—like when you lean too far back on the hind legs of a chair and there is that split second when you don't know if you're going to fall backward or forward. It was like she, and we, were living there for thirty minutes.

Between Michael's Planet and Liz's teetering, it was impossible to fully engage in the ceremony.

While we, mercifully, did not have to rise and sit numerous times like at some Catholic services, which would have been impossible for a third of the congregation and annoying to the rest, we were required to pray frequently. And every time— *every* time—Jane Russell heard the words "Please bow your heads in prayer," she viewed it as an opportunity to reapply her lipstick. Stuffed in her slot, glued shoulder to shoulder between me and Donald Trump, the only movable part of her body was her arms from the elbows down. Like a crab, she plucked the lipstick and mirror from her bag and, unable to raise her upper arms, hunched over and pooched her lips toward the ruby-red stuff while the priest gave thanks to God. I, personally, could not have been more grateful. After the fifth or sixth prayer, Jane's lips could have served as a location device should it have been necessary to pinpoint the wedding from outer space.

Finally the big moment arrived and it was time for the vows: *Do you take this man? Do you take this woman? Do you promise to love, honor, and cherish? May I have the rings?*

Nothing.

Michael was still listening to the music and comedy show in his head and Elizabeth was out cold. Marissa finally nudged Elizabeth, who woke with a start and a grunt. "Whaaa?" The bridesmaids gestured that it was time for the rings and Elizabeth, who was apparently the ring bearess, rose to the occasion. Or at least to an upright sitting position. She hefted her purse from beneath her chair and began to dig through it while we waited. She pulled out tissues, a compact, a prescription bottle, a Milky Way.

Finally, she found the small black velvet box and went to open it but couldn't quite figure out how. She pulled and pried with no success.

"Michaaaaaael!," she stage whispered in a coarse, breathy voice, as if she could go unnoticed and wasn't Elizabeth Taylor calling for Michael Jackson at Liza Minnelli's wedding in front of eight hundred and fifty people. "Michael, help me!"

Michael's eyes opened for the first time since he'd sat down and, Pavlovianly, he responded to the voice of his best-friend-in-need. Seeing that Liz was at her wits' end in her rigorous struggle with the tiny box, he rose and walked past the groom and bride, across the altar, to assist her.

No luck. Clearly this was not the kind of thing that either of these people did in their regular lives, where surely there must be servants more expert in such matters, because neither of them could figure out how to open a goddamn ring box.

The crowd fell silent, thunder-struck. We wondered if this was what it was like *all* the time. Liza caught my eye and jerked her head in the direction of the commotion as if beckoning me to get up and help, and a honk of a laugh jumped from my throat before I could catch it, echoing in the hush. Danny hit me on the arm and Liza nearly burst out laughing herself. Finally, someone else stepped in, I don't recall who— Tito, Guido, it could have been anyone. Shirley MacLaine. LL Cool J. How many megastars does it take to open a ring box?

At last, the rings were exchanged, Liza and the groom did their I do's, and the deed was done.

Almost.

Liza took his hands in hers, gazed into his beady eyes, and

declared, "You don't ever have to live life without me." She could have added, ". . . and I will soon wish you dead, so that will work out just fine," but it would be another month before she would fully come to that epiphany.

"Can I kiss you, then?" he responded.

And he went for her like he'd just come off a vegan diet and she was a Quarter Pounder with Cheese. His mouth widened and his swirling tongue was visible to the back pew as he chewed and chomped. I wondered if it was his first kiss, like when you're twelve years old and you're playing spin the bottle and you try to reenact what you've seen on TV.

It was grotesque. And Liza knew it.

She pulled back, and not wanting to humiliate her newest husband, smiled coyly at the crowd as if to say, "Isn't he . . . committed?"

The priest pronounced them husband and wife, and the audience erupted in an ovation reminiscent of, well . . . a Liza Minnelli concert. Having spent a life on the stage as the recipient of thousands of ovations, and, still trying to recover from the awkward mauling, Liza did what she knew to do to save the day. She grabbed the arm of her husband and costar and together they nodded at the crowd in gracious appreciation. House left—house right—then center. The applause crescendoed as they headed up the aisle. When she passed me, seemingly gleaming, our eyes locked and then she crossed hers, saying everything we both knew.

Jane Russell had just applied her nineteenth layer of lipstick, which was now smeared beyond the margin of her mouth and dotted the end of her nose. She turned to me and said, in her gruff, smoker's voice, "That's show business, kid."

And it was.

The reception was held at the Regent Wall Street Hotel

and the newlyweds entered the ballroom in a spotlight as ex-Queen rocker Brian May sang "We Are The Champions." Liza wore a sumptuous red sequined miniskirt, and the Man Whose Name Shall Go Unmentioned wore sunglasses. At his wedding reception.

He wore sunglasses at his wedding reception.

The party went on until very late. Carol Channing spent much of the evening on the dance floor boogie-oogie-oogie-ing with Snoop Dogg. By this time anything could've happened. I wouldn't have been surprised if they'd announced their engagement.

The Man Whose Name Shall Go Unmentioned and Liza received visitors and congratulations at their center table in front of the thirty-piece orchestra, as the music continued: the Doobie Brothers, Donny Osmond, Natalie Cole, me. The Man Whose Name Shall Go Unmentioned told me that they'd decided to adopt four children as soon as they got back from London, finished a satellite interview with Larry King, and wrapped up redecorating Liza's apartment. Liza leaned behind him out of his view and, eyes wide, shook her head, "nooooooo!" And then Gloria Gaynor joined the orchestra and belted out "I Will Survive." Coincidence? I thought not.

Upon leaving the reception, we were all given heart-shaped boxes of chocolates with "Liza & The Man Whose Name Shall Go Unmentioned" printed on top, and cookies with a portrait of the newlyweds painted in icing. I tossed out the box of chocolates and I ate the cookie, beginning with his head.

It was evident in the following months that the marriage wouldn't last, and over the next year it flared and sputtered, making the sinking of the *Titanic* look like a round of Milton

Bradley's Battleship. When the last Shirley Temple doll had been wrapped in tissue paper, boxed, and sent to cold storage, Liza emerged somehow better than before. And funnier. And we were even closer, once again bonded through our mutual teeth-gritting drive and the ability to shuffle off disappointment and put on a new show—both the literal and figurative kind. Always. No matter what.

One night in the aftermath, when our normal was restored and we were propped up on her king-size bed—which always seemed bigger than king-size, probably due to the enormous amount of stuff that was always present: legal pad lists, DVDs, CDs, a boom box, faxes, Marlboro Lights, several working and nonworking lighters, a dozen working and nonworking pens and highlighters, an ashtray, three pairs of glasses, a mug of iced coffee, a cell phone, a box of tissues, a tray of dishes from dinner, four TV remotes, seventeen pillows, and a dog—Liza and I discussed the difference between regrets and mistakes. Neither of us had any regrets, really. Whatever got us here got us here. But we'd both made plenty of mistakes. God knows she'd been there through mine. And what mattered, we said, was that those mistakes be acknowledged, so as not to be repeated.

Suddenly, Liza smooshed a heap of the bed stuff to one side and asked me to sit on my haunches and face her, eye to eye. Then she made me raise my right hand and take an oath that if she should ever again fall for anyone remotely like the Man Whose Name Shall Go Unmentioned, that I would have her retested for encephalitis, lock her up with no Charles Aznavour records, bind her with a Halston scarf, and slap her until she regained her senses.

That's what friends are for.

4. Odd Man In

When I was three, I choked on an Oscar Meyer wiener and lost consciousness, turned blue, and was ambulanced to the hospital, where I apparently flatlined and then came back from the dead, according to my Memo, who swore that the doctor told her as such but kept it from my mother.

At the very least, oxygen did not get to my brain for many minutes. I overheard the doctor say something to my parents about being lucky I wasn't a vegetable. I wondered what kind—cauliflower, string bean, yam? But I got the idea when, for the next year, appointments were scrupulously scheduled and my hair was shaved into a burr so electrodes could be glued to my scalp to check for brain damage. I sat on the edge of a padded examination table and watched electronic waves jiggle and jaggle on the tiny black-and-white monitor, hoping I wasn't retarded. For years, I wondered how I might have been different were it not for my tragic wiener incident: smarter maybe, quicker. Normal.

Studying basic math in first grade, I couldn't grasp the simple concept of even and odd numbers. For everyone else it was a breeze, ho-hummingly spouting the answers to Mrs. Ellis's oral pop quiz:

"Dee Dee, five?"

"Odd!" Dee Dee chimed.

"Teri, twelve?"

"Even."

"Chris, seven?"

Chris rolled his eyes. "Odd."

"Sam, three?"

I sat frozen.

"Sam, three?"

Clearly this was rudimentary and I could sense judgment at my hesitation. But what made some numbers "odd"? What did they do to suffer such a label? Weren't they just numbers like all the others? I fought my anxiety and pretended that I could see the oddness in what seemed ordinary. But I knew I had a fifty-fifty shot and, thankfully, guessed the right answer.

There would be a lot of guessing for years to come.

I suppose everyone looks back on childhood and remembers feeling odd and bizarre and deviant, misunderstood, and potentially involved in some cosmic galactic mishap that resulted in a baby exchange with a perfectly normal earth-child, who was just as bewildered on some faraway planet.

In truth, I wasn't all that different from the other kids. Except that I wanted to be Jewish and blind and sing like a fat black woman.

And I was "squirrelly." But I didn't know what that meant yet.

I spent my wonderless years in the small town of Sand Springs, peculiarly named, as there was neither sand nor springs anywhere in the area. But the name "Red Clay Dirty River" doesn't roll off the tongue quite so trippingly. Sand Springs was a blue-collar, union-labeled, staunchly Democratic, religiously conservative burb, where everyone's parents worked at the steel mill or the glass plant or the box plant, and it was generally expected that our generation would, with pride, continue the tradition. It boasted the title "Industrial Capital of the Country"—home to more manufacturing plants per capita than anywhere else in the USA. All the pollution of a big city without a single perk.

I came from the sturdy stuff of American grass roots. My parents, Bill, pronounced "Bee-ill," and Carolyn, pronounced "Care-lin" (all words in Oklahoma are pronounced with two syllables), both grew up in Cushing, Oklahoma, a town birthed in the oil boom of the 1920s that has been dying a lethargic death ever since.

My grandfather, Ira "Whitey" Harris, whom I called Paw Paw, had an easy bearing and an enviable hairline. He lived in a well-worn pair of overalls and smoked a pipe, toiling at an oil refinery, where he died of a heart attack when he was sixty and I was three. My grandmother, Floy May, whom I called Granny, was just under five feet tall and just under four feet around. She preferred bright red pantsuits, giving the impression, from a toddler's perspective, that a giant tomato was rolling toward you. She kept a picture of a very Caucasian Jesus on her living room wall and her gallstones in a baby food jar that hung from a pink ribbon on the bathroom doorframe. She would touch them, like a mezuzah, when she went in for her "BMs," which were a favorite and frequent topic of conversation.

When I was left in Granny's care, she often secretly dressed me up in frilly aprons and fluffy house slippers and spouted terrifying tales about my father, all ending with his burning in hell because he used the Lord's name in vain. She would stoop down to me, nose to nose, the glint of her black, rhinestone-dotted, cat's-eye glasses adding a twinkle to her eye, and whisper, "The crows are gonna peck your daddy's eyes out!" I would invariably shriek with horror, which would cause her to let loose a crazy, high-pitched staccato cackle.

Granny had a gifted ear for music and played an upright out-of-tune piano but only used the black keys, so her repertoire was limited to "When the Saints Go Marching In" and a few hymns. Her mind flitted like a drunken hummingbird, and she regaled me with allegories of death and carnage, like the time a cat crept into her infant cousin's crib and "sucked the breath outta him." She acted it out, playing the cat and the suffocating infant, finally falling back on the sofa in a dead heap. When I was sufficiently in a state of terror, her eyes would pop open and she would release that high-pitched cackle and waddle away, humming "Jesus Loves Me."

I am convinced that her parade of activity and prattle did not rely on the presence of others.

My mother's mother, whom I called Memo, was a Texas girl, raised without a father. When she was an infant, her father had abducted her two older sisters and brother and left for parts unknown. She met him only once, at twelve years old, when she heard tell of his whereabouts and took a train to his general store several hundred miles away. She walked in and straight up to a mustached man in an apron stocking a shelf. "I'm your daughter Mary," she said, "and I just needed to see your face." Then she turned heel and took the train back to her mother.

Memo married my grandfather Sam when she was a mere fifteen years old. He was twenty-five and had fought in World War I—a man, strong-willed and solid. They moved to Cushing in the mid-1920s, and Sam operated a taxi stand in a town that didn't support a taxi stand. Its primary purpose was to run bootleg gin during Prohibition and thereafter in the dry state of Oklahoma. Patrons called for a "pick-up" and got a "drop-off" from the trunk. Memo owned a café, which was celebrated for her homemade bread, desserts, and a visit by the gangster Pretty Boy Floyd, who flirted with her while she served him peach cobbler and coffee, after which he walked across the street and robbed the Cushing Bank. Memo said he was, indeed, pretty—and he tipped well.

She'd rejected her generation's idea that a woman's place was in the home and regularly rose before dawn in preparation for her eighteen-hour day. Her challenging schedule didn't really have any wiggle room for my unexpected mother, who was born years after a son had been raised and a daughter had been buried. There was a business to run and others already relied upon her.

My mother was forced to be her own caretaker as soon as she was able, getting herself up and ready for school in the mornings and often not seeing her mother until suppertime, when she ate in the back room of the café before walking across the driveway to their apartment to put herself to bed.

As a teenager, she was a beauty, with chocolate-colored hair that fell in thick, wavy ringlets around her graceful face and sorrowful mahogany eyes. Basically unchaperoned, she could have gone good girl or bad, but chose precision over defiance, becoming her own disciplinarian and homework monitor. She excelled in drama class and dreamed of becoming an actress—maybe even in New York or Hollywood.

My father was a fiery, strikingly handsome rebel with a love of music that never compromised his cool-man, jeans-clad, cigs-rolled-in-the-T-sleeve persona. The trumpet was his instrument of expression and he spent endless hours nestled next to their wooden-cased Motorola radio, devouring jazz and classical music, aspiring to one day join a symphony, or tour with big band leaders like Stan Kenton or Billy May.

My parents were high school sweethearts—an unlikely match since my mother was the perfect student, cheerleader, yearbook editor, and school actress and my father was James Dean with a trumpet. They married during his junior year of college and three years later, when I was born, my father gained employment as high school band director in Sand Springs. There would be no symphony or big band tour or New York or Hollywood. But it was an accessible, responsible career in the field of his passion. And my mother was determined to be the caretaker she never had.

By the time I was a toddler, my dad had become somewhat famous in the tristate area for his marching band style, which incorporated a heart-stopping goose step that brought the crowds to their feet. During the orchestral season of the school year, he conducted concerts on the auditorium stage and, as if a great sorcerer, when he tapped his baton on the metal stand, magic would ensue. I was awash in sound—dramatic and elegant and exquisite—and I watched the back of his head and shoulders rise and release as he waved his arms in a powerful and fervent dance. This was his element, his symphony.

My father brought the love of music to my life. To the lives of many. He was the go-to guy for students and parents alike, the favorite teacher, the giver of advice, the shoulder to cry on, and a source of encouragement. But he was all used up by the time he got to us.

During the rare daylight hours that he was home, my father's moods would swing, alternately and without notice, from playful to fractious. Peripherally glimpsing his hand coming toward me could mean a tussle of the hair or a pop on the head with his ring finger, seemingly without provocation or warning. I mostly saw him on weekends, when he would mutely seclude himself with a ball game on television, prompting my mother

.8.6 .88

to beg thousands of times, "Go be with your father." "Be with your father" meant sit in the same room with him in the dark for twenty minutes while he sat glued to the Cardinals or the Cowboys. My presence was seldom acknowledged and I exited as unnoticed as I entered.

My father was, and is, a good man with a giant if not articulate heart, and we have since developed a strong relationship; but during those years he was driven and career-focused and his best was reserved for others. Mothers were for raising children.

I remember being three—sitting, spinning, waiting on a tall stool at nursery school, the last child to be picked up. I clutched a collection of heart-shaped, crayoned Valentine's Day cards with anticipation. Today was a big day. My dad was taking me to see the movie *Mary Poppins*. Just me and Daddy, father and son. My teacher was as eager for me to leave as I. She was a billowy woman with a mountain of dreary, unfriendly hair that exploded from a priggish bun to a demented puff of white by the end of each school day. Like Santa Claus upside down. My father arrived and she pressed a box of SweeTarts into my fist and nearly shoved us out the door.

We sat on the far left side of the theater in the haze of the smoking section and my father constructed a hump from our coats to prop me up for a better view. He went to the lobby and returned a few minutes later, juggling popcorn and Milk Duds and pop, a cigarette dangling from the corner of his mouth and a trail of smoke stinging his squinted left eye. It was a grand day indeed. I was grateful we'd arrived before the movie started. It was customary for my family to choose a "show," and just go to the theater with no idea what time it ran. We would walk in midway through a film, watch to the end, and then sit through the next showing until the movie got to the point at which we'd arrived.

This time was different. My dad and I saw *Mary Poppins* in order, from the splendorous overture to the final credits. We'd found a common passion—no real interaction, but a bond all the same. This time I was thrilled to "go be with my father" and sit silently to watch something in the dark. I begged to see the movie again and he said yes and we remained in our seats for a second full showing. It is the only time I can remember from my early childhood that my father and I shared something alone, together: a recollection so precious that I have sometimes wondered if I made it up.

But my mother tells me that upon arriving home early that evening, I sang the entire score, reenacting the story of how Jane and Michael Banks didn't see much of their father and then Mary Poppins came and they visited wonderful places and the daddy smiled and everybody flew kites together.

A year later, when *The Sound of Music* came out, my family watched it from the bed of our red-chipped Ford pickup truck at a drive-in, complete with lawn chairs, blankets, and our own popcorn. The actual sound of music tinnily eked out of a wired metal speaker, no better than a transistor radio, but I was just as taken with this movie—same theme, different characters. However, a few days later it went a little sour when my father caught me in the garage with my mother's skirt on my head as a makeshift nun's habit, singing "I Have Confidence."

Having a high school band director for a father, however, had its advantages. I was only two when he plunked me in front of a microphone at a football game and I sang an iron-lunged, on-pitch "Star-Spangled Banner" to the cheers of the stadium. In the next years, it was common and convenient for the teachers' own small children to participate in coronations for homecoming queen or basketball queen or wrestling queen or band queen or debate queen. We'd be dressed up in little suits with hook-and-bar bow ties, or crinoline stuffed dresses with shiny patent leather shoes, and were pushed onto the field or court or stage carrying velvet tasseled pillows with tiaras tied on. Or throwing rose petals before the feet of wrestling royalty.

I'd pomped and circumstanced several times, but I hit the jackpot at age five, when I got to play little Jerome de Beque, one of the two mixed-raced Polynesian bastard children, in the Charles Page High School production of *South Pacific*. I wore a flowered loincloth, full body paint (Max Factor Egyptian Tan No. 5), and eye makeup that looked more like Agnes Moorehead in *Bewitched* than anyone remotely Polynesian.

On opening night, I made my entrance from up left in all my Polynesian Bastard Child Glory, hand in hand with Dee Dee Shields, who played my sister, ready to slay them with the song "Dites Moi"—in *real* French.

Unbeknownst to me, in the prior scene, one of the actors had dropped a drinking glass, which had shattered all over down center. As we began the song, Dee Dee and I walked, barefooted, toward the audience and after only one verse, I stepped onto a shard of broken glass, which drove straight up into the arch of my foot. I felt the hot bite of penetration and looked down to see a pool of blood spreading around my feet on the mottled wooden floor. I gasped and, for a split second, fell behind on the phrase of the song. A voice from within spoke loud and clear—some five-year-old-version of *Suck it up, Harris, you're in show business!* I lifted my chin as Dee Dee glanced down to identify the wet stuff seeping between her toes. She screamed. I squeezed her hand like a vise, a warning, then smiled at the audience—row after row of silhouetted heads and shoulders in the hazy streak of the spotlight—and finished the song alone as Dee Dee wept. The applause was better than first aid. I loved the purpose and the drama and I knew Dee Dee would never make it in show business.

The next scheduled production was *The Miracle Worker*. I became fixated with Helen Keller. Anyone with that many handicaps was not only captivating and heroic, but could relate completely to the tribulations of the human spirit. And who, better than I, to understand the complexities? As it was a high school production, both six-year-old Helen and her twenty-year-old teacher, Annie Sullivan, typically would be played by high school girls of the same age and size, making the dining table scene where Helen eats from everyone's plates look like a teenage food fight, and all but destroying the famous water pump "wa-wa" scene. A sixteen-year-old would just look and sound stupid and Helen Keller was anything but. Because of my triumph in *South Pacific*, I was certain I would land the role of Helen. I understood her—and I was short.

I began staggering about the house with a dish towel tied around my eyes and toilet paper stuffed in my ears to simulate blindness and deafness. I thudded into furniture and knocked over lamps. I stumbled to the smallish avocado-green Formica kitchen table, which was scrunched between the refrigerator and a doorframe against a wall, though an actual full-size dining table, exclusively reserved for holidays, sat only four feet away. I squeezed myself into a chair and, just like in Helen's family, my mother insisted I eat with a fork. Still, I was surprised at how messy pancakes and syrup can get when you can't see where the fork is going. Finally, she'd had it.

"Take that rag off your head and eat like a person!"

"Helen Keller *was* a person! How can you say that?"

"You're not Helen Keller!"

"I *could* be if they'd give me a chance!"

My father entered and exited with one sentence, ripping the cloth from my eyes. "Take off the goddamn rag and eat your goddamn pancakes and don't talk to your goddamn mother like that."

I removed the toilet paper from my ears, but had memorized my senses so I could still pretend to be blind and deaf.

I'd auditioned for *South Pacific,* even though Dee Dee and I were the only ones up for our roles, and on the day of tryouts for *The Miracle Worker,* I begged to go—even though I'd been told a part was being given to me.

I had other plans.

I walked confidently onto the auditorium stage and friendly voices welcomed me from the darkened house. Then Miss Young, the drama teacher and director, said, "You didn't need to come, Sam. We already know you're playing Percy."

"I wanted to come. I want to read for Helen."

Read for Helen. Helen didn't have any lines. But I was prepared to convincingly stare blankly with my eyes slightly crossed and bump into furniture.

They didn't even attempt to stifle their titters, which quickly grew into full-out, patronizing "isn't that cute . . . and strange" guffaws. Despite my pleading logic, I didn't get to bump into anything.

I was cast, instead, in the tiny, silent, and pajamaed role of Percy, "a little Negro child," who mostly slept. I couldn't understand how they could see me as a *Polynesian* child and a *Negro* child, but insisted on casting a *non*child in the most important part. The girl who played Helen Keller was gangly, with full-on breasts, and somehow managed to "wa-wa" with a southern accent. Dreadful. I knew she wouldn't make it in show business either.

My disappointment was not discussed at home, but after a few days, I heard my name called with a tone that I knew meant my dad had been inspired to offer fatherly, sage advice, which would fit perfectly into a commercial break from a game.

"Turn down the TV," he said. I knew this must be really important. When the room was silent, he pulled back the handle on his recliner, rocketing him to an upright position.

"Son . . ."

He leaned forward and paused to shuffle a cigarette up from the pack, grip it in the corner of his mouth, and light it with a Zippo.

"Life . . ."

He snapped the lighter shut with an emphatic clink and took a long draw, letting the smoke fill every cell of his lungs, then finally exhaled, slowly, deliberately, until the last foggy fume was purged.

". . . is a bowl-a shit."

He took another puff and tilted his head, squinting for emphasis. Then through the exhale: "And we just stir it up."

He let the words hang in the air alongside the smoke. Then: "Turn the TV back up."

I did, and the baseball game resumed as he jutted himself back in his recliner and I went back to practicing my autograph. Hoping what he said wasn't true.

My mother also had a motto: "Don't expect anything and you won't be disappointed when it doesn't happen."

She was a full-time mom/housewife who, I suspect, would have pursued the arts had she not fallen prey to the confines of the small-town women's mentality of her era. Her overly regulated and expertly organized household, PTA meetings, and Mothers' Club were a cloak for an often desperately misunderstood and suffocated soul which erupted in dramatic weight fluctuations, bouts of anxiety and depression, and, years later, her late-blooming alcoholism. The family doctor prescribed the popular weight-loss one-two punch: amphetamines and sheep urine injections. It was like Dr. Feelgood meets Dr. Doolittle.

It was not uncommon for her to raid my bedroom at three o'clock in the morning and tear through my toys and books, forcing me to reorganize them. My homework was meticulously checked, not only for errors but for evidence of *corrected* errors. If there was an eraser smudge, it was shredded and I had to redo it, so that the illusion of perfection was intact.

Given that her veins were coursing with speed and sheep pee, I think I got off easy.

Beneath it all, my mother and I had a covenant, and one Easter we unknowingly began a tradition. While unpacking groceries, she stopped to remove the cellophane wrapping from a package of those marshmallow peeps. Suddenly, violently, she ripped the head off one of the little chicks. Gummy innards stretched like a rubber band and then snapped. There was a moment of silence as she waited for my reaction. I took the box from her and ripped another head off. Then she. Then I. We began laughing hysterically, uncontrollably, all of our pent-up angst of perfection melting away with each sugary, sticky headless chick. The perpetual thin ice on which we circled my father was the silent glue of our alliance.

In these many years, the ice has thickened, my father has grown into a sentimental pussycat, and my mother has decades of sober recovery behind her, but the ritual of ripping the heads off innocent chicks remains. We don't necessarily celebrate the resurrection, but come Easter, my mother and I exchange a box of marshmallow peeps, knowing their numbers are up.

I believe my young parents found themselves in the middle of a cultural crossroads, when their 1940s–50s upbringing and postwar nationalism were being challenged left and right—mostly left. But race riots, Kent State, and the multiple political assassinations of the day were somewhere far, far away, and squirrelly little Sam was right in their own backyard, singing "Stormy Weather" at the top of his lungs.

And meaning it.

Though my mother had learned not to have expectations for herself, she had a great deal for me. She recognized me, not for what she could never have, like some stage mothers, but for what she knew I already had.

When I was seven, she enrolled me in a children's acting workshop at Tulsa University—a six-week program that culminated in a single performance of a fifteen-minute play: *Stone Soup.* I starred as the Traveling Stranger who convinces the selfish starving townspeople to collectively make a stew by contributing bits and pieces of food to his pot of water with a stone in it, so that everyone would eat better. It was kind of like *The Music Man* meets *The Galloping Gourmet.*

My father had an upcoming out-of-state band competition, which was also to double as a rare family vacation. The destination was Canyon City, Colorado, home of "The Royal Gorge—Colorado's Grandest Canyon," featuring soaring granite cliffs that towered a thousand feet above the rushing Arkansas River. We'd collected brochures and pictures and I had looked forward to visiting the awe-inspiring natural wonder for months. There were no awe-inspiring natural wonders in or around Sand Springs, though people did travel upstate to the Tall Grass Prairie to see tall grass.

As for heights, in nearby Tulsa, there was the semi-awe-inspiring *un*natural wonder of the Prayer Tower at Oral Roberts

University—a sort of Jetsons-meets-Jesus edifice that more resembled a ride at the county fair than a place of reflection.

The Royal Gorge was going to be a once-in-a-lifetime adventure, and I secretly planned to paint my name on a rock and, when the aerial tram was suspended high above the gorge, throw it over the side so that a part of me would be there forever.

Coincidentally, my single performance of *Stone Soup* fell right in the middle of the band trip. My parents were still only in their twenties, but they somehow found the wisdom and respect to give me the choice: I could go with them or stay and do my fifteen-minute play, miss the vacation, and be separated from my family for a week for the first time.

I chose to stay and do the play, under the care of Memo.

Getting to make that decision forced me to attach a value to my love of performing. At seven years old, I knew what I wanted to do.

I could not get enough of music and theater and movies. I spent much of my days escaping over a turntable, listening to a peculiar amalgam of blues and R&B (Billie Holiday, Jackie Wilson, Aretha Franklin) and musical theater (*Mame, Oklahoma!, Funny Girl, Gypsy, Carousel*); and many weekends watching MGM musicals on television (especially anything with Judy Garland, Gene Kelly, or Fred Astaire).

Unfortunately, my immediate area didn't provide much for the young thespian. The closest thing Sand Springs had to community theater was the living nativity scene that took place each Christmas in the "Triangle," a grassy median across the street from the library and catty-corner to Taco Town. I had to think outside the triangle.

I began putting together neighborhood extravaganzas, mostly revue in style, which featured the Broadway and pop hits of the day. These were performed in our unfinished basement—with a cement floor, wood-framed ceilings, and two weight-bearing metal poles in the middle of the room, which proved perfect for hanging a backdrop and provided a backstage, quick-change area. The cinder block walls made for excellent acoustics.

I thought the shows were wonderful, and after I'd mounted a few of them, I decided they needed to be seen by more people than no one, which had been the sum total of our audience thus far. But I was concerned that the entertainment palate of my fellow Oklahoman neighbors wasn't sophisticated enough for the type of fare I was serving, so I knew I had to come up with a marketing scheme to snag them. Something they could relate to. After careful thought, I had an idea.

I spent the afternoon handwriting flyers on construction paper and distributed them in a three-block radius, inviting one and all to an "Evening of Music . . . and Bowling!!" I set up two two-by-fours on the concrete floor for lanes and used my toy plastic ball and pins. And the people came! It was a tremendous success—the applause of nine or ten adults bouncing off the cinder block walls sounded like my idea of Carnegie Hall.

My appetite had been whetted and the neighborhood kids on my block were too small in number for the kinds of spectacles I was envisioning. I wanted more! But how?

The answer came one day in second grade. A classmate, Jennifer, was—well, she was fat. Undeniably and inarguably fat by anyone's standards, though today she would be considered merely plump. She preferred plaid tunic dresses with wide pilgrim collars and plastic belts to accentuate her waistline, and wore egg-shaped glasses to accentuate her egg-shaped face and egg-shaped body. Our classmates, being seven years old and therefore cruel or honest or some combination of the two, ridiculed poor Jennifer without pause.

One day, when we were learning how a caterpillar becomes a butterfly, our teacher, Mrs. Maule, who knew that Jennifer was an exceptionally gifted artist, asked her to illustrate the process on the blackboard, handing her a box of colored chalks that had been purchased for this very occasion.

It took a half an hour at least, which is like three days in kid time—but we watched as Jennifer painstakingly drew the caterpillar on a leaf, the caterpillar in a cocoon, and the beautiful butterfly emerging. Restless and bored at first, the class was slowly captivated by her skillful hand and careful eye as she shadowed and detailed, bringing the metamorphosis to life. I exchanged looks with Mrs. Maule, realizing what she had planned. Jennifer *was* the butterfly. A plaid, egg-shaped butterfly. She had a talent we didn't possess and, therefore, was special. She was still fat. But talented and fat was much better than just fat. We never looked at her the same way again.

Seeing this as an extraordinarily intuitive and caring act, and realizing that Mrs. Maule was dedicated to recognizing our individual gifts, I decided business was at hand. I asked her if I could use some class time and perhaps recess time and perhaps lunch time and perhaps before and after school time to direct a production of Rodgers and Hammerstein's *Cinderella*. She gave me the thumbs-up and told me she'd suspected something like this was coming when, a month before at show-and-tell, whereas most kids had brought a terrarium or their favorite toy truck, I had taken the words much more literally. For the "show" part, I performed the Act I finale quintet from *West Side Story*. For "tell," I explained how all the songs fit together in counterpoint, leaving the characters conflicted at curtain.

My script, which I'd typed on our manual Smith Corona at

home after memorizing the TV movie, was ready and I began auditions the next day.

I had no desire to be in the show. Prince Charming was a dull and thankless part and my plate was full, trying to figure out how to make the switch from Cinderella's peasant rags to her ball gown with the wave of a wand and no time for a costume change. I solved the problem by double casting Cinderella. Teri Mullins was my best friend and bore a striking resemblance to Benjamin Franklin, so she was cast as the plain one. Cheri Craddock was the pretty one, though less talented (a combination I found to be true more often than not later in my career). When the Fairy Godmother cast her spell, all I had to do was flick the classroom lights off and on to create a very slow but dazzling strobe effect, while plain Cinderella spun off as pretty Cinderella spun on. It was as if the Fairy Godmother had granted her a wardrobe upgrade *and* plastic surgery.

I cast Lance Cheney as Prince Charming. He was dashingly handsome and probably my first crush. More thrilling was the fact that he was one of the few kids in our class whose parents were really and truly divorced. It was exotic and dangerous. His mother was beautiful, independent, and strong-minded, and she was always fashionably outfitted in the way I imagined stewardesses dressed when not in uniform as they sipped olive-brimmed martinis and drew on Virginia Slims. On top of all that, she worked in politics, causing the housewives of Sand Springs to actually whisper in her presence. "You've Come a Long Way, Baby" could have been her theme song.

I was highly attracted to Lance's scandalous family history, his mother, and, well, him. Even at seven years old, he had a dry, witty quality and I could picture him in a smoking jacket with a satin lapel and really shiny shoes. He had a rebellious devil-may-care attitude, so he was the perfect person to understand my deep concern about morning prayer in school ending with "in Jesus' name." He supported me when I complained to Mrs. Maule that the Jews and Muslims were not represented so I didn't feel comfortable joining the class in the ritual. After reminding me that there wasn't a Jew, Muslim, or anything other than Southern Baptist Christians in our little town and no one was being excluded, I think she must have admired my gumption, so she allowed me to sequester myself in the bathroom during the prayer. I took Lance in tow and we practiced tying our shoes until the reverent "Amen" was heard through the door.

More and more, my father was a stew of confusion. While I sensed that he was proud of my talent and that I questioned the status quo, he looked at the extremity of my obsession as something that made me different from the other kids, rather than simply unique. It's one thing for a seven-year-old to love the stage—it's another for him to spend hours a day perfecting an Anthony Newley impersonation and then performing it door to door for confused neighbors. When I was eight, my dad signed me up for Little League baseball and, wanting to please him, I dove in full force.

Our coach was Mr. Flynn. He was broad and tanned and manly. His wavy black hair fringed slightly over his ears and into jaw-length sideburns that framed his chiseled, pockmarked face. He dressed in an adult version of the Little League uniform, which I suspected he wore at home, where I imagined he also slept with his mitt under his pillow and ate all of his meals from an actual home plate. He *was* baseball.

Coach Flynn felt that the tradition of tryouts and winning a position on the team was important for morale, so every afternoon that week, all of us pitched and caught and batted and

Sam Harris

grounded and fielded. I hadn't much experience at this kind of thing but was a fast runner—if not a great pitcher, catcher, batter, grounder, or fielder. Still, I gave it my all.

At the end of the week, we gathered in the dugout as Coach Flynn called out our names one by one.

"Morgan!"

Russell Morgan threw his cap in the air and ran to the field, overjoyed. "Patterson! Cook! Moss!"

They tossed their caps and joined Russell to play catch with boyish elation at being chosen. *Chosen?* We were eight years old, who wouldn't be chosen? It was the ritual, the accomplishment, the deserving of the title. Finally all the names had been called. Except mine. With the cheering boys in view, playing in the background, Coach Flynn swaggered up to me and bent down, placed his palms on his grass-stained knee breeches, and, in a broad and tanned and manly whisper, said, "You can be water boy if you want . . ."

My father was parked fifty feet away in our imitation-wood-paneled Ford station wagon. I glanced over in time to see him absorb what had happened and then drop his hands and head onto the steering wheel in disgrace or submission or something in between. He didn't get out and question the coach. He didn't put his arm around me and offer me a Life Saver. He didn't even look at me. I picked up my mitt and walked to the car, and we drove home silently, staring straight ahead, never speaking of it again.

I didn't care if I ever played baseball, but I think it killed my father that day. While he had never been the kind of dad who tossed a ball or practiced batting with me, this moment was not about athletic preparedness. It signified that he wasn't the only one who knew I was different. Odd. Not like the others. The secret was out. I don't think he ever blamed me. He was just sad and disappointed, afraid that if I wasn't like him, my life would be hard and lonely. He saw how the misfits were treated and he didn't want that for his son.

Suck it up, Dad, I'm in show business.

A few days after the Little League tryouts, my father called out my name, hoisted himself forward from his La-Z-Boy, turned down the TV, and put on a record of classical music. He asked me to close my eyes.

"What do you see?" he said.

I listened and concentrated and let the music create a picture in my mind. "There is a graveyard. And it's cold and windy . . . and foggy. And there are old headstones."

The music changed. "What else?" he asked.

"Now there are skeletons dancing around the cemetery. They're celebrating a new dead person. They're flying around. The dead person is alive again with them."

Rather than attaching a story to the music, it was as if I was making the music happen! By the time the symphony ended, I was enthralled. I understood that music came from intention and not the other way around. I could escape to anywhere I dreamed. I could create my own world. With underscoring.

I was the muddled concoction of my father's contradictions. The same man who warned me that "life is a bowl-a shit" was the channel to my bliss. The infection and the cure. He was, at once, the drought that left me parched and gasping, and the rain that nurtured the single blade of grass, pushing itself up from between the jagged cracks in the sidewalk, and into the sun.

5. The Zoo Story

My four-year-old son, Cooper, and I have little in common.

When he was born, I was the primary caretaker. It was a natural role for me, and Cooper and I had an immediate, primordial bond. I was scheduler and night feeder, burper, soother, then organic baby food maker, onesie stocker, BPA-PVC-phthalate-free checker, lead tester, baby proofer. Toppling stacks of baby books, each over a foot high, were piled on and around my nightstand and, though previously a voracious reader of fiction and biographies, I did not open a single nonbaby book—all highlighted, underlined, and dog-eared—for nearly two years.

Danny was head-over-heels in love and couldn't get enough of our son, but as he bounced the lumpy lox of a do-nothing infant who just ate and pooped and gurgled and spit, I could tell he was eager to get past this stage so they could climb trees and play catch and destroy things. When Cooper took his first wobbly steps, Danny immediately wanted to take him Rollerblading. I kept saying, "Don't worry, there will come a day before we know it where it's all about you guys."

Call me clairvoyant. As Cooper has grown into a full-on

little boy, I may remain the go-to guy for meals, boo-boos, permission, daily organization, midnight fevers, developmental research, hard-ass rules, and "feelings," but now, well, Danny trumps all. His time has come. He is the fun one. He is goofy and crazy and Cooper laughs a particular sound of pure joy that is exclusive to Papa, which is what he calls Danny. I'm Daddy. Daddy is fun, but not that kind of fun.

I go with Cooper's lead and we have a great time, but I have found myself searching for activities that interest us both. It's hard. Very hard. I get bored. Very bored. Not with him, but with what captivates him. We sip from different sippy cups of tea.

Cooper loves cars, jets, monster trucks, and motorcycles. All the time. I hate cars, jets, monster trucks, and motorcycles. All the time. Or rather, I have no real interest unless I build a mini-racetrack out of empty Amazon.com boxes complete with a service garage painted in watercolors, where lunch is served at a juice box picnic table with an affixed cocktail umbrella. But I am not remotely drawn to the actual races or endless crashes—and least of all to the cars themselves.

In real life, when asked what kind of car I drive, I say "a Lexus Nebula" because that is the given name of the color. Nebula actually means "an interstellar cloud of dust" but it rings like the name of an Egyptian prince. I do not know the model of my car and I often get SUV mixed up with SVU. I did not test-drive the vehicle before I bought it. It was a Lexus and it was pretty. Nebula.

There are many more differences.

I hear about kids who painstakingly choose their clothing. Cooper has favorite colors and superhero shirts, sure, but comfort is his criteria and he doesn't give a crap about coordinating. It is my duty to let him express himself *his* way, so I gulp a little as he romps out of the house in plaids mixed with checks and stripes and Spider-Man socks and Velcroed sneakers on the wrong feet because "I like them that way."

Danny and I have always put looks before comfort. Danny is a button-down, dress-shoes man and has never left the house without checking his hair at least three times; then he continues to monitor it in any and every reflection or slightest facsimile thereof: a storefront window, a hubcap, a puddle. I swear I once saw him spit in his hand and gaze into it, tilting his head for adjustments. I admit that if I have no plans to leave the house, I don't care what I look like and have gone for days without seeing my face. However, I weigh myself at least twice a day, no matter what, and even when alone, I wear heavy luggish boots because they add two inches to my height and allow me to buy jeans longer than my legs, which gives me a better line. I feel happier when I feel thinner and I am much more pleasant to be around.

When I was doing *Grease* on Broadway, I wore a cinch corset under my skintight, black-and-white, horizontally striped Lycra shirt to smooth the slightest side bulge that might've pooched over my high-waisted jeans. It didn't matter that I couldn't breathe. It mattered that I was V-shaped.

I considered having ribs removed.

I like clean lines and clean rooms and clean drawers. Cooper makes enormous messes, emptying bins of die-cast cars, action figures, minuscule pieces of Legos, and collected rocks, acorns, and dead leaves.

When I was his age, my toys were categorized and color coded.

Cooper loves firemen, policemen, football players, paramedics, and wrestlers—any man in a uniform.

So do I, but for different reasons.

He talks of blood and bones and guts and boogers. His

figurines engage in battle, and the fatality list is long. Detailed explanations of appendages severed with knives and saws and lasers and axes abound. We don't watch violent TV shows nor do we have any remotely weaponlike objects, except for a water gun, which we renamed a "water-blaster."

I brought up my concerns at a preschool parent coffee. The girls' parents were clueless, as their little princesses were already painting in oils, publishing short stories, and crafting. They *did* have guns—hot glue guns. The boys' parents, however, nodded in exhausted agreement. With seemingly no influence whatsoever, the boys' expertise in savagery is something they just . . . know. No one knows how they know, but they know—as if they receive secret messages from an alien informant through a frequency that only four-year-old males can hear. Like those dog whistles, inaudible to humans, but containing pertinent, violent information. We agreed it's part of their Neanderthalic DNA . . . unless they like to play a lot of dress-up and their favorite song is "Defying Gravity," in which case it's another kind of DNA. Cooper is among the rescuers, soldiers, explorers, hunters, gatherers—with just a smidge of potential serial killer.

"I'm gonna cut off his head and the blood is gonna spill out everywhere all over everything!"

Apparently that's all quite normal for his age. It was also normal for Jeffrey Dahmer.

Danny laughs. I pretend to.

Once, during a family trek up the trails of Griffith Park, recent rains had left the paths and porous bluffs in partial ruin. There were gullies and chasms and mounds of soft dirt lying at the foot of root-exposed summits. Danny and Cooper found long sticks and bludgeoned the vulnerable walls, watching them crumble onto the path like Zeus on a bender. "BAM!" "KAPOW!" "ZONK!"

I desperately tried to stifle my tongue, but after fifteen massacring minutes, I finally blurted out in a calm but pointed tone, "Cooper, do you know what *erosion* is? It's when weather breaks down the hill, gradually destroying it for us and everyone who wants to come here. Forever! You and Papa are not helping. You are doing more damage than a tsunami. Please stop tearing down the mountain."

Danny and Cooper rolled their eyes in unison as if to say, "Daddy spoils everything."

I tried to redirect his interest. "Cooper, come over here and look at this black beetle. Notice how, when I put a stick near him, he turns around and raises his bottom in defense. He is planning to either sting or spray his attacker. Isn't the insect world amazing?"

Cooper crouched down to get a closer look.

"Maybe he's just gonna fart."

I try to encourage creativity over destruction. I once used his Magna-Tiles, Lincoln Logs, Legos, and blocks to build a four-bedroom, three-bath dream house with gardens, a spacious kitchen with an island, a media room, a pool, a four-car garage, and a gift wrapping room, stocked with tiny rolls of real paper and ribbon. Eight seconds later, Cooper bombed it with a "meteorite" pillow followed by the proclamation "Everyone is dead."

This behavior is so far away from my boyhood that I cannot relate. However, if I make the stretch, in the same way that Cooper can fashion a gun out of anything—a stick, a piece of cardboard, an apple core, a used tissue, bent and formed with the epoxy of fresh snot—I can walk into any kitchen, be told there is nothing to eat, and find enough stuff to make a scrumptious four-course meal that could be photographed for *Food & Wine* magazine.

Cooper and I do share a love of fine cuisine and I would

define him as a miniature foodie. He has never met a calorie he didn't like. He partakes in all cultures: French, Latin, Indian, Moroccan, Thai, Chinese, Italian (not spaghetti and meatballs—osso bucco with gremolata). He doesn't like indigenous British food, but then no one does, not even the British. He loves sushi. Steamed mussels. Burrata with heirloom tomatoes. Pomegranate sorbet. He has a rare passion for raw oysters with just a touch of lemon. He loves tapas and is particularly fond of manchego-stuffed dates wrapped in rasher bacon. He has been known to request balsamic vinegar and can tell the difference between Himalayan and Mediterranean salt. This is due, in some part, to the policy in our house since he graduated from pulverized carrots and gooey oatmeal to real food: *Eat what I make or starve.*

Children's menus in all restaurants offer the same things: hot dogs, mac 'n' cheese, spaghetti, chicken nuggets, and grilled cheese. Kids seem conditioned and enabled to avoid real food. We don't order from children's menus and I have explained to him that chickens don't have nuggets. There is no part of a chicken that is considered a nugget. I tell him, "Don't ever order a meat that you can't trace to an original body part."

But sometimes I think it's all for naught. Truthfully, Cooper could eat potato chips and waffles at every meal and be happy. His palate is not so sophisticated as it is driven by his endomorphic *need* for food. While I strive to cultivate his appreciation for varied cookery, which is artfully served on white mini-ceramic plates that match our larger versions (never plastic for dinner), there are personality issues that make me fear he will one day drink Coors from a can.

For instance, he is quite fond of the words "fart" and "penis" and is obsessed with asking us to smell his feet. He thinks belching is the highest form of comedy.

I make up songs with inner rhymes:

Cooper is a super trouper,
A loop-the-looper, a sometime blooper,
Hula-hooper, secret snooper,
And he makes me laugh!

"Now your turn—make up a verse!" I say. Cooper responds with:

Cooper is a pooper and he has a stinky butt.

Boy, is he a boy. And Danny loves it. At heart, Danny is a boy too. They have their own language. They wrestle, smash toys against walls, smash themselves against walls, belch, fart, and hike. They are magical together, and it relieves my concerns around Cooper being an only child.

More than once, they have entered the front door after one of their "adventures" with the singsong announcement "Da-ad! Don't worry, we're oka-ay!" so that I am not shocked when I find them muddied and bloodied from that slip down the hill that was "a little steeper than we thought."

But with me, the apple seems so far from the tree. From a different orchard, even.

As my criteria for things in common widens with desperate necessity, I realize we do share an unnatural love for chocolate, but I don't think it's something we will look back on as a bond. If he didn't like chocolate, I would consider it an aberration much greater than his fascination with blood and gore, and I would send him to a psychologist. I don't trust people who don't like chocolate or people with very thin lips, which often go hand in hand.

And books—we both love books. He's a bit of a research freak, like me, and wants to know about everything, but with a particular interest in knights and volcanoes and dead skin cells.

And we do love playing out wild, ridiculous stories and characters in imaginative situations, although Cooper has most of them end up with casualties. Cooper "Tarantino" Harris-Jacobsen directs with meticulous, seemingly scripted detail and many retakes. "No, not that way, Daddy. Go out the door and come back in and die. Slower."

It's not that we don't have a good time. We laugh a lot. And I am astonished by his infinite mind and freaky memory and extensive vocabulary. He uses words like "exasperating," "transformation," "paleontologist," and "cinematographer." The word "awesome" was used only once, as it is strictly forbidden in our household. I explained, "The aurora borealis is awesome. The Grand Canyon is awesome. A gummy bear is not awesome. Getting a parking space near the entrance of Toys"R"Us is not awesome."

After a series of stinky-butt and amputation references, I am mollified by phrases like "It's spring so the jacarandas will be blooming" or, to our talking GPS, which we named Shirley, "Shirley, we're almost home so we are no longer in need of your assistance." And when he says "Please turn off your cell phones and unwrap any hard candies before the performance," I wipe a prideful tear from my eye.

Still, I look for any potential pea-to-pod-ness, and one night I thought I'd hit upon something.

In addition to an obsession with dinosaurs, Cooper loves animals of the current, Cenozoic period. He has lots of stuffed bears and tigers and alligators, which he animates with distinct personalities. And he loves dogs. He *loves* dogs. It occurred to me that if I shared my history with animals, it would give us another common passion.

At bedtime, after reading *The Courageous Captain America* for the seven thousandth time, after which I wanted to stab out my eyes with an ice pick, I said, "Cooper, you know Daddy loves animals like you do. I've had so many different pets. Would you like to hear about them?"

"Yes, Daddy. What kind of pets?"

I had him! I started at the beginning:

"When I was a baby, Nanaw and Bubba got a little white poodle for our family named Jimmy-John."

Cooper thought that name was very funny.

"Jimmy-John liked to have his tummy scratched."

"What happened to Jimmy-John?" Cooper asked.

I hadn't thought this part would come up. Jimmy-John was only with us for a year when he got a rare cancer and died.

"Jimmy-John had to leave us . . ." I stuttered, "but we got another dog right away. His name was Duke."

"Where did Jimmy-John go?" He wouldn't let up.

"I think to another family that needed him more. But then we got Duke! Duke was a mutt. A crazy brown big dog that"— *jumped the fence and never came back. Shit!*—

". . . visited us for a while and then went on an adventure."

I remembered we got two more dogs that we also named Duke, both of whom escaped and were never seen again. We just kept replacing the dogs but maintained the name so as to live in denial and not have to fix the fence. I skipped the extra Dukes. I didn't want him to think we might replace him with another Cooper.

There was also a psychotic beagle we named Columbo because he had a slightly wandering eye like Peter Falk. He yelped and yapped fourteen hours a day while constantly racing the length of the backyard fence. He couldn't jump over it, but his OCD pattern soon created a balding runway that became a dusty trench deep enough for him to crawl *under* it. My father fumed and steamed. "That goddamn fleabag's days are numbered." One day, Columbo was just gone. No explanation.

Next came a scroungy mutt called Furfy, whose name I really wanted to share with Cooper because it was so funny, but I didn't know how to explain that she bit the mailman and my father drove her to a wooded area twenty miles away and abandoned her there. Or that she somehow miraculously returned to us months later, exhausted and mangy and pregnant, and bore a litter of equally scroungy puppies, all of whom were suspiciously given away in one day, along with Furfy. I suspect my father actually crossed the Oklahoma border this time.

"Then we got Noni," I said, skipping to a dog I could talk about. Once again, Cooper laughed at the name.

Even though we'd had Jimmy-John and Duke and Duke and Duke and Columbo and Furfy, Noni was the first dog around long enough for me to develop a real relationship. She didn't jump fences or yelp or bite mailmen. Hers was the name I used when asked to create a stripper name, which is based on your favorite pet and the street you grew up on. I would be Noni Washington. Great stripper name. Or it could be a prostitute name, but it sounded more to me like a heroin-addicted lounge singer with sleepy eyes, who wore dulled lamé tunics with sporadic wiry threads popping up here and there, and seams stretched beneath armholes and at the hips. Noni Washington would kick off her shoes and sing songs of unrequited love and pain and torture and misery and despair. I could actually picture myself as some version of Noni Washington in the future. And it wasn't bad.

"Noni was a sweet dog," I said to Cooper, snuggling close to

him. "And she loved to chase cars and she slept in the garage . . ."
Damn it!

Once again, this wasn't going well. What decent person would let his dog chase cars? Noni had, indeed, been run over several times, suffering broken bones and hemorrhages and everything but death. As a result, she had a noticeable limp and always veered to the left. She had to aim right to go straight. I didn't want to portray myself or Cooper's grandparents as irresponsible, or as people who kept their dog in the freezing garage in the winter with a metal pan of ice-capped water. If Noni was thirsty, she had to lick her water like a Popsicle from November to March.

I changed gears.

"One time I found a baby bird that had fallen from its nest and broken its wing. And Nanaw and I mended the wing and made a nest in a shoe box and fed it oatmeal and worms until it was big and strong enough to fly away. When living things can't help themselves, we help them."

"What was the baby bird's name?" Cooper wanted to know, hoping it was also funny.

"Um, Harold. The bird's name was Harold." I paused for a giggle. "And every year Harold returned to our house and sang on our windowsill."

Now I was just making shit up.

I flashed on the number of creatures who hadn't made it. And the animal cemetery across from our house under a streetlight at the top of the woods. Dozens were buried there. Not only family pets—any creatures, critters, varmints, or strays that we found—birds, squirrels, rats, snakes, an opossum, an armadillo. Anything dead. If the area were ever excavated, one would think the Pol Pot of the animal kingdom had stormed Sand Springs.

I held a funeral for each animal and was obsessed with ceremony. There were songs and eulogies and robes draped from bedsheets. Tears were shed. Memories of beloved pets were shared and unfulfilled lives of strangers were mourned.

"We never knew his name. But this snail brought happiness to our neighborhood." I'd gathered other snails and placed them at graveside, and when they drew themselves into their shells, I imagined them weeping.

Flowers were laid and crosses were planted. I decided the armadillo was Jewish so I built a crude pine box, chanted the Mourners' Kaddish, tore my shirt, and sat shiva.

I fast-forwarded.

"When I was fifteen and I moved to my own apartment, I couldn't have a pet and I was so sad."

But I did have a sort-of animal mascot. I lived in a nondescript suburb of St. Louis off I-44 that had no road signs or any indication that it existed. You had to live there to know it was there. Driving home from work, I often missed the unmarked turnoff and had to backtrack, slower, to find the narrow gravel road that led to my tiny apartment. A couple of weeks into the summer, as luck would have it, a dog was run over on the shoulder of the highway at that exact intersection, and the carcass became my landmark: Dead dog—Turn right. The dog was never removed, and as it rotted in the equatorial heat, the corpse finally decayed into a discolored oily spot, which I still relied upon as my marker: Dead dog oily spot—Turn right. If not for the poor animal, I might have gotten lost, run out of gas, and wandered on foot along I-44, only to be hit by a car and become a discolored oily spot landmark for some other geographically challenged traveler. I was glad the dog was dead.

I skipped that story.

I also skipped the one about the winter I returned to Sand

Springs and, late one night, skidded on a sheet of ice in front of our house, unsuccessfully avoiding a cute little cottontail bunny. I sprang from my car, slipping and sliding, and found the poor thing panting its last pants, the steam of its body heat rolling up like a funeral pyre, all eerily lit by the glare of my headlights. I lifted the limp ball of sticky fur and placed it gently in the snow as if that would help. It sank into the drift and its crimson blood seeped into the ice like a carnival snow cone. The rabbit died almost instantly, probably hastened by the shock of freezing snow after being plowed over by my beat-up Gran Torino, which I knew only as "my red car."

The next day I made the mistake of sharing the saga with friends in journalism class, and Sheilah Nobles, standing stiffly in her calf-high, turd-colored leather boots and cowl-neck macramé sweater, leered at me through gigantic plastic-framed glasses that looked more like ski goggles than prescription eyewear. Then she murmured, "Rabbit Killer!" with a wicked, depraved snigger that grew into a howl and was soon joined by everyone in class, their mouths wide with laughter. Then the chanting began:

"Rabbit Killer!"

"Rabbit Killer!

"Rabbit Killer!"

Most of these kids were from families who regularly shot and ate rabbits, wore their pelts, and carried their sawed-off feet on key chains, but because it was sweet little sensitive me, I was now known as "Rabbit Killer" until I left home again, months later and for good, confident my work as a professional performer would supersede my reputation as a murderer. Still, when I received the token senior yearbook a year later, signed by all my classmates as a surprise, most of the personal notes started with "Dear Rabbit Killer . . ."

Cooper was losing patience for my silent, agonizing trip down animal lane and I knew I had to get to a good story quickly.

"And the *next* place I lived wouldn't let me have a dog or a cat and I *really* wanted a pet, so . . . I got a snake!"

"A snake?" Cooper asked with wonder. "Was it poisonous?"

"No. It was a baby boa constrictor and his name was Joey."

"Joey the snake! That's funny."

"All my pets' names are funny. That's part of why we have them. Because they make us laugh."

"Did he eat snake food?"

Joey ate little white mice. I bought two and put them in a cage right next to the snake aquarium. In retrospect, it was a horrible thing to do—giving the furry little creatures a 24/7, up-close-and-personal, wide-screen view of their ultimate nightmare. I might as well have placed a giant stuffed hawk on the other side. In the blink of an eye, the mice population rose to fourteen, probably nature's instinct to build an army in defense. Oddly, fourteen was the exact same number as was in the cast of the show I was doing. I named each mouse for a member of the troupe and every week, when I fed Joey, I would report, "Nancy is dead" or "Jeff was swallowed whole."

I obviously couldn't share this either.

"Yes, Cooper, I fed him snake food," I said instead.

I recalled when Joey seemed to slow down, which is hard to detect in a snake, and soon after died of pneumonia. Boa pneumonia. I'm sure it was my fault and that his aquarium must have been left in a draft or something. I thought creatures of the wild would surely be made of sturdier stuff. Like there aren't drafts in Nicaragua or Peru or tropical rain forests?

Desperate for a happy, uniting pet story to share with my son, suddenly I was questioning my love for, or at least my care of, all my pets. By the time I was sixteen years old, every creature

I'd been associated with had fled or died or been abandoned or fed to someone else. Noni still lived with my folks but she was getting old, and at any moment could be walking seemingly straight but veer left into the street and get hit by a pickup truck. My parents would probably just get another dog and name it Noni, hoping I wouldn't notice.

"Let's see, what other *great* pets did Daddy have? Hmmm . . . When I was in college and I shared a house with Uncle Bruce, we got a kitty," I said to Cooper with a cheerful cadence.

"Was it a boy kitty or a girl kitty?" he asked. "What was its name?"

"Her name was Frances," I said. "After Frances Farmer."

The actress who went insane. I couldn't know how tragically fitting the name would be. We had her only for a day. Frances was a scrawny muslin-colored rescue with a dire but curable case of worms. I wanted to save her, and we were given a box of pills and instructions for her healing. We confined her to the laundry room and made a small bed of fluffy towels with kibble and water in reach before taking off for Musical Theatre Workshop at UCLA. When we returned, several hours and a medley from *Guys and Dolls* later, we found the pitiful pussy extended in a gruesome and heartbreaking frozen pose, covered in diarrhea, clenching the corner of a towel in her teeth, countable ribs barely rising. She was deeply comatose. We rushed her to the emergency vet. The doctor took one look at her and said, "What in God's name did you do to this poor animal?!" We explained that we'd followed the prescription instructions. Frances was put on an IV but never regained consciousness.

She was the Sunny von Bülow of felines and there was no choice but to pull the plug.

"What did Frances do?" Cooper asked, eyes aglow.

"Not much," I said, and quickly moved on. "Then we got two more kitties. Their names were Shana and Esther."

"Shana and Esther are funny names." Cooper laughed.

"Shana means 'pretty' in Hebrew, which is practically Daddy's second language, and Shana was sooo pretty."

"What does Esther mean?" asked Cooper, wide-eyed and hanging on every word.

"Well, Esther is a Persian name from the Bible, who was originally called Hadassah. Hadassah means 'myrtle' in Hebrew, which is an equally funny but hideous name. The Book of Daniel has stories of Jews in exile being given names relating to Babylonian gods—for instance, Mordecai means 'servant of Marduk,' who was a Babylonian god. Esther came from the Proto-Semitic name 'Morning Star,' which comes from the Babylonian empire in 2000 BCE, not to be confused with the Chaldean empire or the Persian empire. Got it?"

"Got it," said Cooper. "Was Esther pretty too?"

"No, she was a dog. I mean she was a cat but she was a dog."

"Which one was she, Daddy? A cat or a dog?"

"She was a cat . . . but she was a dog. Not pretty. And since Shana was so beautiful, Esther sometimes got a little pouty and whiny and self-pitying."

I couldn't tell him the truth: that Esther had committed suicide. One day when Bruce and I were sunning on our foldout rubber-ribbed chaise lounges, lathed in baby oil—which is like a wish for cancer—in the driveway of our small house, known as Tara, Shana was strutting around with her nose and tail in the air, in applause of herself. Esther, on the other hand, was glowering in the garden, jealous, a woman biologically wronged. She emerged and crept solemnly to curbside. Bruce and I watched. She looked to the left. Then to the right. No traffic. She remained still and focused. In the distance, the rumble of a truck could be heard approaching. Esther sunk low onto her haunches, waited until the truck sped directly in front of Tara, and then bound into the street—a clear choice for all to see— me, Bruce, and, most important, Shana. The truck never slowed and Bruce and I ran to Esther's body, which spasmed, springing and bouncing off the asphalt like a demon-possessed wind-up toy, finally landing with a splat.

Shana took a few steps toward the street, at first, we thought, out of sisterly concern. But when she turned heel and trained her puckered ass in Esther's direction, we realized it had been for confirmation. She wanted to make sure the whiny hag was dead.

I couldn't share this part with Cooper either. Suicide stories are never good just before bedtime.

Shana remained with us until I woke one morning to find our landlady, Pat Chiang, leaning stiffly over my naked body with an accusatory Asian glare, accentuated by strict eyeliner lunging to her hairline like black knives. This wasn't the first time I'd been awakened in this fashion—she felt she could come and go as she pleased—but it was always a startling way to begin the day.

Her accent was thick as hoisin and her voice scraped the air like chopsticks on a chalkboard. "Ma h-h-h-husband saw white cat in your guys' window! *No cat allow!*" she shrieked. "That Helen Funk in a-pot-ment in back have cat, I say *no cat* too! That Helen Funk, she a dirty woman. She have account at Kentucky Flied Chicken . . ." Pat Chiang paused, then added, inquisitively, "Your guys have pot parties?"

We were forced to give Shana away and hoped the new family didn't have other pets with suicidal tendencies.

Cooper caught me choking back a tear but I put on a smile, continuing with a good story at last.

"My next pet was a dog. His name was Larry."

"Larry is my favorite name so far. I love Larry the dog," Cooper said with glee.

"I did too," I said, relieved. "I had him for fourteen years."

Larry was a dog's dog. A man's dog. Scruffy and ragged. He was an old soul. My friend Delia gave him to me, and when Larry and I saw each other on the street for the first time, we ran together like slow-motion lovers in the movies. "He was the best pal ever. And then Uncle Bruce wanted his own dog and so he got a Yorkie named Ethel."

"Like Lucy's friend?" Cooper asked. I was pleased at the reference.

"Well, she was named after Lucy's friend, but she wasn't much like her."

Ethel was not an old soul. She was an idiot. She was in constant frenetic motion and always underfoot. She ran haphazardly into walls and furniture. When anyone entered the room, she choked and threw up from the excitement and then dashed to pee on their shoes. Ultimately, she was the reason I left Tara. "This house isn't big enough for the both of us!" I declared to Bruce, though Ethel was only slightly larger than a field mouse.

On a weekend trip to Big Bear in a car stuffed with five people and Larry and Ethel, I knew it would be a horror show and begged Bruce to get some doggy downers for Ethel from the vet. The dosage was based on weight, and Ethel didn't fit into even the tiniest category, so I gave her half a pill. I swallowed the other half and another three or five. Somehow, I ended up with Ethel on my lap and an hour into the trip, I noticed she was strikingly still. I knew that Ethel was never motionless, even in sleep, her paws quivering as she dreamt of running into walls and furniture and vomiting and peeing on shoes. But now, draped across my lap, she was inanimate and her breathing was undetectable. When I lifted her tiny eyelids, I saw that her pupils had rolled back into her head. I didn't want to alarm Bruce so I asked that we pull over to let the dogs pee and get some water. When I opened the car door and nudged her, Ethel fell onto the pavement flat, facedown, with an indistinct thud, her legs splayed symmetrically like a miniature bearskin rug.

I didn't know what to do. In a moment of subdued panic, I took a sip from my drive-thru Diet Coke and the liquid caught in that hollow place in the back of my throat like an emotion. The bitch was going to die and I knew Bruce would blame me. She needed mouth-to-mouth resuscitation but I couldn't fathom how that was possible. Her entire head would fit in my mouth like a cupcake. I chewed on my straw and got an idea: straw-to-mouth resuscitation! I parted her black lips and found ample options to place the straw in the spaces where her teeth were missing—a result of too much Chinese food—specifically, General Tso's Chicken.

I tilted her head back and placed my pinky over her scaly, dry nostrils and blew several spurting breaths through the straw along with a few remaining drops of Diet Coke. Her golden chest rose. I located her sternum and slightly pumped it with my thumb, then alternated with the straw breathing. In a few moments, her eyes fluttered and her beady pupils returned to center. I'd saved her.

I'd almost killed her but I'd saved her.

This was yet another story I couldn't share with Cooper. But I knew the next one was surefire fun.

"A few years later, I got a pig! A Vietnamese potbellied pig named Lillian."

Cooper screamed with laughter. "A pig? A real pig? Was Larry the dog there?"

"Larry the dog was there. He didn't like Lillian very much, but he put up with her."

"Why didn't he like her?"

"Well," I said, "she was a pig. Lillian wasn't really a dog person. I mean a dog pig. She wasn't really a people pig either. She made rash decisions. She was bossy and pushy and she bit choreographers."

It was true. Lillian bit five people in two years and they were all choreographers. She could sniff them out like truffles and she hated them. Lillian possessed an almost human opinion about nearly everything and I thought perhaps she resented that her stout frame would never allow her to be a *real* dancer.

One day, I arrived home and the Nicaraguan housekeeper gravely and wordlessly gestured for me to follow her to the guesthouse in the backyard, where she lived. She showed me that Lillian had figured out how to open the sliding glass door, enter the kitchen, open the refrigerator, and raid its entire contents. Broken dishes and plastic wrap and empty Tupperware containers littered the floor. In the adjoining living room, Lillian lay at the base of a rough-hewn wooden altar that displayed a dozen burning Sacred Heart veladoras for the Virgin of Guadalupe. I wondered if she'd lit them herself. She was on her side, her bloated belly extending past the length of her stubby legs, which made it impossible for her to stand. Still, she appeared virtuous, saintly even, but for the sickly green foam that frothed from her snout and lips. The housekeeper pointed to a particularly ravaged, crumpled scrap of foil. "*De puerco,*" she spat with disdain. Lillian had eaten her own kind.

"What happened to Lillian the pig?" Cooper asked.

"Well, I realized she needed to be with other pigs, and people in show business were not enough. So I took her to a place called Hog Heaven, which was a special farm for potbellied pigs, and she was very happy."

She was very happy because the moment she arrived, she was eagerly surrounded by a small herd of male swine parading corkscrew pig penises that twirled and twisted like a power tool demonstration at Home Depot. She engaged in group sex within seconds. I waved, misty-eyed, calling, "I love you, Lillian!" She never looked back. She was, indeed, in hog heaven and the word "pork" had an entirely new meaning.

"What about Larry the dog?" Cooper questioned.

"After a long, long time, Larry got very tired and his body wore out. And then, when I met Papa and fell in love, we moved to New York and got Zach and Emma."

Zach and Emma were very old when Cooper was born. As a younger pooch, Zach was a handsome, brindle shepherd-Dane mix, and the best dog anyone could want, sweet and playful and solid. Emma joined us a year later when a neighbor, fiercely dedicated to rescuing basset hounds, asked if we could foster her for a day or two. She'd been in three different homes in the past month. Danny made me promise it would be temporary, but I knew the moment I saw her that she would be ours. She weighed sixty-five pounds and thought she was a lap dog, and we related. She arrived on Thanksgiving Day to a house full of friends, including Liza, who brought Lily, her cairn terrier. Lily knew Zach well and felt safe with him. Emma, on the other hand, was more volatile, and after dinner, when the turkey carcass was tossed into the trash bin, Emma positioned herself next to it and bared her teeth like a tigress, then attacked Lily by the scruff of the neck and shook her as if she were a stuffed dog toy.

I made the excuse that Emma was a victim of the system and never knew where her next meal was coming from.

I didn't tell Cooper any of this, of course. Near-death Thanksgiving tales aren't good before bedtime. But I did share that "Emma was fond of costumes." I never understood people who dressed their animals, but I explained to him that she actually begged to wear strands of pearls and fur capes and a particularly alluring jeweled and beaded headdress that made her look like a canine Cleopatra. He thought this was a scream.

"She was also quite famous on the Upper West Side," I went on. "She could sense when someone was feeling badly and she would walk up to them and press her forehead against their legs until they felt better." She was a healer. People we didn't even know would see her in the park, approach reverently, and say, "Why, you must be Emma," recognizing her miraculous aura. Or it might have had something to do with the Cleopatra headdress.

I skipped the story about the time I opened the dog food bin and dozens of mice sprang out and scuttled into floor cracks and secret passageways in bubonic plague numbers. I considered various traps and decided on the most humane—the kind in which the mouse is caught live to be released elsewhere. For three days I carried expensive little plastic containers of squeaking, claustrophobic mice to Riverside Park. But I couldn't keep up. Finally, I broke down and bought glue traps, which turned out to be teeny-weeny torture devices. The little furry rodents nearly tore their little brown bodies from their little gray legs in desperation. The instructions said to "simply discard," which meant tossing them in the garbage and leaving them to die of thirst and starvation. I knew I couldn't do that.

I picked up the first glue-padded mouse and slowly lowered it into the toilet bowl to drown the poor thing. Little bubbles pop-pop-popped to the surface and I sobbed, begging for forgiveness from the mouse, God, mankind, the entire animal kingdom. The next drowning was painful, but a little less so. The third was more brisk—just put it out of its misery. By the tenth mouse drowning, I was dunking the pests into the john like dipping ice-cream cones into sprinkles. It was an assembly line of death and I was the executioner who disengages for his own emotional survival as he indifferently releases the guillotine blade. My cold-blooded apathy grew into a sense of powerful purpose and I became drunk with it. I was the great protector and these disease-carrying vermin would contaminate my dog food no more! *So long, little fuckers!*

Cooper probably would have liked that story, but execution tales before bedtime are never a good idea either.

"A few years later we moved to Los Angeles and Zach and Emma loved it. They could run more and play more and it never snowed."

I flashed on the first winter Danny and I spent in Los Angeles. Zach could get anxious sometimes. His brow would furrow and he would look troubled. One night, what started as a worry became a full-fledged nervous breakdown. His eyes darted from corner to corner, ceiling to floor, and he began pacing in circles with a thin, inconsolable whine. Soon he was drooling dementedly and his big, sad eyes started rolling around, unfocused. It was three o'clock in the morning and he was clearly having a seizure. Danny and I rushed him to an emergency veterinarian. After a quick examination, the doctor took us aside and said, slowly, seriously, thoughtfully, "Is it possible . . . that your house . . . is haunted?"

"Beg pardon?"

"I asked if your house could be haunted?"

"This is your professional medical diagnosis?"

"Have you seen anything strange?" he continued. "Heard any peculiar sounds? Felt a frigid presence? Has anything mysteriously moved from one place to another? I'm just asking if it's possible."

"Is it possible," I responded, "that you have a degree and a license to practice medicine?"

We were, indeed, in California.

It turned out that a tree was scraping slightly against our Spanish roof tile in the wind and Zach had freaked out. We gave him sedatives until we could arrange for the tree to be trimmed to the tune of a thousand dollars.

We were a family and did what families do for each other. At the depths of my alcoholism and accompanying depression, when Danny was often traveling extensively, my obligation to feed and walk Zach and Emma was the sole reason I got out of bed. They were there when I was broken, and they were there through my frazzled recovery. Stalwart. Unconditional.

When Cooper was born, the dogs instinctively stepped up to a new level. "Cooper, did you know that when you were a baby, Zach would sleep outside your bedroom door to protect you at night? And Emma would lick your face and push her forehead against you if you were crying?"

"And then they went to heaven, right, Daddy?"

"Yes, Cooper. But they loved you very much."

After fourteen healthy years, our baby dogs declined, seemingly overnight. Their joints became arthritic and their eyesight and hearing deteriorated. Taking them for walks, carrying them up and down steep stairs, and hoisting them into the back of the SUV or SVU was painful for all of us. And maybe, with a new infant at the center of our world, they felt their task was done. Not in a sad way. In a complete one.

One night, Danny and I got down on the floor with Zach

and Emma and said, "You have been the bestest dogs ever. And we know you're hurting. Please feel free to leave the party at any time. We'll be okay."

Not long after, Emma had a really bad day that revealed a ruptured tumor we didn't know she had. And we had to put her down. Then, three months later, Zach had acute renal failure and left us as well.

I've always considered myself a true-blue pet person. But as I traversed the litany of my animal history in an effort to bond with my child, I realized that while it is brimming with love and compassion and laughter and tears, it's also riddled with abandonment, disease, murder, suicide, genocide, and the supernatural—very much like a day in the four-year-old, action-packed imagination of Cooper.

Perhaps my son and I aren't so far apart after all.

Danny and I believe that furry family is essential to a full life. We've promised Cooper a puppy of his own when he is five. He's already considering names: Stinky, Farthead . . .

Danny will probably be the one who takes Cooper and the pooch on hikes and have wrestling matches and play fetch, and I will cook organic dog food and schedule vaccinations and invent funny puppy stories. Cooper will learn from us both.

And the dog.

He'll learn the most from having the dog.

6. "I Feel, You Feel"

Rochelle Chambers had a spectacular voice. She flipped and fluted in a high, playful register like a violinist. A soulful, black violinist. At our high school talent shows, she sang with an ease that escaped me. I was sure she popped up in the morning and just opened her mouth and trilled like some celebratory bird. My singing was effortful and born of a need that surfaced in a cry.

Rochelle, who preferred to be called "Roach," for completely non-drug- and non-insect-related reasons, repeatedly asked me if I'd like to go to church with her some Sunday. It wasn't the kind of invitation that insinuated I needed to be saved. I sensed there was something more—a secret that Roach wanted to share. Finally, I said yes.

The following Sunday, only an hour after a devious sun had sneaked up, uninvited, I showered and stumbled into a pair of black slacks and a white, short-sleeved buttoned shirt. Roach arrived soon after, dressed in a rousing shade of mulberry that matched her mood. Her broadly ruched chiffon blouse both hugged and softened her generous bosom. She looked like she was going to a party.

I looked like I was going door to door to sell Bibles.

We drove down the hill, past middle-class, neatly painted homes with closely mowed, dew-sprinkled lawns and impatiens-lined walkways, and then farther and farther, through the poorer section of Sand Springs: run-down houses and hollow carcasses of cars peering through weeds that shot up between axles and rusted hoods in unwatered yards. Chipped ceramic mules and gnomes aimlessly guarding cracked puzzle-piece front walks. Pebble-covered tar shingles collected upright, like playing cards, in distended rain gutters.

We drove on, crossing the Sand Springs railway track and into an area I'd only heard about. Colored Town. It was a ten-square-block ghetto with no room for expansion—row after row of clapboard houses, barely more than shacks, with narrow, dry clay yards and no trees.

At the end of the road, a wooded area emerged, centered by a small white, plain brick church. In great contrast, parishioners buzzed around the entrance, dressed for show, especially the ladies: in electric tangerine and turquoise and cranberry, stripes and polka dots and presumptuous, architectural hats with matching shoes and gloves, like sapphires sprinkled among dust. Roach introduced me to her family and neighbors and I was greeted with grace.

Once inside, she left me in a worn pew and joined the choir behind the pulpit. And then the spirited rhythm of a small band started—no single, solemn organ here—and the congregation rose and sang:

Ain't gonna let nobody turn me roun',
Turn me roun',
Ain't gonna let nobody turn me roun'—
I'm gonna wait until my change comes!

The sound had nothing to do with any church I'd ever attended. There was no attempt to create a pleasing, ethereal, homogenous blend. *Real people* were singing without apology.

Don't let nobody turn you roun',
Turn you roun',
Don't let nobody turn you roun'—
Wait until your change comes!

It was loud and untamed, a united glorious noise built on vastly individual voices, each with its own story, celebration, and pain. I sang along in my head but dared not join in.

I promised the Lord that I would hold out,
Hold out, hold out!
I promised the Lord that I would hold out—
Wait until my change comes!

A nearly carnal joy rose slow and hot in the back of my throat, swelling until I could no longer contain it, and I opened my mouth and let it pour from me.

I say I'm gonna hold out!
Hold out,
I say that I'm gonna hold out!
I'm gonna wait 'til my change comes!

Until now, the closest thing I'd experienced to this kind of liberation was alone in my room, singing along with Aretha. Except. Except—this was about more than a "chain of fools" or "respect when you get home." The people in this black church seemed to have a direct connection to a happy God, who surely danced, and an unbridled belief that change would come and suffering would end through faith and action.

It had only been thirteen years since the Civil Rights Act had been signed. It was all still hot and messy and red and personal, like a fresh wound, purposely inflicted. Things were changing, indeed, and I was standing in the middle of it. I didn't know the songs, but the choruses were simple and easily memorized, and I lifted my voice and sang along as if I'd known them since before forever. I felt that perhaps I had.

An old woman next to me took notice of my full-throated enthusiasm and seemed to know everything about me in a single moment. She was ancient and ageless and beautiful— her crinkled face read like a history map, and her eyes, which had surely witnessed more than they should have, glimmered beneath the ghost-colored haze of cataracts. She was standing in the middle of even more change than I. And now, a flush-cheeked white boy was singing gospel at the top of his lungs, right by her side, in *her* church. She grabbed my hand with her crocheted glove, wrinkled her nose with approval, and shouted a "Hallelujah!"

Roach smiled at me from the choir. She'd shared her secret. She had let me in.

Even though I was no more black than I was Jewish, I had found yet another tribe that seemed more natural to me than my own.

And it changed the way I heard music and sang from that day forward.

Rochelle Chambers released something primal inside that set me on a trajectory, for the next several years, of leaving home and defining myself through a fusion of theme parks, rep companies, college musicals, black-box revues, and dumpy nightclubs. And then, after a few performances on a national television show, my anonymity gratefully expired and I was suddenly thrust into the spotlight I had yearned for.

In one moment, I was recognized everywhere, invited to everything, and hobnobbed with everyone. America embraced the little white boy with a big soulful voice dressed in oversize thrift-store tails and Converse high-top tennis shoes. All of the oddities and eccentricities that once separated me from others had become the very qualities that made me original and special.

To my ever-growing astonishment, I was even accepted by many of the legends I had grown up idolizing: I lunched with Lucille Ball! I shared a dressing room with Al Green and improvised with him! I discussed playwriting backstage with Lily Tomlin and Jane Wagner! I was just about adopted by Liza Minnelli and Chita Rivera! I was given song ideas from Bette Midler! I had breakfast with Michael Jackson and Rosa Parks—at the same time! I had dinners with Roddy McDowall and his friends, friends like Bette Davis, George Axelrod, and Lee Remick! I was summoned to the stage at a Patti LaBelle concert and we sang together! I chain-smoked with Elizabeth Taylor! I got a phone call from Stevie Wonder at three o'clock in the morning. He asked me to come to his house to hear a song he'd just written . . . for *me*.

"What?! Really? When?" I asked, suddenly fully awake.

"Now," he replied.

Three in the morning, three in the afternoon . . . it was all the same to him.

And to sing an original song with Stevie . . . it was all the same to me too.

I didn't have much interest in most of my contemporaries and most of them had little interest in me. But I got it where it counted. Backstage, while shooting a television special, Sammy Davis Jr. put his arm around me and said, "You're one of us." Those were the sweetest words I'd ever heard, the kind of old-fashioned showbiz validation every old-fashioned stagestruck kid longs for.

Another time, at a charity event, Gregory Peck walked across a ballroom to my table to tell me he was a fan. How could Gregory "Atticus Finch" Peck be a fan of mine?

It was all overwhelming. Where would it end? Or could it somehow go on forever?

In the middle of it all, Motown, my record company, called to say that a prominent promoter had asked me to open for the great Aretha Franklin in Cleveland. I was told Aretha had specifically made the request and couldn't wait to work with me. I couldn't believe she even knew my name much less asked if I would do a show with her! It surely couldn't get better than this. She was one of my top five idols. Tom Waits was another and I knew he'd never ask me to open for him. The other three were dead.

I'd grown up singing along with Aretha and had learned to place my top notes without straining my voice by mimicking her. Two years prior, when visiting home, my father and I were in the car together and I blasted the radio, belting out "It's My Turn" with Aretha. My father said, "You're a boy. How come you want to sing in the same octave as a woman?"

"Because I can," I replied, and went for the key change.

Listening to Aretha had taught me *how* to sing. Going to church with Rochelle had taught me *why*. The combination of the two had transformed me.

The offer was to do two shows on the same night—8:00 p.m. and 11:00 p.m. I would need to have thirty minutes of music specifically charted at my own expense for Aretha's twenty-piece band. The fee was low, not even enough to cover my orchestration expenses, but I didn't care. I would use the charts again and it was for a concert with *Aretha Franklin*! I was offered one airfare and a single hotel accommodation, so I would be traveling alone with no management on hand, nor my own pianist. But Aretha's conductor was H. B. Barnum and a showbiz veteran, famous in his own right, so I was covered.

Honestly, I would have sung with a kazoo and peddled myself on a tricycle to do this gig.

I arrived in Cleveland the night before the shows and looked for the driver with the "Sam Harris" sign who was to meet me at the airport gate. No one there. I found a pay phone and called the promoter, Jim Welcome, at the hotel but there was no answer. No big deal. A little mix-up. I got my suitcase and box of orchestrations and went outside to find a taxi. I knew I'd be reimbursed later.

It was the dead of winter. As I walked out of the airport, I was accosted by a cruel wind that slapped my face like a jealous lover. My eyes teared and I feared they would freeze over and I would be blinded forever. Yes, I had fantasized about being blind, but not this way—not in Cleveland, at an airport. I ran to the taxi line in my thin coat, dragging my bag and box behind me, and an airport worker in a parka and a ski mask recognized me and threw me in a cab right away.

As we drove into the downtown area, I realized it was only seven o'clock and there was no one on the street. No one. The driver said there was an advisory to stay inside. It was below zero.

"You mean below freezing," I corrected him.

"No. Below zero. Winds are fifty miles an hour off the lake. Add in the windchill factor and it's about twenty below."

I didn't know this kind of cold was possible outside of

77

Antarctica, where people wore body-length flannel underwear and beaver furs insulated with seal blubber.

I arrived at the hotel and checked in. No credit card had been put down for my room, so again I called the promoter, Jim Welcome, and again there was no answer. I was tired and cold and knew I needed to focus on my voice and health, so I put down my own credit card, confident it would be corrected before checkout, and went to my room to thaw and steam and drink tea. My rehearsal was set for 2:00 the next day and I would get a solid night's sleep and be prepared.

The following morning I woke with an excitement that couldn't be dulled by the spiritless, chalky sky. Outside my window, gusts of cutting snow whipped past, parallel to the desolate streets of downtown Cleveland. But it might as well have been spring.

The hotel was connected to the theater so I didn't have to brave the icy tempest and chance frostbite to get there. At 1:50 I grabbed my box of charts and was nearly out the door when the phone rang. It was Jim Welcome at last! He said rehearsal had been pushed to 3:00. Fine. I told him about the missing-driver-credit-card-hotel misunderstanding and he promised he would take care of it later.

At 2:45 he called again to say rehearsal had been pushed to 3:30.

I reminded him that I had all new charts that had never been played and we might have to make corrections. He said there would be plenty of time.

He called again a half hour later. Rehearsal would be at 4:00.

At 3:55 I waited for the phone to ring. It didn't, so I galloped through the hotel lobby and sprang to the theater, ready to sing and hang out with my new best friend, Aretha. I was already imagining harmonies for the possible duets we would sing.

The theater was empty.

There was not a musician, crew member, house manager, or single soul to be found. I walked to the stage for stability, knowing if I stood on the boards and looked out at the empty seats, I would assemble a sense of purpose.

At around 4:30, musicians began to amble to the stage with their instruments and a sound technician began to set up mics. At 5:00, H. B. Barnum arrived and was warm and sure and shook my hand enthusiastically. His assistant took the box of music books designated for each instrument and distributed them as the players unpacked and warmed up. Better late than never.

I was raring to go but alone in any sense of urgency. At 5:30 I asked when we could begin. Barnum said, "Oh, we need to do Aretha's music first."

"But she's not here," I replied.

"She will be. Afraid of planes, you know. Drives everywhere, and with the ice and snow . . ."

"Can't we start my rehearsal and stop when she gets here?"

"Better to keep it clean."

Curtain was at 8:00 and I knew they'd be opening the house at 7:30, or more likely at 7:00 with this kind of weather. But I was new and just a kid and this was a legend and her conductor, so I politely took a seat in the house and waited. The musicians waited. Barnum waited.

We all waited.

A little after 6:00, the front of house door burst open and the Queen of Soul entered in a golden floor-length fur coat, a matching Russian hat, and a gigantic pair of sunglasses that I swear were the same ones she wore on the cover of her *Yeah!!!* record.

She was accompanied by an absolutely enormous man who,

despite the cold he'd just escaped, was sweating profusely. He was also the whitest black man I'd ever seen—whiter even than me. He spotted me and lumbered in my direction.

"I'm Jim Welcome . . . Welcome."

"Nice to meet you," I said, not able to shake my gaze from Aretha, who was sauntering down the aisle toward us, puffing on a cigarette and flinging her ashes on the carpeted floor. She seemed tired. And fat. Very tired and very fat. But I knew the coat added at least a hundred pounds and I was in awe.

As she was about to pass us, Jim gently took her arm and said, "This is Sam Harris." All of my angst evaporated as I clutched her hand.

"Miss Franklin, this is an honor. I am such a big fan and I can't believe I'm meeting you and get to open for you. Thank you for asking me."

She lifted her sunglasses and peered at me with dull eyes and flatly said, "You sing like a black woman."

I presumed it was a compliment and laughed, but her expression remained frozen. She took a long draw from her cigarette and yawned, exhaling a thick, slow-moving cloud of smoke into my face. For the first time in my life, I wanted to smell like someone's smoke. It was Aretha smoke. I decided right then that I would not shower before the show, or perhaps ever again. I'd been anointed.

"H. B.!" she yelled as she walked past me and to the stage. "I want to start with the overture. I need to practice my entrance."

The band pulled out the chart and the music started. I sat in the second row and I could see Aretha waiting just offstage right in the wings. She lit another cigarette. The overture was a medley of her incredible history of hits: "Chain of Fools," "Do Right Woman, Do Right Man" "Ain't No Way," "Think," "Natural Woman," "Spanish Harlem," "Respect"—it went on and on—electrifying and intimidating. And long. I knew it had to end at some point but it kept going for what I guessed was ten minutes. Enough time for Aretha to smoke two more cigarettes and finish off a bag of donuts.

Finally, a series of Vegasy horn riffs built and built, changing keys for what surely would lead to the grandest entrance of all time. "Ladies and gentlemen—the Queen of Soul!" boomed over the system. Aretha crushed her cigarette with a twisted stomp, tossed her hat into the air behind her, and let her fur fall to the floor as she walked from the wings, grabbing the mic from a stagehand who'd been standing the entire time, holding it until she was ready.

Aretha arrived center stage and looked out to the empty theater and said, "I feel. You feel. The important thing is we feel together," as her opening line. The band launched into the iconic introduction to "Respect" but she waved for them to stop. "I want to do that again."

"From your entrance?" Barnum asked.

"From the top," she answered.

They played the overture again. All ten minutes.

"I feel. You feel. The important thing is we feel together . . . Wait a minute. I need to do that one more time."

I shifted in my seat, appearing composed and unconcerned, all the while thinking, *You're kidding, right? Okay, you're Aretha Franklin, the greatest voice in the world, but seriously??!* It was nearly 7:00, the doors were supposed to open in half an hour, and she'd not rehearsed a single song. More important, neither had I. She ran the overture two more times, always followed by "I feel. You feel. The important thing is we feel together."

I was feeling a lot.

Finally, Aretha moved on to "Respect" and in an instant, I was once again transported. I couldn't help but revere her. She was singing to an audience of one. Me. And in a little while, I would sing to her.

Her voice was coarse and smoke-worn. She gave nothing. There was no sense of performance, but it was just a sound check, and I knew she was saving it for the real thing. On her darkest day, Aretha would still be better than anyone else. After the one song, she announced she'd had enough and told Barnum the band could rehearse the rest without her. Jim Welcome hoisted her fur onto her shoulders, and they disappeared behind a veil of smoke before you could say "Rescue Me."

For the next forty-five minutes the band played through the Franklin songbook with a backup singer doing Aretha's part. I looked at my watch every seven seconds. Jim Welcome returned and announced from the back of the house that it was nearly 8:30 and he had to open the doors. People had been dangerously waiting in the freezing cold for hours.

I ran to him and asked about my songs. My rehearsal. My orchestrations. He said there was no time and the band would have to read my charts cold. I was young and vulnerable but not stupid. "There is no way I am going onstage without rehearsing new charts and no one who knows my music," I bargained. "They don't even know tempos!"

Suddenly Jim Welcome began to panic, nervously shaking. In an instant, sweat poured off him as if his skin were a thousand-prick sprinkler hose turned on at full pressure. What little color he possessed drained from his shiny head and dripping face, like some sort of morphing, melanin-free superhero trick.

"You have to go on!" he begged. "More than half the tickets sold are for you!"

"Yeah, right," I countered.

"It's true. It's why we chose you. You're fresh, man. The people want to see *you*!"

I didn't know what to believe. I had no one to step in. No one to stand up for me or insist on rehearsal or see the impending doom that had begun when the driver had failed to pick me up at the airport. All of this was new to me—the fame, the demand—all of which I lapped up hungrily. But I didn't yet understand the power or need for self-preservation that comes with the fame and demand. At the bottom of it all, I didn't want to disappoint the people who were there to see me. Or even just there. An audience in a theater expecting a show.

"Okay," I said. "Here's what's going to happen."

Jim Welcome's eyes popped in desperation, knowing he was on the verge of a deal.

"I will go on—*for fifteen minutes.* I'll make up a story about how my music was lost by the airline and I will sing three songs, a cappella, and make the best of it."

Jim Welcome wept. He hugged me with his three-hundred-pound clammy, colorless body and told me I was a true star.

The capacity crowd had been standing in subzero Siberian winds for much too long. Amputations of frostbitten digits would surely be necessary. I ran backstage as the house was opened and I heard the wretched mob charge into the warm theater. I suddenly remembered that I was still in my rehearsal clothes and had not brought show clothes from the hotel. I rushed back to my room and returned with only minutes to spare.

Once in my dressing room, I breathed deeply and planned my strategy. Under normal circumstances I would have had time to get nervous, worrying about my voice cracking, the dry radiator heat, Aretha's impression of me, the band, the sound, the lighting . . . just failing. But there was no time to do anything but dress for battle and plunge into the front lines.

I could hear the audience on the dressing room monitor. It wasn't the sound of excitement and anticipation. It was the sound of anger. Grumbling, justifiably hostile people whom I would momentarily face to sing a few songs with no band—a meager payoff for the rabble. A riot could break out and I would be the first casualty.

Jim Welcome knocked on my dressing room door. It was time. I walked down the hall silently as if on my way to the gallows. We arrived at the wings and I was handed a microphone. A voice came over the loudspeaker. There was no welcome, no apology, no transition, no explanation or attempt to unite the crowd or create focus. Just: "Ladies and gentlemen—Sam Harris."

A little voice popped into my head that said, *What the hell do you think you're doing? Who the hell do you think you are? . . .* And then I remembered. I marched onto the stage to the accompaniment of nothing, smiled broadly, and yelled, "Pretty pissed off, huh?!"

The mostly African-American crowd answered with a laugh. "I know I would be!" I continued. "Are you numb? Can you feel your feet?" They cheered and howled and stomped on the floor like they were at a national election convention. We were bonded.

"Do you see a band here? Do you even see a piano player? My charts got lost on the plane and I got no music! They made you wait outside in the freezing cold and for what? A little white guy with no music! Don't you worry, the Queen of Soul will be out here soon with a band and backup singers and everything."

"We love you, Sam!" came a voice from the mezzanine.

"Sing 'Over the Rainbow'!"

The crowd reignited in the request.

"You want me to sing?" I hollered. "With no music? You got it! I will do anything you want. I'll sing, dance, tell jokes, make cookies. Hot chocolate. Hot toddies. I am your servant."

I sat on the edge of the stage with my legs crossed, Indian style.

I sang "God Bless the Child."

I sang "I Am Changing."

I sang "Over the Rainbow."

With my voice the only sound, the great hall became an intimate room. Just me and a spotlight and them. It was pin-drop quiet during each song and then an eruption at the end. They were mine and I was theirs. And, shockingly, I was having an amazing time.

After "Rainbow," I rose and took a bow as the audience rushed down the aisles, crowding the thrust of the stage to reach up toward me. I ran the distance of the proscenium, touching as many as I could.

As I headed stage right to make my exit, I saw the gigantic Jim Welcome sweating more than ever, practically translucent. He was giving me the old showbiz signal to *stretch* and was mumbling something I couldn't make out. I strained my eyes to read his lips: "She-e-e-e's No-o-o-o-t He-e-e-e-re. We-e-e Do-o-o-o-n't Kno-o-o-o-w Whe-e-e-e-re Are-e-e-e-tha I-i-i-is!"

You're fucking kidding me.

I knew that returning to the stage after my save-the-day triumph could only go downhill from there. I should have walked off. I should have said that it wasn't my problem. I'd fulfilled my duty beyond-beyond-beyond the call. But something deep inside me, burdened and inspired by my "the show must go on" credo, coerced me to return to the fray and do something, anything, until they could locate the diva and get her onstage. I circled back to the boards, but I knew that I couldn't make the audience think it was my choice.

"They're not ready yet," I said, convincing them the delay was about production and not Aretha, to maintain her innocence. I plopped back down onto the edge of the stage and said, "Any requests?"

"A Change Is Gonna Come!"

It was my pleasure.

I sang a song from my upcoming album, "I've Heard It All Before."

"Anything else? What do you want me to sing?"

"The phone book! You could sing the phone book!"

"Somebody bring me a phone book!" I joked.

A stagehand came out from the wings with a phone book, getting a big laugh from the audience and me. Why not? I was relieved to have a gimmick, a bit, something to take up some time.

I flipped to the businesses that began with *A*. I sang and riffed, musically commenting on each of them. "A-1 Auto Service" had a zippy jingle and "All Saints Funeral Home" had a wailing, soulful mourning vibe. The crowd hollered with laughter and then applauded wildly when I hit a long high note. Just as I got to "Cuyahoga Community College" I spotted Jim Welcome's enormous soaking arms flailing in the wings. He was signaling for me to *wrap it up*. Aretha was standing next to him, smoking in every way, and looking impatient, as if I'd kept her waiting.

I closed the phone book and said, "They're ready now. I have had the best time with you tonight. It was scary to come out here so late, with no music, but this has been one of the greatest experiences I've ever had onstage. Thank you."

I stood up and crossed to the down-center spot and resang the tag of my song: *"If happy little bluebirds fly . . . beyond the rainbow . . . Why, oh, why can't I?"*

I bowed and walked off the stage as the crowd roared. I passed Aretha and said, "They're all yours—Go get 'em!" I was still enamored but digging deep to remain respectful, because what I really wanted to say was "Top that, bitch!" However, I suspected that she would, indeed, "top that," and probably wipe the floor with me.

Aretha Franklin was about to walk onstage and erase any memory of my existence.

Her overture began. I took a seat just inside the wings, two feet behind Miss Franklin, so I could study her every move. She puffed and shifted back and forth, waiting for her entrance. I caught my breath, still tingling from the oddest episode of my career. I took the moment in.

And then I took her in.

Aretha Franklin, who was all of 250 pounds, was wearing a pinkish tube minidress that was tassled from her ginormous, hazardous breasts to her vast upper thighs. No one in her court had told her this was a bad choice and that she looked like a blood sausage stuffed into a 1920s flapper Halloween costume. I remembered the floor-length fur she'd worn earlier and thought that would have been a better option. But it probably would have been equally wrong to flaunt a luxuriously warm mink at an audience who'd been standing in the hypothermic, polar chill for untold hours.

As her overture built to its endless finish, the announcer proclaimed: "Ladies and gentlemen—the Queen of Soul!" Aretha stubbed out her cigarette, pushed up her breasts, grabbed the mic, walked onto the stage, and unemotionally said, "I feel. You feel. The important thing is we feel together."

And then the audience booed.

They booed Aretha Franklin.

She acted like she didn't hear it. The band started "Respect" and she went on as if it were any other night. Maybe it was. But I was sure that once that voice started wailing "*What you want, baby, I got it,*" all would be forgiven. Then, just as she was about to start the first verse, Aretha waved to the band.

"Stop!! Stop!" she said, shaking her head.

Barnum signaled a cutoff and the band petered out in a slow, confused melt of noise. This was it. She was going to face the elephant in the room. The big, pink tasseled elephant.

Then she yelled out, "I don't want to sing that song. I want to sing 'You Are the Sunshine of My Life'!"

Barnum stood, stunned.

"You heard me!" she reinforced, and the band rifled through their folders to find the music while Aretha blithely took a drink of water. The grumbling, confused, occasionally shouting crowd went unacknowledged. Barnum raised his hands and an upbeat introduction began to a song that, to my knowledge, Aretha had never recorded or even sung.

The boos started up again.

And a solid third of the audience got up and walked out, shouting at her up the aisles. Black audiences are the best, most dedicated audiences in the world. They are also the most honest. And they knew. They somehow knew everything. And they were not having it. They were looking for a little R-E-S-P-E-C-T.

Aretha cut her show down to a scant half hour, about the same amount of time I had been on. She sang four or five of her big hits, but the overture was the only true acknowledgment of her extraordinary contribution to the American pop scene. When she finished, the mayor came onstage and awarded her the key to the city. I was called out for a final bow and saw that fewer than half the audience remained. The mayor, Aretha, and I walked off the stage together with nary a word. Then I told her I thought she was the greatest singer ever and she mumbled a simple "Thank you." As we parted to our respective dressing rooms, the next frozen audience was being hustled into the theater while the previous one exited, and I heard Jim Welcome politely ask Aretha if she could please stay at the theater. We'd be going up as soon as possible.

For the second show, I repeated my story about the airline losing my charts and decided to sing "Rainbow" as my opener, thinking the audience would be more apt to accept uncharted (literally) a cappella territory if I gave them something they wanted first. As I was about to begin, the piano player, drummer, and bass player poked their heads from the wings and offered to play. They knew what I'd been through and I was honored to have their support. They were consummate, magnificent, following my every move.

Halfway through the song, I glimpsed over at the wings and saw my idol standing, staring, one hand holding a cigarette, the other firmly on her tasseled hip. This was a major moment for me and I knew it. I was singing for Aretha Franklin. I smiled at her like a smitten schoolboy.

She didn't smile back.

I revved up for the big finish and milked, or rather *drenched*, the last eight bars for every bit of heart I could muster. At the end of the last note, which I held for about as long as Aretha's overture, I gestured the cutoff and threw my arms out and my head back. The audience gave even more to me than I had given them. Yes, I was showing off. I was showing off for Aretha Franklin, for the incredibly patient crowd, and for me. I was showing off to prove that I could handle anything, and that as long as I was honest onstage, it would all be okay.

I looked to the wings for Aretha's reaction in time to see her squash her cigarette under her kitten heel, gesture angrily to Jim Welcome, and turn away.

Her back glared at me.

I took a bow and was about to go into my next songs when

I got the big *wrap it up* heave-ho signal from Jim Welcome. It was clear she wanted me off. Now!

I shouted my good-byes and left the stage. Barnum began her overture. I didn't feel comfortable standing in the wings with Aretha, so I went to my dressing room, shaking and a bit winded.

She hated me.

The dressing room monitor blared her introduction: "Ladies and gentlemen—the Queen of Soul!"

"I feel. You feel. The important thing is we feel together."

The next morning I was assured by the front desk that the airport was open and traffic was moving in spite of the ice storm from the night before. I dashed to the lobby early to meet my driver. He never came. I called Jim Welcome's room from the reception desk. After twenty or so rings came the fumbling of a pickup and a barely audible, groggy "Ehh?"

"It's Sam Harris. My car isn't here and I'm going to miss my flight."

He gently replaced the phone in its cradle, perhaps hoping I wouldn't know he'd answered. I called back and after another ten or so rings, I heard him pick up and clumsily lay the phone down on a table.

I convinced the front desk to give me his room number and I rushed to his door. I knocked! I banged! I yelled, "I know you're in there!! Answer the goddamn door and get me a car!"

I could hear him sweating.

He never answered the door.

I raced back to the front desk and was told there were no taxis waiting and it would take a while to get one. There was no way I was going to spend another minute in this fucking place. I persuaded the hotel manager to let a bellboy go off duty and drive me in his own car. We had to wait for what seemed like hours for the bellboy's broken-down Toyota to warm up while he moved piles of dirty laundry from the passenger seat. I thought perhaps this was his home. Not even the sense-numbing cold could block out the stench of pot smoke ingrained in every pore of the vehicle, and I wondered if he was high at that very moment. More so, I wished I was. The bellboy maneuvered the icy freeway like an Olympic luge racer and deposited me at the airport in the nick of time.

The newspaper carried a large photo of Aretha getting the key to the city from the mayor with an article that mentioned "the show was opened by *Star Search* champion Sam Harris." There was no account of what had happened and I could hardly believe it myself. But 3,500 Clevelanders had been there and I found solace in their anonymous witness.

Back in Los Angeles, I informed my management and record company that I would never again travel anywhere without someone at my side.

I was never paid for the concert, much less reimbursed for my hotel and taxi costs. I'd also thrown in a crisp fifty for the impromptu pothead bellboy shuttle. But the money was nothing compared to the loss of my hero, my idol, my innocence.

I didn't want that to be the ending to my Aretha story.

One night, a couple of weeks later, I uncorked a bottle of wine and dimmed the lights and pulled out all of my old vinyl Aretha records and stacked them in front of me. I sat on the floor next to the turntable and played them, one by one, every song she ever recorded. And occasionally, I sang along.

Me and Aretha singing together.

7. Liver

I have a new fancy washer and dryer. They are front-loading, bacteria-killing, über-environmentally efficient, space-age works of uncommon art.

They have hundreds of options for every possible fabric in the world. You could wash and dry the Shroud of Turin in these things and it would be guaranteed safe. There are knobs and buttons and digital amber lights and delightful little bell tones that ping with each selection, like the sound of an idea, assuring that you have made a good and apparently very happy choice. They even have a "16-Hour Fresh Hold Option with Dynamic Venting Technology." I don't know what that is, but it is a good and happy choice.

When dirty clothes are placed in the washer, the door seals shut like a vault—no "Oops, I found another pair of underwear to toss in." All decisions are final. There is serious work to be done and it begins with a sequence of scientific evaluations. The washer drum tumbles the clothes for a moment. Then back the other way. Then it weighs the contents to determine the exact, proper length of each upcoming cycle for this exact, particular collection of garments. Then it stops again and thinks. You can feel it thinking because it's doing nothing, so it must be thinking. I imagine it analyzing the fabrics: cotton, wool, silk, Lycra, Lurex, nylon, rayon, velvet, mockado, crinoline, angora, chiffon, bombazine, spandex, chambray, crepe, duvetyn, rumchunder, tweed, twill, vicuña, grass, hemp, jute. Hundreds of options. I have no rumchunder and wouldn't be caught dead in bombazine but I appreciate the technology.

After a few empirical, apprehensive moments, the washer has specified the most minuscule amount of water necessary to wash the clothes and save the planet at the same time. It spritzes a fine mist so as not to surprise or shock the clothes. Then it tumbles again. Then back the other way. Then it thinks again. Then it spritzes with a little more pressure. Then a sudden brisk spit. After half an hour of thinking and spritzing and spitting, the silent drum begins to turn with more frequency, slowly at first, so as not to make the clothes dizzy, and then it commits to actual water, or at least the *sound* of water, because you don't actually ever *see* water and it could be another audio accessory like the idea pinging. But you can be sure that whatever water added has been heated or cooled to the exact, perfect temperature for this particular collection of these particular fabrics. It is so environmentally conscious that it can wash a large load of jeans with what appears to be little more than a tablespoon of water. Perfect and perfectly utilized water. As the washer turns, glowing lights fade up from within so that the proud owner can watch the entire hour-long exhibition from start to finish.

I have. With popcorn.

At the end of the final spin cycle, it plays a happy, larkish eight-bar song. It is a merry tune, which brings to mind images of Pan cavorting down a path in mountain wilds and glens, framed by moss-mounded chubby rocks and sprigs of violets and daisies as he toots his fluted pipes. He is followed by cheery cottontail bunnies and big-eyed frogs who smile and nod in rhythm. The internal lights dim. Act One is over.

The dryer is equally theatrical and scientific. Lots of important decisions are made. And it is so quiet that if you didn't actually see the clothes occasionally plopping around between thoughts, you wouldn't know it was on. Until the end, that is, when it offers its own ducky ditty in the same key as the washer. Once, in a miraculous moment of two-load timing, the washing cycle ended just before the drying cycle was completed. It was practically a concert and I nearly applauded.

If this were not enough, the design of the machines is stunningly architectural. So much so that I considered putting the washer and dryer in the dining room just to show them off and also use them as a buffet. I imagined warm napkins plucked from tableside. It seemed shameful to hide these beauties away in a bedroom closet, but I knew I would give tours and demonstrations, inviting friends to come for dinner and bring their dirty laundry.

There is one downside to the new washer and dryer.

They suck.

Our clothes are not clean.

And no matter how small the dryer load, everything comes out wrinkled.

And somehow wet.

A bit of research revealed that the drying-sensor option was made in Korea and the Korean idea of "dry" is somewhat damper than that of Americans. Its detectors are set for a different, clammier culture. Who knew? I always thought dry meant "without moisture." Apparently dry can be damp—at least in Korea. But I have not noticed any dampness or the smell of mildew on any Koreans I know or have happened to encounter.

I've been duped. I don't care how fancy my washer and dryer

are or how many stars they got on Bestbuy.com. The fact is: it is not possible to properly wash a load of laundry with a table-spoon of water. Any idiot knows this.

Well, I do now.

And furthermore, periodical tossing does not make for dry or smooth clothing. Not even with the 16-Hour Fresh Hold Option with Dynamic Venting Technology, which is still a mystery to me, and probably comprehensible only by reading the twelve-hundred-page operator's manual. The guide is offered in English, French, Spanish, and German, but not Korean, presumably because all the presets are already perfect for their version of dry.

Our ten-year-old top-loading Whirlpool combo contraptions had worked perfectly fine. The wash cycle was appropriately known as "agitating." It didn't pussyfoot around. It was agitated. It shook and banged, and the final spin cycle ended not with a song, but a ratchety, mechanical clanking that grinded to a halt with a final, constipated grunt. "I'M DONE!" it bellowed in no uncertain terms. "AND YOUR CLOTHES ARE FUCKING CLEAN!"

Nothing was wrong with the Whirlpools. They were old and noisy and cantankerous and produced beautiful results. Kind of like me and Danny. But I needed a change, so I decided to keep Danny and get a new washer and dryer instead. It has taken me too long to get through his operator's manual to ever consider a different model.

The new dynamos are fool's gold. But alas, they remain. I can't get rid of them just yet. They were hauled through a treacherous and life-threatening walkway and up a spiny, crumbling-rock back staircase into the bottom floor of our hillside house by a trio of shirtless, sweaty men who were tipped well but may never walk again. For the time being, the sting of my disappointment is quelled by my enjoyment of the happy final spin cycle song. And aesthetically, which is almost everything to me, the machines are emphatically beautiful and modern and perfect in every way but actual purpose. I have photographed them.

It's frustrating and confusing. The elements seem right: bells and whistles, knobs and buttons and amber lights. Ecstatic reviews from Amazon.com housewives with soiled construction worker husbands and five filthy children. The package is perfectly put together and impressively marketed. But the machines are charlatans. Imposters. The Frank Abagnale of appliances. And yet I hang on, convincing myself that *this* load came out a little cleaner, brighter, drier. That everything will be better.

And then I recognize that there is a familiar pattern here.

I have often found myself blinded by what could be—*should be*—rather than seeing what *is*. I hear the happy song at the end of the spin cycle and block out the encroaching death march, whether from an appliance, a relationship, an agent, a manager, a project, a business opportunity, a pair of skinny jeans. And my indefatigable tenacity, which has proved winning in so many cases, argues for stick-to-itiveness for things I really care about—despite truth. If success is defined as one percent inspiration and ninety-nine percent perspiration, I rank among the most successful, albeit sweatiest, people I know.

I have always believed that the light at the end of the tunnel is not an illusion; the illusion is the tunnel itself. But then there's the old saying that the light at the end of the tunnel is an oncoming train. Both are possible, I suppose. For this reason, I have been forced to come up with a checkpoint for my life. A simple barometer of sorts. Something I call "The Liver Law."

The Liver Law is basic: *Liver is liver. You can throw on a little bacon. Add some onions. But it's still liver.*

When Danny senses that I am sugarcoating something so far off its original trajectory—affixing myself to the tiniest, most remote glimmer of positivity when everything around the situation spells "run"—he blithely mutters "liver" and walks out of the room. Sometimes his insight slaps me into actuality, but not always. I have been known to stick with certain liver for years after the project or the person has proved rancid. I add a little more bacon. A few more onions. And the acrid smell of sizzling, iron-packed organ meats is perfumed and averted. Temporarily.

I have a long history of liver:

The alcoholic, abusive boyfriend who was not really my boyfriend, who said there should be a "wide load" sign on my ass, while he sat, propped up in bed, devouring mounds of steak tartare between prank calls to televangelists. But he had introduced me to obscure Patti LaBelle songs, which was tantamount to a mountain of applewood-smoked and dry-cured sizzling pork.

The abysmally disastrous mini-tour that I'd suspected would be an abysmally disastrous minitour, but for which I had diced enough onions to sufficiently tear my eyes to a blinding blur. It began in the town of Parole, Maryland, where the sign at the border read: WELCOME TO PAROLE—BETTER THAN YOU RE-MEMBER IT! It might as well have read: WELCOME TO PAROLE—LIVER!

Then there was the other boyfriend who was studying for the bar, mostly *at* the bar, in keeping with my malignant attraction to functioning, bipolar alcoholics. He was so sweet when not drinking—like a Vidalia. And I remained besotted, despite evidence suggesting he was a serial cheater. Little things: secret phone calls, sudden changes of plans, other people's underwear at his apartment. When I casually offered my suspicions, the tables were always turned, ending with an apology from me accompanied by a gift of some sort.

One late night, I was delivering a large bouquet of flowers to his doorstep with a note saying I was sorry that I'd upset him to the point that he had to slam on his brakes, nearly smashing my head through the windshield, and throw me out of his car blocks from my home. As I crept away from his front porch, I saw him drive up, so naturally, I hid in the bushes. Through thorny branches, I watched him emerge with a young blond club-type and stagger, drunk and laughing, to his apartment. He noticed the flowers and foggily read the attached card, then stepped over the arrangement to open the door for his companion. I crawled behind the bushes to my car in tears.

The next day I confronted him and, without the slightest hesitation, he yelled, "That was my cousin! He was visiting from Kansas!"

"*My* cousins are from Kansas, not yours," I reminded him.

"Now you're an expert on my family geography? You have some real trust issues and I don't know if this relationship is going to work."

He was convincing. I knew he'd make a great lawyer. I sent more flowers.

My experiences of career-liver qualify me as a card-carrying member of the North American Meat Processors Association.

Take the legendary record company mogul who told me I was one of the best singers in the world and that he wanted to take me under his tutelage and give me the record career he knew I could have.

Within the industry, he was known as somewhat of a genius. Within the human race he was known as somewhat disgusting. His pudgy frame was ever stuffed into a disheveled five-thousand-dollar suit with his bloated, scarlet face popping above a sweated-out, unbuttoned shirt, offering eye bags so large they wouldn't qualify as carry-on. His balding head rose like a spotted dune from wiry white tufts forever in need of a trim. He reeked of careless money and expensive red wine. He told me I was fat. I starved myself and lost fifteen pounds in a month and was deemed "able to be seen in public." There were many late-night dinners and limos and platinum carrots dangling in my face but no actual contract or music or any work whatsoever.

Just when it was clear that I should get out of the kitchen, he took me to San Francisco, where Madonna was playing her Blond Ambition Tour, with the intention that she and I would meet and write together. He said we each had qualities the other lacked and we would elevate each other. Real promise. No need for bacon or onions.

We limo'd directly from the airport to the venue and were escorted to Madonna's dressing room only minutes before the show. We found her sprawled across a leather couch in her opening costume—a black tailored men's suit with slits cut to expose giant golden cone-shaped pointy breasts that could blind an unsuspecting midget at ten paces. She was glorious. There was only the sofa, no chairs, and she sat up to receive us but outstretched her arms on the cushions to occupy the entire couch, so we had to remain standing.

She was friendly but glib. Low energy, possibly reserved for her minions. She looked me over like I was a concubine and spoke to the record giant in a condescending tone, reducing him to a cocktail of anxiety and indignity that he seemed to enjoy, like a masochist begging for one more flick of the cattail. When introduced to me, she managed a monotonic compliment, but it meant acknowledging she might have watched *Star Search* and that was trickily beneath her.

Her show was amazing. Smart. A collection of historical iconic images from the *Metropolis* set to the Monroe, Dietrich, and Fosse influences that no one in her frenzied audience had ever seen—all reborn with decadence and a modern dirty defiance. It didn't matter that she couldn't sing. I had been smug about her vocal abilities but this production convinced me that she was a true artist. A hardworking, hard-thinking trouper. She loved show business.

I couldn't wait to collaborate with her.

After the concert, the mogul and I went backstage for a quick congratulations and then were off to the hotel he'd arranged for the night. At check-in, I learned only one room had been booked for us both. He claimed it was a mistake, but unfortunately, there were no more available rooms in the entire hotel. The smell of liver burned my eyes and I couldn't help but wonder if the fumfering receptionist had been bribed to confirm the news. All cards had been exquisitely played. In return I played dumb, claimed exhaustion, and slept fully clothed under a high pile of covers on the precipice of the king bed, facing away from him.

I was swimming in a vat of slimy, bruise-colored liver.

But at this point I'd been presented and exhibited and was set up to work with the biggest music star of my generation. A quick trip to the fridge for a slab of fatback and all would be well.

For the next entire year, the game continued. Lots of talk, no music, no contract, no Madonna collaboration. I rummaged the pantry for an onion—yellow, green, red, pearl. Onion powder. A soy bacon bit. Finally, one night at a schmancy Italian restaurant in Brentwood, I gave an impassioned and well-rehearsed speech.

"I want to believe in all of your plans for me, but I need something concrete. I need to make the record."

I punctuated the appeal with a sharp and convincing exhale of my Salem and stubbed it out as an exclamation point.

He leaned forward, as red as the wine and with equal alcohol content, and slurrily said, "Sam, if you'd just followed my lead back in San Francisco, you'd already have a CD out with two top ten hits and a Grammy nomination. I have a way of doing things."

Having driven full speed ahead, hypnotized by the white dashed lines down the middle of the desert road with the oasis ever just around the bend, I had burned out the clutch and run out of gas. A slow, blunt rage rose through me, scraping my throat like a carpenter's plane, and I took a liberal gulp of wine to swallow it down. Then I stood, coolly pushing my chair under the table to signal I would not return. I found a sidewalk pay phone and called a friend to pick me up.

I had been proud that I'd never had to do the Hollywood Boy-Toy Shuffle. My talent had always been enough. As I waited on the curb in the crushing, fleeting strobe of head-lights, I finally broke, not knowing which was worse—the mogul saying what he said, or my knowing it long before he said it.

If it looks like liver and it smells like liver . . . blah blah blah . . .

Sometimes my bacon and onions have come in a form unrelated to the actual liver at hand but are meant to distract, nonetheless. This tactic often reveals itself through my hair, with the thought that a dramatic change in style will alter the rest of my life. However, photographs through the years expose me as severely disturbed and probably schizophrenic with a multiple personality disorder. My hair has been spiked, mulleted, banged, crew cut, Mohawked, shaved, shoulder length, curly, poofed, ponytailed, page-boyed, pompadoured, weaved, and even cornrowed—the last requiring sleeping in a do-rag and not washing my hair for weeks at a time.

Then there are the colors, which have included the entire spectrum from onyx to platinum—the last, a four-hour process during which my scalp was chemically burned to bloody boils, but even that did not deter me from insisting on "one more time!" to get the colorless color just right. This particular fashion choice came with a matching soul patch, which made me look like I'd just eaten a white cat and couldn't find a napkin.

Liver is a cruel mistress.

Like the time I hired a publicist for the release of a CD. I'd used this guy before, when I was on a sitcom, and he'd gotten me a few good features and made sure I was included in all the studio publicity. He quickly provided a list of the publications that would review the CD, as well as the radio interviews he would schedule, the *Los Angeles Times* feature with photos he had all but secured, and a trip to New York to appear on *The View*, reaching millions. I'd done the show twice before and had a great time with the girl gang. They were smart and funny and I knew the power of their ratings.

The record came out. Dates for the interviews were pushed and pushed but never materialized. The few reviews he acquired were from easily dismissible sources: Howard's CD Blog wasn't exactly *Rolling Stone*. The publicist seemed to be scrambling, supplying his own heaps of fancier prosciutto and shallots, but I did all the cooking. A photographer supposedly from the *Los Angeles Times* came to my house for a photo shoot but arrived with the faint smell of fresh liver. I pushed back the cloying notion that the publicist had just hired someone to *pretend* he was from the paper. But how could that be true? Who would possibly go that far in lieu of honesty or accountability? The interview was supposedly scheduled and canceled five times.

With newly born Cooper and our supernanny, Blanca, in tow, I flew to New York to do *The View*. Upon my arrival, the publicist and all information suddenly went missing. His assistant passed on a few minor questions about a car service pickup for the show and song length, but she seemed to be stalling and I couldn't get any facts. Then, suddenly, the appearance date itself was in flux. Still, I hung on through what was clearly a shell game as the publicist's absence became more shrouded in increasingly odd and inchoate excuses: His cat was in the emergency room—for two days. Then his sister apparently broke out with a bad case of cancer and he had to fly to her.

"That's awful," I said to the assistant, feeling suddenly small and shallow and guilty. "What kind of cancer?"

"Liver."

"Come again?"

"Liver."

"You're kidding."

"Why would I joke about something like that?"

"You wouldn't. It's not funny. Nothing about this is funny."

"Okay, Sam, I'll be in touch."

"Wait a minute," I jumped in. Then, "Could you say it one more time?"

"Say what?"

"The kind of cancer."

"Liver."

"Thank you."

The universe was yelling at me.

The excuses were dubious at best, but no decent person with half a heart could question sick cats and cancerous sisters. I was starving, the dinner bell was clanging, liver was on the table, and it was too late to change entrées. I had no choice but to remain in New York with infant and nanny—stuck, stymied, and cuffed, but clinging. Surely I'd not been sent there for nothing.

Who would possibly go that far in lieu of honesty or accountability?

Two nerve-wracking, pointless days later, I finally called Joy Behar, one of the cohosts of the show, and asked if she knew any particulars. She was an old friend and did some checking and called me back and said, kindly, "Sam, you are not scheduled to be on the show. An appearance was discussed but never set and we are solidly booked. We'd love to have you another time."

I realized in that moment that the publicist was a fellow liver smotherer. He *had* tried to book me and had gotten close enough to believe it would come together in time so that I would never know there'd been a glitch. And when it didn't, there was nothing for him to do but flee.

I flew back to Los Angeles and shaved my head.

Sometimes a hairstyle change wasn't enough. During a particularly liverish time in my life, I once went to a prominent cosmetic surgeon for a new nose, gargantuan and angular with a Roman bump at the bridge and devious alignment that suggested a former boxing career. I love big noses. I think they're sexy and rugged. The surgeon looked at me cross-eyed and explained he'd have to graft it from pieces of my femur.

"No problem," I said, "I'm free Tuesday." He politely asked me to leave.

I've never once looked at the menu of life and said, "I'll have the liver," and yet I nearly salivated when my enthusiastic and trusted friend Rhonda innocently set up an opportunity in Florida for me to pitch my screenplay to a suspiciously "wiseguy" shipping magnate for financing.

There is nothing about the previous sentence after the word "opportunity" that sounds like a good idea. Beginning with Florida. Nevertheless . . .

I took my longtime pianist and musical soul mate, Todd Schroeder, and my producer, Effie Brown, with me, telling them that before we pitched the movie, we had to attend the magnate's daughter's thirteenth birthday ball, as I had agreed to sing as a favor, even though it was a job I would not have done for money. I shared that he'd asked me to invite Selena Gomez. "And could you get Justin Bieber too?" he'd thrown in. "I'll pay a hundred grand." I didn't know Selena Gomez or Justin Bieber but I knew people who knew people who knew their people and I actually made calls.

That was when I'd first fired up the skillet.

The party was held in the ballroom of a chain hotel, which was decorated in Art Nouveau Ongepotchket, in keeping with the Florida aesthetic: *If it's really shiny, it must be expensive.* The place was overrun with rich, entitled, and already cosmetically altered teenagers, and three hundred or so relatives and friends, who were dressed to compete with the decor.

I was the warm-up act for the birthday daughter's musical debut, and I barely got off the stage before a taped explosive introduction reminiscent of the *2001: A Space Odyssey* theme heralded the entrance of the plain, blank girl, who was incredibly thin and somehow paunchy at the same time. It was her slump, I think—like a double-shift waitress at an all-night diner. A rhythmic pop track blasted at a thousand decibels and she sang-ish a song especially written and produced and coached by a team of Top 40 hit makers.

Inappropriately underclad teenage backup dancers strutted and licked their teeth between each lip-synched phrase. Strobe lights blinked and wind machines blew back their weaves.

The three-minute spectacle had cumulatively cost hundreds of thousands of dollars, yet the little darling evoked an attitude that said, "Doing this full-out would make me really really supertired." On the final musical cutoff and provocative pose, I joined the screaming crowd with simulated enthusiasm, and the shipping magnate shrugged as if to say, "Whaddaya gonna do?"

The evening ended with his standing in the ballroom vestibule surrounded by dusty plastic palm trees and ferns, pointing at his ex-wife as if casting a pox, and screaming, "You're a whore!!" Then he threw his hands to the heavens and bellowed, "You're killing my mama!!" before storming away. Mama, all of four feet six inches, hovered near the bar, uncomfortably spangled for the occasion, and I sensed she'd rather have been in a black kerchief, hunched over a wood-burning stove, stirring rabbit ragù with a stick. She didn't speak a word of English, but she got the general idea.

The next morning, Todd, Effie, and I arrived at the magnate's house to pitch the movie as planned, and pretended nothing odd had happened the night before. He lived in a luxuriously tasteless McMansion, complete with Venetian-themed muraled, double-storied ceilings, mismatched imported marble, and ostentatious gold-leafed everything. It was like Versace and Napoleon had teamed up for a garage sale. There were Roman busts and glass mosaics that, if you looked closely, might have borne the likeness of our host. The hallways were lined with framed photos of Al Capone and James Gandolfini as Tony Soprano, and *The Godfather* lobby posters—the kind of characters, real and fictional, who he was rehearsing to be—all underscored by the gurgle of countless gasping, peeing cherub fountains. It was all too much.

Part of me was afraid he would say yes and that I would

have to see him and his horrible house again. But I wanted my movie made and, looking through the rose-colored Murano vase that sat between us, I decided that our shipping magnate was a sentimental fool, smitten with his vacuous daughter and old-country mama, whom his whore of an ex-wife was trying to kill.

Add pancetta, cipollini onions, and stir.

I pitched and sang and clutched and shucked and jived and hoped. Todd was strong support and Effie was on fire, spouting numbers and locations and Sundance deadlines. I noticed our host never looked her in the eye. After two hours, he saw us out with a handshake and a smile that shone like the gold chain on his exposed chest.

The following days brought a multitude of questions, not about the movie but about Effie, a fiercely intelligent African-American woman with exceptional credits. Finally, he decided to pass, choosing to invest in his daughter's singing career instead. We both knew there would never be enough. I also suspected that the real reason for his pass was Effie, the triple threat: Woman, Black, Smart.

Ix-nay on the ack-blay oman-way. Don Vito Corleone would never approve.

I wouldn't consider replacing her and he wasn't the kind of person I would ever want to be in business with. Plus his house was stupid.

Of the vast variety of recipes in my *Joy of Cooking Liver* cookbook, my biggest glob of personal liver and my greatest attempts to cover it up would undoubtedly be my alcoholism. Alcoholism didn't *happen* to me. No one led me down a garden path or lied to me or bamboozled me into becoming a pathetic drunk. My drinking was a seemingly calculated, entirely self-motivated attempt to cover my liverish life with distilled, fermented, and inebriating bacon and onions. Then my *drinking* became the liver and my *life* became the bacon and onions. And then it all stewed to the point of an unrecognizable goulash of delusional gook.

I told myself if I could run five miles in the morning and never drink before a show, I couldn't possibly be an alcoholic. When that criteria couldn't be met, I simply stopped running and stopped doing shows.

Pesky near-death stories kept popping up: Like the night I supposedly stepped onto a Juliet balcony on the twenty-seventh floor of a hotel and was climbing over the railing until Danny woke up and pulled me back. Or the time I came perilously close to falling onto a subway track seconds before the train rushed by and Danny pulled me back. Or the time I methodically filled a sink with toiletries, including a blowing blow-dryer, and was about to turn the water on until Danny pulled me back. Ironically, I had no memory of any of these dramatic stories, and Danny was curiously the only witness in each one. How convenient. I'd seen *Gaslight*. But it would take more than a few slightly unbelievable tales to convince me I was in trouble.

Or less.

It was finally the obese, inescapable burden of sadness—such a simple word—that finally led to acknowledging and treating my malady. And the beginning of my deliverance from liver. At one of my first 12-step meetings, a guy I'd never seen before said "I hoped you'd end up here" and described an alcohol-fueled night of decadent debauchery a hundred years ago, of which I had no memory. I wondered how many others there were. People I passed on the street, in grocery stores, at the dry cleaner, Starbucks. Intimate strangers.

Denial ain't a river in Egypt was an apt, albeit corny slogan.

So was *Wherever you go, there you are,* though I wasn't sure if it applied if you actually had no idea where you'd been.

My name is Sam and I'm a liverholic.

And acid reflux, like hangovers and hindsight, is twenty-twenty.

Liver or not liver? That is the question. Nearly all of the successful projects and relationships in my life are the result of long-term trust, high hopes, and steadfast grit. So, does the wisdom lie in pressing on or putting the dog to sleep and out of its misery? It is the rut that agonizes. But I can't expect to vanquish the pain of loss unless I also forfeit the thrill of hope, and it's not worth the trade. In the end, I would rather be bruised than cynical, trusting than suspicious, disappointed than apathetic.

At this time in my life, however, there is less liver than ever before. Part of it is the wisdom of time and experience. Part of it is a sense of priority that comes with sobriety and parenting. Part of it is sheer exhaustion. And part of it is the growing consciousness that reality is okay, that fixating on a specific goal with inflexible criteria prohibits me from other, much larger possibilities unavailable to the myopic eye.

More and more, I can smell the Big L at a mile and even when underemployed, my liver litmus comes with a shorter clock. For instance, I get out as soon as anyone asks me to invite Selena Gomez or Justin Bieber to a debutante ball in Florida. Liver and learn.

Also, the stakes are no longer as extreme. They fall more often into the category of things like . . . appliances.

My washer and dryer are liver. I know it now. In a little more time, I will donate them to my pediatrician's outer office, where they can be made into stunningly, internally lit architectural aquariums, complete with a 16-Hour Fresh Hold Option with Dynamic Venting Technology. I will include the manual in the event they want to know what that is, in any of a number of languages except Korean.

Liver is liver. But sometimes I will still hold out for paté.

8. Crash Course

By the time I got to the hospital in Amsterdam, Jerry had already died.

He'd been my director, writer, mentor, friend, and father figure since I was nineteen, and now, nearly ten years later, I'd rushed to catch the next plane from Los Angeles upon receiving the call that "it's almost time." But I had missed the moment.

For the two years before I met Jerry, UCLA had given me opportunities that far exceeded anything remotely scholastic. When I was a sophomore, my housemate and best friend, Bruce Newberg, and I were so enthusiastic, obstinate and unrelenting about getting to write and produce our new musical—*Hurry! Hurry! Hollywood!*—that the dean of fine arts at UCLA actually allowed us our ambitious request in lieu of taking courses. I was given fake classes and fake grades and never met a professor. It was like they knew I was never going to graduate—or at least they hoped I would leave after I had exhausted everything the music and theater departments had to offer.

I thought this was how show business and, well, life worked:

you insisted on what you knew would be wonderful and people let you do it. I couldn't imagine getting a finer education or anything more from UCLA unless they named a campus theater after me, so immediately after the curtain fell on our show, I left college to pursue my own course.

I had other, bigger projects to beg for and get.

I found family in a gang of young singers and comedians at a crusty Santa Monica club called the Horn, where we clumsily chiseled and hunted out our stage personalities, experimenting with new material and singing backup for one another in multiple sets, four or five nights a week, for twenty-five dollars a night and free drinks.

The Horn was a dingy and dreadful and depressing place. Everything was painted black: the walls, floors, tables, chairs, bar, the stage. Not a chic, shimmery, lacquered black—a dull, gloomy black that made you want to drink the moment you stepped in. The only reason the place stayed open was that between the black everything and the dimmest murmur of lighting, no one was ever sure if the people they saw there were actually there. Hence, it was a magnet for a low-life clientele of barflies and cheating out-of-towners.

What the Horn lacked in charm it made up for as a stomping ground for talented, young hopefuls—none of whom were getting anywhere. After I'd played there a few months, a stunningly beautiful cocktail waitress named Paris Vaughan told me, "My mother would love you. I'm going to bring her to see you." The following week, she did.

"Hi, I'm Paris's mom, Sarah."

I did the math. Paris Vaughan . . . Sarah. Vaughan. Oh. My. God.

If I'd known beforehand that she was the plump woman in the silk caftan and turbulently crested wave-shaped wig, I doubt

I could have sung. My dad had all her records and I'd grown up singing along, emulating her phrasing, tone, vibrato.

"That was fuckin' real, white boy," she said, and wrapped me in her arms. She hadn't been called "Sassy" for nothing. Sarah Vaughan liked me, and I was confident a pat on the back from such a legend would mean immediate stardom.

Not so much.

Record producers, A&R guys, and Vegas bookers occasionally came slumming, but glimmers of possibilities were always snuffed out like the messy tabletop candles in cheap red glass jars after last call.

My father recognized and related to my fierce drive and, in a remarkable act of true belief, he decided I needed professional help (the show kind, not therapeutic, though it could have gone either way). If success in this business was what I craved, then my father wanted to help me get it faster, and the encouragement he was still unable to verbalize was voiced through action.

By day, I worked part-time in the office of City Councilman Zev Yaroslavsky, and also in the office of television producer Pierre Cossette, and learned that politics was show business and show business was politics. During a visit from Oklahoma, my dad requested a meeting with Pierre and his associate Dee, and asked them who the best person would be to guide my particular talents.

They gave him one name: Jerry Blatt.

Jerry had been with Bette Midler since her bathhouse beginnings and had basically cocreated her Divine Miss M persona with her. He wrote and then directed all of her shows—and not just the funny stuff. The stuff that made you hurt. They said he would "get me."

Jerry came to hear me sing at the Horn, and the deal was done that night in a chafed red pleather corner booth, thick with smoke and plans. My father hired him to write and direct an act for me that would attract Hollywood big shots and record companies. I knew he was the guy. What I didn't know was that he would become the single most important influence on the way I think and create and perform, and the greatest gift my dad, or anyone, ever gave me.

Jerry was twenty years older than I, and two inches shorter than my pint-size five-foot-eight. His muscled, gym-rat upper body was perpetually stuffed into T-shirts sized for a teenager, in odd contrast to his spindly legs. He wore a curly, full beard and his hair may or may not have been streaked with a dash of purple or lime green. "It's *lypple* green!" he would specify. His intelligent eyes were framed by round wire glasses, which, despite his attempt at a worked-out, punk-haired, über-now image, recalled a scrawny little Jewish boy, perpetually studying for his bar mitzvah.

Jerry taught me to find the extraordinary in the ordinary and see the world as art. On a stroll through Greenwich Village, he would point out the way the sunlight hurtled between two buildings and splashed against a widowed tree next to a stump, to create a thriving jagged shadow on the pavement. Or the incongruous beauty of a vigorously painted red wall as the backdrop for a street crazy peeing on the sidewalk. He introduced me to Tom Waits and Jean-Paul Goude and taught me how to make perfect sautéed mushrooms. He took me to the Horn of Plenty nightclub to see Cissy Houston, whose opening act was a hypnotist (I was the volunteer) and whose guest was her daughter, an eighteen-year-old, unknown Whitney, who sang "The Greatest Love of All." He told me about the 1960s experimental theater movement in New York, describing a particularly fabulous production in someone's West Village loft apartment in which the first act was a man carrying around a bag of dirt and carefully sprinkling it all over the furniture, and the second act was the same guy vacuuming it up.

Jerry thought everything was important, but he didn't take anything very seriously.

He believed that singing is just storytelling and the opposite of trying to create a specific outcome, or, worse, trying to *re-create* a specific outcome. He made it clear that in stepping onstage, I had to surrender to the terrifying, dangerous process of preparing thoroughly and then releasing the preparation, like blowing a kiss, not knowing where it would land or what would happen. The biggest lesson he taught me—to which Bette was a testament—was that if you tell the truth onstage, you can do anything. Try anything. If you feel like standing on your head and it's authentic, it will work.

My first show with him was called *Sam Harris and Fries to Go!* Fries to Go were my backup singers. Because of my youthful, corn-fed appearance, Jerry decided they should be old white ladies wearing flower-patterned housedresses, church hats and sensible shoes, as if they'd chaperoned me by bus from Oklahoma and their presence was the only condition under which my parents would let me leave. After numerous auditions, we realized that actual old white ladies couldn't sing the ripping gospel parts we were creating, so we settled for young women who *dressed* like old ladies in flower-patterned housedresses, church hats, and sensible shoes.

With Jerry, I turned my soulful style into the theme of the little white boy from the sticks with the big black voice. The first song in the show said it all: "Bless My Soul, Mama, You Got to Know There's Love in Them There Hills." We rehearsed at a hole-in-the-wall space in East Los Angeles with decades-old, nasty stained carpeting and chipped, lead-loaded, mud-brown-painted walls. When Jerry and I rehearsed alone, we both moved pianos and chairs and speakers, but when anyone else was present, he would not allow me to touch a thing. Even in this hovel, I was the star and "stars should not be seen *schlepping*."

My debut was in a dump of an Italian restaurant on Sunset Boulevard called Gio's. There was a tiny squibble of a listing in the *Los Angeles Times* announcing that I would play there for a month of weekends. It was my first mention in a major newspaper, and I felt as if I'd been knighted. The restaurant included a small, dreary room adjacent to the dining area with scarred wooden tables, a few dozen rickety cane-back chairs, and a tiny platform stage at one end. We brought in an entire band, the girls, and me—all costumed and choreographed and charted to the gills. There were only three small stage lights and no gels, so Jerry took red straws from the bar and lined them up in the barn-door frames for mood.

We were ready for the masses. There was no backstage, so I paced nervously in the alley outside the kitchen, surrounded by garbage cans puffing wet, rancid food smells, and a couple of illegal immigrant busboys on a smoke break. Jerry burst outside with excitement in his eyes and said, "Think of it as a rehearsal!"

"What do you mean? We've been rehearsing for weeks," I said.

"The house is small."

"How small?"

"Very small."

"How very small?"

"No one is in the audience."

I stood in a pool of some sort of leakage and took in the news.

"No one? Not one person? No one?" I begged.

"Sean is here," Jerry offered with a positive grin.

Sean was Jerry's lover/partner/appendage who had so much brain damage from the festival of drugs he had taken throughout his life that it was more like having half a person attend my show. He was missing important teeth. But you didn't notice right away because his broomish mustache hung over most of his mouth and was always littered with remnants of his last meal. Not crumbs. Enough to qualify as leftovers. I loved Sean. He taught me about gardening and did a dead-on impersonation of a Shasta daisy, but he was hardly enough audience. Besides, he was photographing the show for my archives. Up to this point I didn't have any archives so this would be my maiden archive. What a start.

I unstuck my shoes from the alleyway goop and bummed a smoke from one of the busboys. I hadn't asked any friends to come, as I wanted a few performances under my belt before their scrutiny. Now I wished I had.

"What are we going to do?" I asked.

"Well, we're doing the show."

"What do you mean, *we're* doing the show? You're not the one who has to play to nobody!"

"You are getting paid, not much, well, you're losing money, but you are billed and you need to fulfill that promise . . . Think of it as another rehearsal."

Gio's was supposed to be the next step toward my destiny of stardom. I wanted to be famous. So famous that I would be vehemently hated by all the people I admired most. I wanted mobs of fans to remind me that I was not alone in the way I felt about myself. I wanted to complain that the tabloids were printing *Lies! Lies! Lies!* but I would know it was all true. Suddenly, as I was standing in a stinky alley outside an audienceless cheesy Italian restaurant, an avalanche of reality and doubt invaded my head and I feared that I would never reach my full potential because I was disillusioned about the potential of my full potential.

I did the show. Full-out. The manager of the restaurant didn't even pop his head in to see if we were there. Midway through the first act (yes, there were two acts with an intermission), a slob of a drunk staggered in, slouched into an unsteady chair, sucked down most of a cigarette, and left. I played an entire comic monologue to the gray plume that continued to rise from the ashtray. Sean's effortful cackle landed at all the punch lines. I looked to him for support and when he lowered the camera from his face, I saw from his mustache that he'd just had veal parmesan, a side of linguini with clam sauce, sautéed spinach with garlic, and a cannoli. It just made the whole thing all the more pathetic. At the end of the first act, Jerry switched off the three stage lights for a lackluster blackout and I returned to the alley for a costume change.

At the end of my first show, Jerry grabbed me and held me tight. He had tears in his eyes. He was *kvelling*. Fifteen minutes later, I was fired for singing too loudly. "People can't digest their food in the next room with all that noise," the manager explained. It would have been kinder to bring up that I hadn't brought any business, but for some reason he wanted to make it personal.

Jerry and I began working in every awful club in Los Angeles. I am not a "club" person. I don't do well with vomit-stained greenroom sofas and low-ceilinged rat holes that shouldn't be seen in the daytime—call me a snob—but Jerry said we were building something and we needed places to fail. After two years, and with no Hollywood big shots pounding on my door, I needed a *proper* place to fail, and found a fifty-seat venue called Theatre/Theater, where I convinced the owner to let me play for six months. The show was called *Sam Harris: Out of Control.*

Just as we were about to begin rehearsals, Jerry got a writing gig in New York that actually paid, and announced he was moving back, tossing me out of the nest but leaving me with a vision.

My backup singers were now known as the International Pancakes and each had a character name and nationality: Leipi von Biesterfeldt—from Germany; Zorova Petrova—from Bulgaria; and Fiore Bellini di Vicci—from Italy. They wore black corsets and puffed taffeta skirts with picture hats and stilettos and lace gloves. Ann Marie, who played Leipi, made all of their costumes by hand with a budget of nothing and added some sparkle to what would be my look: a pair of 1940s dark teal, pleated trousers with a pencil-thin, pink pinstripe, a white cotton fake-front dickie covered by an oversize tuxedo tailcoat, and a pair of black high-top Converse sneakers. All but the tennis shoes were from thrift shops. Ann Marie sewed on a sad, slightly tattered silk gardenia to the lapel and sequin piping to the tails. I looked like Groucho Marx meets Magic Johnson, with a little Cher thrown in for good measure.

The set was inspired by Grace Jones. Jerry loved Grace Jones and she was a huge influence on both of us. It was easy to steal from her because no one would ever think of me as anything like her. She was statuesque and angular and dark black and enigmatic. I was more like Edith Piaf with baby fat and a mullet. Grace had one particular video that Jerry and I were mad for called "My Jamaican Guy," in which her single set piece was a large black staircase. I lifted the idea outright, but decided my staircase would be multifunctional. It would have stairs that could flap up, individually, on hinges, so that I could open the show by emerging from the inside, bound in a straitjacket (which I had to special order from the Humane Restraint Company), as the Pancakes whispered from offstage: "I tried to warn you . . . I tried to warn you . . ."

The staircase would also be used in a number called "You Don't Have to Be Nice to the People You Meet on the Way Up—If You Ain't Coming Down," in which the Pancakes crouched inside with their heads appearing to "sit" on the steps as I walked on top of them. It would be arch and bent and theatrical!

We rehearsed daily, but as our opening date approached I was still unable to find anyone who would affordably build the staircase. The best price I got was from the scene shop at my alma mater, UCLA. They wanted a thousand dollars! Inconceivably out of my budget. A hundred dollars was inconceivably out of my budget.

I called Jerry and said, "I don't think I'm going to get the staircase."

"You have to have the staircase."

"It's too expensive. Maybe I can just use a stepladder."

"The whole show is about the staircase."

"I thought the whole show was about me."

"Of course it's about you . . . but it's really about the staircase."

Ann Marie hooked me up with two young entrepreneurs who might loan me the money. She deposited me at a house in West Hollywood at two o'clock in the afternoon and fled suspiciously swiftly after minimal introductions. They were a couple, one being short and round and Jewish and the other tall and cut and German. The living room reflected their 1980s success: everything matched in airy pastels, offset by a glossy plastic round-cornered coffee table and a glass-front entertainment cabinet, with all the latest stereo and VHS equipment in view. Deco-framed Nagel prints hung on every wall.

They offered me noshes and a lot of drinks, and then sandwiched me between them on the kind of soft, low leather couch that's easy to fall into but impossible to get out of without a crane. They lit and passed a joint, getting up close and very friendly, gushing about how they'd like to be a part of the show. Then one of them pushed play on the VHS machine and the *bomp-chicka-bow-bow* of '80s porn blasted from the screen.

I called Jerry and told him I got the staircase. Just not how.

Out of Control opened and we began to attract a local following that *Los Angeles* magazine dubbed "Harrisites." Talent scouts from a new television show called *Star Search* were looking for contestants and came to see me at Theatre/Theater. I was asked to audition and went to a production office in Hollywood where I sang for nine or ten people crammed into a room so tiny that I had to perform in the doorway with the piano in the hall. I sang "I Am Changing" from *Dreamgirls* and was promptly rejected. Too theatrical.

A few weeks later I got a call informing me that they'd reconsidered and wanted me on the fourth episode. I learned that two of the talent scouts had fought for me, saying I was different from the cookie-cutter wannabes, but knowing there was a very good chance I was a "what-not-to-be."

I called Jerry and told him I would be on the show.

"Are they letting you sing what you want?" he asked.

"Yes, I get to choose my own material."

"Good. Don't let them dress you. Wear what you've been wearing," he insisted.

"My crappy thrift shop tails? But they have a whole fancy wardrobe department."

"It's all about the crappy thrift shop tails."

"I thought it was all about me."

"Of course it's about you . . . but it's really about the crappy thrift shop tails."

With Jerry's advice under my 1940s-narrow belt, I won the

first show. And then the second. And then the third. During the day, I went to the TV studio for rehearsals, band prerecordings, and tapings, and at night I performed *Out of Control* for the "Harrisites." A few weeks later, my episodes began to air and we had to stop doing *Out of Control* because the box office was just that.

Bigger things seemed on the horizon.

Today, with the number of television reality talent shows springing up like medical marijuana clinics in Los Angeles, it's a different, slicker animal. On *Star Search,* there were no coaches or stylists or mentors—we were on our own. The judges changed each week, so it was never about them. There was an innocence about the show that revealed raw, often hokey entertainment. I was definitely raw and hokey. But I meant every word and every note. I found a formula in which I sang an emotional ballad, put a key change after the bridge, held out a long note, and finished big. Today, if you line up the recordings of my performances one after another, you'll see that they're all the same arrangement in the same key. Yet 25 million people a week couldn't get enough.

After sixteen appearances, I won the title of "Grand Champion," which is the same title awarded to winners of the American Kennel Club dog show. Suddenly, fame kissed me, or, rather, stuck its tongue down my throat. I was an answer on *Jeopardy!:* "Who is Sam Harris?" I was impersonated by Dana Carvey on *Saturday Night Live* and I was jabbed on MTV's *Beavis and Butthead.* But having fought so hard to claim my individuality and fearing it would be stripped away, my ego wouldn't allow me to be led by people smarter than I, with more experience. And pretty much *everyone* was smarter than I, with more experience.

Jerry was the only guide I would follow. He hated *Star*

Search. He was beyond happy for my new success and knew that it gave us the opportunity to play large venues, but he was afraid that since I'd won the hearts of Middle America, I would sell out to a common denominator and become too commercial and homogenous. Jerry wanted me to be an artiste!

On a January afternoon, Sam Riddle, the producer of *Star Search,* took me to lunch and asked, "How would you like to play Carnegie Hall?" I lost it on the spot.

The event was announced and sold out in three hours. Thanks to the growing number of Harrisites, we could have played for weeks. Jerry came back to Los Angeles and we went to work. The International Pancakes would be making their Carnegie debut as well, and this was our chance to show America the Sam beyond the two-minute, money-note power ballads.

We wrote, arranged, and rehearsed nonstop. Jerry had Bette pop in now and then to offer ideas and a little confidence bolstering. We used the same cheap costumes Ann Marie had sewn for the fifty-seat gig, only my dickie-tuxedo shirt was upgraded, with white and translucent sequins, like shiny scales, now making me look like a combination of Groucho Marx, Magic Johnson, and a flounder.

Jerry, the girls, and I arrived at JFK and piled into a waiting giant black stretch. When the legendary twinkling skyline appeared to us from the Triborough Bridge, we knew it had been lit just for us. As we neared Times Square en route to our midtown hotel, I opened the enormous sunroof and the girls and I stood, squeezing our upper bodies through the portal, and waved like grand marshals in the Macy's Thanksgiving Day Parade. We yelled to Times Square, "How do you get to Carnegie Hall?" and a few New Yorkers actually yelled back, "Practice! Practice!"

The next day, I entered the stage door for rehearsal with the reverence that some might feel entering the Vatican. I was shown to my three-room suite with a Steinway in the corner of the guest area and a little window that looked out over the audience. At a break during rehearsal, Jerry left me alone on the empty stage and told me to take in all the ghosts: Gershwin, Bernstein, Callas, Ellington, Garland, Holiday. I was next. I did a time-step in my Chuck Taylors and could hear the sound of rubber taps pinging back from the tiers of seats that would soon be filled.

Flowers arrived by the truckload and were endlessly lined along the hallway outside my dressing room. The old stage doorman, who had been a fixture since the late 1950s, said it was the most flowers he'd seen since Judy Garland in 1961. Jesus Christ.

As it got closer to showtime, I began searching through the arrangements. Some of them were from friends and family, most were from people I didn't know—supportive TV viewers who saw me as the American dream, and celebrities whom I'd never met. But none of them were from the guy I was dating in Los Angeles. His name was Stephen and he was an entertainment lawyer and I was planning on spending the rest of my life with him. We would be a historic team like Norma Shearer and Irving Thalberg, which he didn't know yet but would find out soon enough.

At the half hour call, instead of preparing for the biggest night of my life, I was tearing through the flowers like a madman and the hallway looked like a gardener had gone on a psychotic mowing rampage. But there was nothing from Stephen. It occurred to me that Jerry had hidden the flowers to sufficiently freak me out and give me an edge for the show. It would be just like him to try to make me vulnerable so that I went on *in need*.

I pushed him up against the dressing room door, put my nose to his, and growled, "Where. Are. My. Flowers?!"

I went on in need.

The show was otherworldly for me. And a bit jarring for the audience at times, especially the part where I pulled a gun out of my tailcoat breast pocket at the end of "God Bless the Child" and shot myself in the head. Then the Pancakes entered in Pierrot costumes and masks, holding bouquets of colored balloons on long strings, and we sang a song about being committed to a mental institution.

The audience was *farmisht,* as Jerry would say. But they were willing.

After "Over the Rainbow," they rushed the stage and I exited to find Jerry in the wings, jumping up and down. I knew I was going back out for an encore, but he said, "Let 'em beg." He pushed me by the shoulders down the hall and, in our euphoria, we somehow walked *out* of the stage door and onto Fifty-Sixth Street. The door slammed behind us, jarring us into reality. I turned the brass knob to get back in. Locked! We rattled. We banged. We screamed. Nothing.

The crowd was chanting inside and I was trapped outside! After several minutes of kicking and shrieking, the old stage doorman, who'd been watching from the wings, came to look for us and heard our desperate calls.

I ran back to the stage and as I was about to go on, Jerry stopped me and said, solemnly, "I really didn't take the flowers. Stephen didn't send any. He didn't send any flowers, Sam."

Jerry knew what he was doing. And I knew what he was doing. And he knew that I knew that he knew what he was doing. But it still worked. My encore was the Janis Joplin song "Cry Baby"—all about being treated like shit and still remaining a doormat, and I'd practically had the word "welcome" tattooed

on my chest when it came to relationships. I gave the performance of my life and ended in a melodramatic puddle on the
floor at its finish.

After the show my mother and brother and closest friends,
who had flown in from everywhere, came to my dressing room.
I realized my father was missing, and my mom told me he
thought it was too crowded backstage. I left my guests and,
after a lengthy search, found him smoking in a hidden alleyway,
where he could tell me that I had done good without the dis-
traction of other compliments.

A downtown hotspot hosted an after-party and I barely
slept before being interviewed on the *Today* show, and then
rushed to the airport to get back to Hollywood in time to shoot
a variety television series—all in twenty-four hours. I was already feeling like the overextended, poor-me, piece-of-meat,
nobody-suffers-like-Sam-does lonely star who is used up. I'd
been rehearsing that role since I was twelve and I was finally
getting to play it, complete with episodes of secluding myself
in the bathroom only to emerge hours later smelling of Jack
Daniel's and Cheez Whiz.

Jerry loved and played into the drama, but he was mostly
protective. He stayed with me in Los Angeles to write my first
concert tour show while I finished my first album. One Sunday
morning, I ambled into the kitchen for coffee and found Jerry
sitting in the breakfast nook reading the *Los Angeles Times*. I sat
next to him and flipped through the Calendar section. I'd had a
feature article the Sunday before and I was eager to see if there
were any comments from readers.

The "Letters to the Editor" page was curiously missing.

"Where's the rest of the paper?" I asked.

"I don't know what you mean," Jerry mumbled, his face buried in the sports section, which I'd never seen him read.

"Part of the paper is missing."

"I didn't notice."

I was disheveled and morning puffy, but I jumped into my clothes, still pooled on my bedroom floor from the previous night, and headed to the corner market called World's Finest Meats. They weren't the world's finest meats. They weren't even the block's finest meats. In fact, no one was quite sure what animals their finest meats came from. But they also sold sundries and newspapers, so I ventured in and began leafing through the *Times*.

"Hey!" came a voice from in front of the world's finest meat counter. "Hey!! Sam Harris, is that you?"

I looked up to see an African-American of Amazonian proportions and questionable gender, wearing a yellow tube top and a pair of capri pants that wouldn't capri on anyone shorter than six-foot-two.

"Good morning." I smiled.

"I thought that was you. My sister said she saw you in here once. She was so excited. But now that I see you for myself—you just an ugly little thang."

I didn't know what to say. Somehow this person felt that because she had seen me on TV, I must not be an actual human with actual feelings.

"I'm sorry," I actually said, throwing money on the counter and tucking the paper under my arm as I hurried out.

I walked in the door of my house in a daze. Upset. But more so, perplexed. Had a woman-who-might-have-been-a-man just said to me "You just an ugly little thang"? And she-he-whatever was black! Black people were my people! How could this be?

I told Jerry what happened and took a shower to collect myself. Once dressed, I returned to the breakfast nook and found the paper neatly folded. I flipped through the Calendar section but, once again, the "Letters to the Editor" page was missing.

"This can't be happening!" I complained in disbelief.

Jerry was washing morning dishes with a casual homey air that brought to mind Aunt Bea from old episodes of *The Andy Griffith Show*—if Aunt Bea had been a muscled, bearded gay man with a streak of lypple green in her hair.

"Wha-at?" he said in singsong innocence.

I knew something was up. I'd seen the *Lucy* episode where she cut an article out of the newspaper to avoid Ricky's wrath.

"Okay, where is it?" I demanded.

"Where is what?"

"Where is the page? I know you took it."

He was drying a pan. "You know, if you turn the flame off right after you put the eggs in, they don't overcook and they stay really fluffy."

"You're hiding something from me! Where is the paper?!"

Jerry reluctantly reached under the sink and pulled the missing section from the very bottom of the trash can. It was covered in soggy coffee grounds and gooky eggshells. He wiped it off as much as he could and shyly handed it to me. I scanned the page and found it:

Dear Editor,
Why are you wasting valuable column space on Sam Harris?
I don't get it. He sounds like a cross between a police siren,
Ethel Merman, and Arnold the Pig.

I paused to absorb the full effect. Then I turned to Jerry, who was standing sweetly with a dish towel in his hand.

"I CAN'T BELIEVE YOU LET ME READ THIS!" I screamed, and stormed out of the room.

• • •

When Jerry was diagnosed with AIDS in 1988, he and Sean moved to an apartment they'd taken on a picturesque canal in Amsterdam. He was writing a movie for Disney that was to star Bette, and the disease was so mired in taboo that he was afraid he'd be fired if they found out. If anyone found out. Bette, her husband, Harry, and her business partner, Bonnie, along with me and my partner, Ed, were the only ones who were privy to the shameful secret. We flew to Amsterdam several times to see him, swearing to keep quiet, even when it came to our closest mutual friends. As autumn descended into winter, each trip was a progressive snapshot of a weaker, more aged, insufficient Jerry. "I had to get AIDS to get a jawline and cheekbones," he joked, grinning, from his hospital bed.

I could not show my grief to him, nor Sean, nor anyone back home, so from Amsterdam, I found myself traveling to Auschwitz-Birkenau for some sort of cruel sanctuary, to experience the concentration camp in the biting, opiate cold, at its worst. Anything green would have seemed wrong.

The camp was oddly unsupervised and I saw only two other visitors, as silent as the white, dead sky. I wandered throughout the desolate place, row after exacting row of rotting bunkers among a geometric landscape of teetering brick chimneys rising like Legos from naked cement foundations.

I found the exact spot in front of the train tracks where boxcars of unsuspecting Jews and other outcasts had arrived for selection, and sat on the frozen ground among footprints, petrified like muddy fossils, left from tourists on warmer days. I lay in a bunk that was cramped, even by myself, with oddments of stubborn straw poking up from between the wooden planks. In the museum, photos of skeletal prisoners with lifeless eyes looked too much like Jerry. But that's why I'd come, I supposed. For the injustice.

Several weeks later, on January 18, Sean called me in Los Angeles at 4:00 a.m. and simply said, "It's almost time." I got the first flight out of LA to New York to London to Amsterdam and I rushed from Schiphol airport to the hospital. But I missed Jerry's passing by an hour. For nearly a decade, he had been there for me at every important moment of my life, and I had failed to be there for his last.

A doctor led me to a strikingly white room where a gauzy lemon haze of sunlight formed a trapezoid through a single window. Jerry would have totally loved the light. And that I noticed it. In the center of the room was a waist-high wooden slab of birch or ash or beech. Jerry lay on top, covered with a sheet as white as the walls. He didn't have his glasses on and it seemed wrong. I would need to find his glasses.

Sean insisted that Jerry be laid to rest in their newly adopted country, and we were joined by Jerry's mother and father and sisters and Bette later that day. He was buried the next morning in a Jewish cemetery dotted with lopsided headstones dating back to the eighteenth century, etched with weathered Dutch names like von Hofwegen and Klerx. It was surreal—like some kind of foreign period-piece indie film. The air was sad. Black, naked trees reached down like knobby-knuckled, arthritic fingers. Six pallbearers, dressed in formal gray tails with gloves, spats, and top hats, silently carried the pine casket in procession as a bell heavily tolled over and over again. And over and over again. And over and over and over again. We walked behind the casket, led by Sean, who had planned the whole thing with the funeral director like a Dutch Jackie Kennedy. His mustache revealed a breakfast of *suikerbrood* with *hagelslag* and hot chocolate with *slagroom*.

"What the fuck is this?" came a voice from behind me. It was Jerry's seventyish mother. "Stop with the bell already."

At graveside, Bette sang "I Think It's Going to Rain Today," and I sang "The Boat Song," which Jerry and I had written together. Both had been requested by him—or so Sean said. I didn't believe Jerry ever acknowledged he was going to die so I couldn't imagine him making funeral plans, much less this version. It was all too maudlin. And just too Dutch.

The only thing remotely Jerry was the headstone, which Sean had had engraved with a line Jerry wrote for one of Bette's shows:

DID I SING THE BALLAD YET?

WAS I WONDERFUL?

Memorials were planned to celebrate Jerry in Los Angeles and then New York. The LA ceremony brimmed with so many people whose lives had been touched by his genius, including a very mournful Marc Shaiman, the composer, who was incensed at the secrecy of shame that had cheated him out of saying good-bye to his good friend.

The New York memorial would be the most important. It was Jerry's city and his people. The Actors Playhouse was the venue, a few short blocks from the apartment on Bleecker that Jerry had rented since the 1960s. Bette and I and a few others arrived early to place flowers, the piano, a podium, and the screen for the slide show.

When nothing was left to be done, there was still time to spare and I was anxious and needed an activity. I looked down and noticed that the carpeting was nubby. I found a pair of scissors in the box office and began crawling on the floor, row by row, seat by seat, snipping clots of carpet. I knew it was stupid and fairly pointless but it was the kind of thing Jerry would have done—like using red bar straws as gels in the crappy Italian restaurant where we started together. Lost in my own world, my head suddenly bumped against something. I looked up and it was Bette. We were nose to nose. She had a pair of scissors and was crawling on the floor, row by row, seat by seat, snipping clots of carpet. We smiled at the improbability and of-course-ness of the moment. I wanted to believe in an afterlife where Jerry was laughing at the extraordinary in the ordinary.

One way or another, he had trained us well and we were products of his neurosis.

That night, after the memorial and the family get-together at the mandatory Chinese restaurant on Seventh Avenue, Sean, Jerry's sister, Cynthia, Bruce, and I went to the apartment to recover and reminisce. I felt blank. Jerry's influence and friendship was so large that I couldn't find specific memories. There was no place to begin. I couldn't get past the end. His gaunt face. The bizarre Dutch funeral. And more than anything, that I wasn't there for his death. That I had missed the moment.

At about two in the morning, a scream of sudden brakes and the squeal of skidding tires were followed by a metallic crash that broke our reflection. But no one moved. We were spent. It was New York. Things happen. Then I found myself racing down the stairs and out to the street.

The accident was bad. The car was buckled around a street-light, which was akilter but still illuminating the scene. The warped passenger door fell open and a man covered in blood, probably in his thirties, crawled out slowly and fell to the street. I ran to him and, with the help of another man, carried him a few feet to the small set of stairs at the entrance of the corner building. His head was a pincushion of tiny shards of glass and blood streaked his face and hair like red ink. There were no visible major wounds and he was breathing fine, if not talking.

Someone called an ambulance and a small crowd gathered, but no one with any medical knowledge came forward, so I sat with him on the stairs. He edged himself up and lay splayed across my lap, and I wrapped my arms around his chest.

And then he died.

There was no gasping last breath or final, wisdom-filled declaration. No fluttering of the eyelids or clawed outstretch of hand. No moan or even the raising of his chest for a last, releasing exhalation.

He just . . . died.

I remained with him until the ambulance came and then I went back upstairs, covered in the blood of a stranger, and remembered Jerry.

9. Ham

I fear that my karmic lesson in this lifetime is humility. And I think that lesson is beneath me.

It was the tradition at Central Elementary that the role of Santa always be played by a third grader in the annual Christmas show, so, as a lowly second grader, I was relegated to a mere elf in the chorus. Our music teacher, Mrs. Fisher, who was also my private piano teacher, wrote an inspired original show with original songs every year. We didn't live in New York City, or even Tulsa, but come the holidays, the Sand Springs grade school Christmas show had a world premiere. That year, the story line was that Santa had disappeared, and all of the North Pole was desperately searching for him in time to save Christmas. Penny Bare played Mrs. Claus. She was given a powerful scene near the end in which she wished and prayed for her husband's safe return. When the phone rang, rather than answer, she stared at it, unable to pick it up, and sang a song contemplating the caller, hopeful that it was Santa or at least someone with information as to his whereabouts.

I'd loved the song since the first time I heard it when Mrs. Fisher taught it to Penny, along with our backup elf parts. Mrs.

Fisher conducted, the flab under her upper arms swaying in time to the music, creating a fleshy metronome that was both mesmerizing and slightly disconcerting. But the tune had a catchy hook:

> *Ting-a-ling-a-ling, my phone is ringing.*
> *Ting-a-ling-a-ling, who can it be?*
> *Ting-a-ling-a-ling, dare do I answer?*
> *Ting-a-ling-a-ling, I sweetly sing.*

Its melody haunted me day and night and I crooned it around the house and school yard, nonstop.

On the night of our single performance, my elf-mates and I wore little outfits made of green felt, with red spiked trimming around the collar and matching hats with silver bells sewn at the end. We entered in a line and stood just downstage of a flimsy cardboard flat, broadly painted as a wintery candy cane workshop. One sneeze from a sniffly elf could have taken the whole thing down.

Penny began her monologue and I looked out into the audience of radiant and proud parents. The Clauses' phone rang on cue and the pianist began the musical boom-chuck introduction. Penny registered all the angst and anticipation of the caller and Mrs. Fisher nodded for her to sing, dictating the strict tempo with dangling upper arms.

There was absolutely no premeditation.

Yes, I'd sung it a thousand times, and perhaps had even fantasized about playing the part myself. So I . . . just . . . started . . . to sing her song. Not humming along, lost in my head. Loudly. Like there should be a spotlight on me.

> *Ting-a-ling-a-ling, my phone is ringing!*
> *Ting-a-ling-a-ling, who can it be?!*

Mrs. Fisher frowned and discreetly shook her head. I didn't know why. Penny didn't come in at all. She just turned to me and glared. It was then that I realized I was singing. And Penny was wondering why a fucking elf was upstaging her big number.

Ting-a-ling-a-ling, dare do I answer . . . ?

I trailed off on the last line of the stanza.

Ting-a-ling-a-ling, I . . . sweetly . . .

I knew I had done something terribly wrong. Suddenly, I thought of the audience and considered their quandary of why a backup elf was so concerned about Santa's whereabouts in the eleventh hour. Did they think there was a shocking plot twist introducing a new character? Who was this troubled elf? A heretofore unknown relative? A disgruntled employee? And what was he doing answering Mrs. Claus's personal phone?! The piano continued to vamp the plodding boom-chuck boom-chuck for what seemed hours as I rummaged my elf-index for any possible dramaturgical justification to save the show. Unlike with my glass-in-the-foot show-must-go-on experience two years earlier, there was no way out of this. My singing was obviously an appalling mistake and my actions were unforgivable.

In the most unprofessional move of my seven years, or any time thereafter, I began to cry and ran off the stage.

I buried myself in the black drape bordering the stage-left wings until a teacher came and pulled me away and down the few stairs to the classroom hallway, where I could no longer sabotage the production. I sobbed and blubbered as Penny finally got to sing her song. At its finish, even from the hallway, I could hear the deafening applause. I knew it was not so much for her performance as in support of her ability to go on with the show after an upstart elf tried to abduct her moment in the sun . . . or the snow, as it were.

I sat, alone, in my second-grade classroom for the remainder of the show. I didn't return to the stage for the company curtain call, afraid I would be booed or, worse, patronized. It wasn't cute. I changed into my civilian clothes and waited in the parking lot by the car for my parents to take me home.

Twenty-five years and several thousand performances later, I played the title role in the national tour of the Broadway production of *Joseph and the Amazing Technicolor Dreamcoat*. It was the best financial deal of my theater career thus far and I called my parents to share the good news: an incredible weekly salary, a percentage of the box office, merchandising. After a long silence, my father said, "You know, if you were a professional baseball player, you'd *really* be raking it in." If I had called to tell them I'd become a professional baseball player, he'd probably have said, "You know, if you were emperor of the world . . ."

Undaunted, I heartily dove into the Andrew Lloyd Webber show, which was based on the classic Bible story but was really about my being practically naked in a loincloth. At least it was for me. I spent more time doing crunches and push-ups than singing.

One of the unique elements of the tour was that we picked up about forty local kids in each city to participate onstage with singing and some dancing. They were cast months in advance and were rehearsed prior to our arrival. They ranged in age from about eight to thirteen and, often, by the time we actually rolled into town, some of the girls had blossomed into young women—tall young women—with large breasts. They were placed in the back row and their chests were strapped down with ACE bandages and hot glue. The short, innocent, and innocuous were positioned in the front. And then there were the parents—hovering, crouching in the shadows like vermin.

For some reason, certain cities produced an astounding number of stage parents who encouraged their moppets to mug and upstage other actors, seeing this as their wunderkinds' big break into show business. Little tykes would come to the put-in with enough makeup to make Courtney Love look like a PTA president—and some of the girls wore makeup too. I recall a sweet boy, undersize for his eleven or twelve years, with a real sparkle about him, who was always practicing little pirouettes in the wings. Unlike some of the other mothers, his was unassuming and trying to honor her child's hunger for the stage, though she didn't quite get it. I wanted to say to her, ever so gently, "You do realize that little Brian is a big queen, right? Be understanding with him. Norfolk won't be . . ." But I bit my tongue and gave him the thumbs-up. He returned the signal and landed in splits.

I would receive notes, drawings, and little gifts backstage from the kids. Most were lovely: "Dear Mr. Harris, this is my first show. It is so exciting. Break a leg!" Little Brian wrote: "Dear Mr. Harris, how often do you work out to get your chest like that?"

I once actually got a note from a child that said, "I need some advice about agents. Can we have coffee between shows?" *Agent advice? Coffee between shows? From a ten-year-old kid?* A mother was clearly involved. I wrote back, "I never have coffee between shows. It keeps me awake during Act Two."

Truly, though, I did enjoy them. They were, for the most part, ebullient and joyful. However, when you're on the road, a lot of enthusiastic screaming children can be trying, especially when you're hungover and still have hundreds of crunches to do before curtain. I fantasized that they could be chained up in the boiler room when not onstage. Occasionally, there'd be a child who had "it"—that special inner light and inherent need. And I knew they'd been a backup elf in a Christmas show somewhere, desperate for a solo, and that they were destined to make this their life. When I saw that spark, I would make a point to spend time with that child and let them know I recognized their calling.

At the end of the show, I sang an encore of "Close Every Door," which had a dramatic key change and final note that never failed to ensure a standing ovation. The kids were staged to sit on the floor around me and gaze up with their sweet little faces and sing their sweet little *la-la*s in the sweet little interlude. One night about a year into the tour, a talented and highly driven ham of a child, who was positioned directly at my feet, kept smiling straight out to the house instead of up at me. Then, during the song, he somehow edged in front of me so that he was center. At the key change I would always walk down a few feet for the big finish, but with the kid there, I had to climb over him so as not to step on his hands. After the first show, I asked that he politely be told not to crawl in front of me. It was reported that his reply was, "I'm so sorry. I didn't realize I was doing that." Sweet thing. It can be confusing out there with all those people staring.

The next night, he not only made his way in front of me but took to sitting on his haunches so that he was tall enough to be in my light. It was as if he was possessed. Clearly, whoever was talking to him about this problem was not making headway, so I asked to speak to him myself. He was brought to my dressing room, where I told him that I was concerned that I might step on him when I moved downstage and would hate for that to happen. He was quite mannerly, said he hadn't realized he was doing it, and then asked if he could try on my gold finale headdress.

Since the poor kid had been admonished twice, I thought it was the least I could do.

The next night, little Hormel edged his way down center, rose to his knees, smiled out front, and now I could hear him *singing my part!* Just as I had done to poor Penny Bare. But this kid seemed intentional, calculated, and I knew I should never have let him try on my gold headdress—the showbiz equivalent of smack to a junkie.

When the key change came, I had no choice but to cut him off, cold turkey, so I stepped forward onto his little hand, not giving it my full weight . . . well, most of it, and without letting the audience see, I shot him a death stare intended to stunt his growth.

It suddenly occurred to me that I was competing with a little kid for my place on the stage and how pathetic that was. What did that say about *me*? *My* ego? *My* ham-dom?

That was when I stepped on his other hand.

He had a choice: either see it as an opportunity for *more* attention by jerking back or crying or running off the stage—or get the message, suck it up, and learn to be a pro, kid. He chose the latter.

After the show, I told him how sorry I was for stepping on his little hands, but he'd somehow *accidentally* gotten off his mark and I couldn't see him *all the way down at my feet* for the glare of *my* spotlight. We stared at each other for a moment. Then he said, "It's okay, I didn't really feel it, with all the applause and excitement and everything. Hey, did you hear that audience tonight? I think they were the best yet. A little slow in the beginning but by the end they were like putty."

This kid had it bad. I predicted big things.

• • •

After fifteen thrilling and arduous months with *Joseph,* I was ready to move on. Keeping my weight in constant check had resulted in choosing alcohol as my primary means of caloric intake. I'd also decreased my sit-up regime and had taken to drawing on abdominal muscles with brown eye shadow. I was grateful to hang up the loincloth at last. A new chapter was at hand: Danny and I were getting ready to move to New York as a couple!

We had met on the show. I was taken with him on the first day of rehearsal when the cast took turns introducing ourselves and he cleverly said, "I'm Daniel Jacobsen and I'm playing Daniel, Jacob's son."

He was ruggedly handsome in a Marlboro Man way, but with the naive, jocular smile of a boy, and he drew my eye against my will. I was officially still in a ten-year relationship that was suffering a sad, irreversible rut, but I swore it would not be a casualty of the road. I chose isolation and discipline. Still, as the tour progressed, Danny pierced my defenses, unknowingly ripping me from my settlement of routine and an overall solemnness that had bound me to the known and prohibited me from spontaneity for so long.

I left my hotel room.

We explored cities and jumped in lakes and hiked up mountains, we made up songs and talked with silly accents, we shared our fears and expressed our hopes and we lived. And somewhere along the way, I discovered and returned to myself, concurrently. It was as consuming as a storm in the way it drenched me. It was as unpredictable as tears in the way it surprised me. And it was as sturdy as courage, in the way I said yes.

Danny would have no part in the collapse of my marriage, and I tried desperately to deny that I was meant to be with this shining, beautiful, charismatic guy who was playing my brother.

Ultimately, incest would triumph. We resisted during the Northeast leg of the tour, platonically courted on the Eastern Seaboard, and consummated in the Deep South. My previous relationship legitimately ended in the lower mountain region, and Danny and I moved in together in the Pacific Northwest.

Now we were moving into a grand nineteenth-century brownstone on the Upper West Side of Manhattan. During our travels, we had shopped for furnishings, which had been stored in various cities, and now crates containing sofas, lamps, tables, carpets, collectibles, and art were arriving from all over the country. It was like being in our own, at-home version of *Antiques Road Show*.

Only three weeks later, I got a call from Garth Drabinsky, the producer of the Canadian company of *Joseph*, which had been touring for several years and starred Donny Osmond. It seemed Donny had ruptured a vocal cord and would be out for a week, maybe two, to recover. I was asked to fill in for the last week of their run at the Colonial Theatre in Boston and *possibly* open the show in Detroit at the Fox for the first week.

The last thing in the world I wanted was to go back to the road and play this role again. I'd already gained five happy pounds and the only sit-ups I did were to reach for a box of Cheez-Its, an ashtray, a TV remote, or another glass of wine. However, the offer was lucrative and donning the loincloth would be like slipping on an old shoe—a bun-hugging, abdomen-revealing old shoe—and I still had a large supply of brown eye shadow to paint on abs as necessary.

Also, I'd been in show business long enough to know that it was an ever-changing climate of wet and dry spells. I'd been quenched and parched my whole professional life and, having been out of the New York scene for nearly two years, with Danny and I living large and no prospects on the horizon, I remembered the motto of a good friend: "When a limo pulls up—get in."

I said yes, with the provision that if it turned out to be more than a week, my fee would increase substantially. If it was more than two weeks, it would increase again. And again after the third, fourth, fifth, and so on. I knew that the healing of Donny's ruptured vocal cord was not something that could be rushed, and once I was in, it would be hard to desert the show.

My stint with the Canadian company turned into six weeks and my salary provided a year's worth of living expenses in our fancy brownstone.

During the final two weeks of my run, Donny flew to Detroit and started hanging around the theater. I had been a fan since I was about ten and had seen him and his brothers on tour three times, and was thrilled to find he was one of the kindest, sweetest, most genuinely gracious people I'd ever met. His relationship with the company was playful and there was no star ego whatsoever. Though he'd been road weary and injured, he missed his traveling family and was eager to get back to work.

Donny was on strict vocal rest and wrote everything on a pad to communicate. I'd been in that position myself and knew how grueling and frustrating it could be. Writing conversation is belabored, kills any sense of comic timing, and arguments are next to impossible. Once, while on voice rest myself, and using a pad to communicate, a friend and I got into a fuming squabble and I began writing every furious word in all caps. He grabbed the pad and said, "Stop yelling at me!"

Donny wasn't yelling at anyone. He was all smiles all the time. He started visiting my dressing room before the show and then hanging out backstage, playing pranks on cast mates and joking with the crew, but always watching me from the wings during primary scenes and songs. Finally, he was given the thumbs-up to return to the show, but Garth decided that I should finish the run in Detroit. The reviews had been stellar, the show had sold out, and it had become "Sam Harris as Joseph." For press, for ease, for everything, it was just cleaner to put Donny back in at the next city.

To assure promoters that he was returning for the remainder of the tour, and to create some extra publicity, the producers decided to put Donny in the curtain call. I was happy to comply, though I thought it odd that I would work my ass off (and abs, painted on or otherwise) for two hours and then Donny would come out for my bow, fully clothed. But I was trying to get the bigger picture and be a mensch, so I came up with a solution that I felt would serve us all, and everyone agreed: rather than having Donny enter *during* the bows, I suggested that we separate his appearance from the show to *after* the bows. I would make a curtain speech saying that I'd had a great time with this company and that Donny was healed and returning but was still on voice rest.

"He can't speak or sing until next week," I said to the crowd. "But he wanted to come out and say hello."

Donny entered and waved and smiled, a treat for the people who'd bought tickets with his name on the bill long before his vocal injury forced him out. Then we played a little vaudeville act. Voiceless Donny stood down center with me directly behind him, mostly hidden, and I slipped my arms under his. Then I sang "Puppy Love," one of the big hits from his *Tiger Beat* childhood career, while he mouthed the words and I gestured. Our ventriloquist schtick was silly and stupid and the audience ate it up. Then Donny blew a kiss to the crowd and exited, leaving me onstage for the final bow as the orchestra began the play-off.

Afterward, Donny was like a schoolboy. He loved being

onstage. He'd been playing to the masses and on television since he was a very small child, and even coming out after not having done the show was like oxygen for him.

One night, after curtain, Donny came to my dressing room and told me they'd forgotten to arrange his car service and asked if I could please give him a lift to his hotel after my driver dropped me at mine. "Of course," I said. "Not a problem at all."

The only catch, he told me, was that it would be awkward for him to come out of the stage door to waiting fans and not be able to communicate with them, being on voice rest. So could we please just make a quick excuse and get in the car and take off all in one swooping motion. I told him it was my policy to always meet people at the stage door to say hello and sign stuff, but he begged me to give that up, just this once. It seemed odd to me, but he was a fellow trouper and I wanted to be gracious, so I agreed to make the fast getaway.

The crowd waiting outside the stage door was the same size as usual, but there was a special excitement when the two Josephs emerged, and cameras snapped and flashed as they called out "Sam! "Sam!" "Sam!" "Donny!" My ego noted that there were three "Sam"s for every "Donny." It made sense—I'd just performed and he hadn't.

"Hey, everybody," I shouted, as we kept in motion toward the waiting Lincoln at the curb. "We'd love to stay and say hello, but we have to run. Donny is on voice rest and I have to get him out of the night air. But thank you for coming. I'm so sorry!"

I felt horrible. We waved to the fans and dashed to the car. Donny opened the back door for me and I slid in first. Then he lowered his head inside and said, "I just saw my driver. He's here after all, my mistake. You go on and I'll see you tomorrow." He shut the car door and turned around with a wide grin and open arms.

"I'm not supposed to talk," he practically yelled as he walked to the crowd. "But I know you've been waiting and I couldn't ignore you!"

I'd been played. He stole my people. I felt like an asshole, having sacrificed my stage door policy to protect him, and now I looked like a selfish schmuck.

But I knew that he needed them. He'd been watching me play to *his* audience, dress in *his* costumes in *his* dressing room, aided by *his* dresser. He saw that in six weeks I'd developed my own relationships and jokes with *his* company.

But when it came to the fans, he couldn't let me have them.

I was shocked at his behavior. And yet . . . and yet I understood him. Donny and I and the kid who hogged my spotlight were all very much the same. None of us could help it. We *needed* the audience. Without them we were nothing.

My driver pulled away and I looked back through the tinted windows to see Donny surrounded, smiling, laughing.

He was happier than I'd seen him since we met.

10. Drilling Without Novocaine

"Mr. Harris," roared the voice over the outdoor PA system. "Mr. Bill Harris. Your wife just called and your house is on fire."

Mom was standing next to us, holding my five-year-old brother. She couldn't have called. The townsfolk chuckled at the joke. We had gathered to watch the ribbon cutting for the new Sand Springs Airport, which was basically a paved strip in the middle of a thirsty field of cudweed and sand burrs. Fifteen minutes later, the voice came again: "Mr. Harris. Please go home. Your house is on fire."

My father decided we'd better go.

As we drove toward our block, I could smell the smoke before I could see it. We arrived to find six fire trucks and twenty neighbors clustered on the street in front of our house. A heavy, peppery steam spiraled skyward and the remains of our house spit and stammered like the last stubborn kernels of popping corn. Everyone was so sorry. The rock structure of the house was standing, but what wasn't burned was ruined by water and smoke damage. The fire had started in the basement from an electrical-wiring malfunction and gone up from there. My underground neighborhood productions would be over and my collection of Gene Kelly pictures was surely gone forever.

We sought comfort in Lot-A-Burgers, bought toothbrushes at a local store, and drove fifteen miles to Tulsa, where we stayed at the Camelot Inn: a big pink hotel complete with turrets, a massive iron gate, a moat, a drawbridge, and a swimming pool shaped like the top of a medieval spear. We'd lost the house but we were moving into a castle. A big pink castle. All we needed was someone on a purple unicorn to ride up and rescue us.

A week later, we moved into a small trailer home across the river on the outskirts of town. At first, we were a coalition of survivors—a family, hand in hand, bonded. "It's just stuff," my mother would say. "We're all okay and it's just stuff." But the glass half-full soon evaporated and was shattered on the gravel drive that led to our mobile home.

At first I blamed the mounting tension on the trailer itself. The exterior was bad enough—metal-sheeted in a migrainey white. But the inside was a foulmouthed assault on the eyes, much too much to take in all at once: A tiny space with a vast sea of browns and more browns, matching harvest gold shag carpeting and pleated half-drapes, rudely interrupted by a pumpkin kitchenette and a dining area with a foldout table that featured built-in cup holders sized for beer cans, and framed by checkered, padded bench seats. I didn't mind the individual trendy components. It was just that they were so condensed. Like walking into a swatchbook. Once, when my grandmother entered in a paisley caftan, I nearly went to the built-in knife block and gouged my eyes out.

It was also an assault on any sense of personal space. My brother and I shared a bedroom that was *exactly* the same size as the double bed inside it, so that you opened the door and climbed directly up onto the mattress like one of those blow-up bouncy houses at children's parties. I figured it must have been dropped in before they attached the roof. We had no clothes so closet space was not an issue.

The thin walls, which could not even be considered fake wood paneling—more like a photograph of wood, with grooves cut in the laminate—were not nearly enough to muffle the accelerating arguments between my parents. As the weeks wore on, the Great Wall of China might not have done the job. Money, insurance, doubts, jealousies. The precariously stacked cinder blocks supporting our tin home became an appropriate metaphor for our family foundation.

I felt it my duty to do my part, to not make waves, and to be as strong and perfect as I could. At a dentist appointment for a cavity filling, in order to prove to myself and to my mother that I was tough and could handle any challenge, I declined the Novocaine before he drilled. The doctor insisted, but I was unrelenting. It was a filling, after all, not a root canal. He finally gave in, thinking I would cave when he began.

I found a focused spot on the wall, concentrating with all my might to block out the pain as the high-pitched buzzing drill invaded my mouth. The voices in my head played over and over: *This is a test. For the next sixty seconds you will endure intense pain. In the event of a real emergency you will be prepared. This is only a test.*

I didn't give in.

I began to wear shoes and boots that were too small for my feet so that I would have a constant reminder that I was tougher than outside forces and I could block it out. At the end of the day, when my feet and toes were released from bondage, there was a surge of rapturous relief, a rush, a secret reward for suffering. Totally worth it.

I asked God for greater challenges to endure.

I should have been more specific.

• • •

Like every other year in Oklahoma, spring brought fields of dandelions, chiggers, and tornado season. One night, the sky grew dark with twisted spokes of low, smoky clouds. Then an angry rain came, heavy and unyielding. Though we all knew what it meant, Indian legend was that tornadoes flew *over* Sand Springs but never touched down. Still, basements and cellars were the routine, only this time we didn't have a cellar or basement. Trailer homes don't have cellars or basements. Memo was with us as we huddled around the TV set, adjusting the antennae to watch for weather warnings. The electricity went out. The tornado siren sounded. The rain pounded on the metal roof like a thousand machine guns. Then it stopped as if someone had turned off a switch.

Silence.

Then a series of sounds, as if instruments in an orchestra were being added, one by one:

The discordant wail of the faraway siren.

The crescendo of a slow, whooshing noise, as if heading toward a waterfall.

Then the low, tympanic rumble of an oncoming freight train.

Louder and closer. Closer and louder. Deafeningly louder.

Then it hit.

The trailer was slapped and kicked like a discarded Chef Boyardee can, tossing us about the tiny living room. Blown off the cinder blocks on both sides, but with the center ones remaining, we teeter-tottered up and down, side to side, as the furniture flew. In the strobe light flash of exploding electric lines, I saw a trailer roll, longways, outside our window. Hulking sheets of metal, entire sides of trailers took wing while my father held on to us with a strength greater than the force of God. Then, just as suddenly, it stopped.

Stillness.

Silence.

The siren trumpeted the cyclone's exit.

And the rain came again.

Tornadoes, like Baptists, travel in groups, and there was no time to wait for the next wave, so my father gathered us up to find shelter. Memo opened the screen door and it blew off its hinges, taking her with it a good ten feet. My father raced to her with my brother in his arms and scooped her to her feet. My mother grabbed my hand and, together, my family plodded through the rain and flood, knee deep, to a brick laundry facility a hundred yards away.

Inside the sturdy building, we joined other families, bleeding, crying, and in shock. The harsh fluorescent light sputtered on a woman with a great gushing wound on her forehead who refused to go to the hospital until she found her dog, which was probably somewhere in Oz by now.

My family was intact and unharmed, and I found myself disengaging, sort of floating above the crisis, observing the calamity all around me like a dream. It was as if I were invisible and had slipped into a book or movie without playing a part.

This is only a test.

The next day was sunny and breezeless and smiled with no accountability. And our family was united again. We were kinder, more available to one another and to everyone else. Together, with our neighbors, we scavenged through the debris, searching for clothes, photos, dolls—odds and ends and crumbs that could be salvaged of their lives. My tomboy girlfriend, Jonnie Tedford, and I rifled through the wreckage and would triumphantly hold up an unchipped cup, an unbroken picture frame, or a slightly bent tricycle to return to its grateful owner. Entire families were uprooted and destroyed and we were playing treasure hunt in the aftermath.

The night came, and we caught lightning bugs in a jam jar and used it as a lantern. Jonnie ripped the tails off the little insects and rubbed the glowing gunk on her face like war paint. I became enraged, transferring my silent anguish of the tornado disaster to the injustice of her senseless torture.

Big things were endurable, little things were hard.

Several months later, we moved into our rebuilt house, which was decorated with the latest trends in design, including green shag carpeting, a gold crushed-velvet sofa, a striped velvet La-Z-Boy, and a marble coffee table supported by scrolled, gold-painted legs. Hanging macramé netting held a vineyard of golden glass grapes at the entrance and clown paintings added a homey balance. The decor was not unlike the trailer's, but more spread out and with no built-in beer can holders.

We began anew, immersed in our own beautiful White Trash Versailles.

It was a guise of normalcy, and moving back home relieved no pressure. Family time was the occasional convergence around the dinner table, always hurried and awkward, singularly purposed for fueling.

More and more, my little brother and I would press our ears to the basement door as our parents fought below. Mostly that meant my father yelling and my mother crying.

One day, I came home from school with severe stomach cramps. My mother rushed me to the town doctor, who prodded and poked. I moaned in agony. My father met us at the doctor's office. This was becoming a big deal. I moaned a little more. And a little more.

As the attention and tension mounted, an odd unity developed: my parents had lovingly joined forces because I was the common concern. I squirmed, crinkling the sterile paper atop the cold examination table, and they stood on each side, holding my hands and gazing at me with tight-lipped smiles and reassuring nods. But I could sense their stolen looks to each other, their fear, their love, their apology. The doctor shook his head, as if I had only an hour to live, and they all left the room to confer and, presumably, make funeral arrangements.

Lying alone, I felt a rumble and then a gurgle and then suddenly released a great, voluminous bubble of gas. Elephantine. The table shook.

And the pain was gone.

I was in a panic. The pain couldn't go away! It *had* to get worse to justify the drama—to justify my mother and father coming together. I waved my hand furiously to clear the air as my parents and the doctor reentered with a diagnosis: acute appendicitis. I would rupture if I didn't have emergency surgery immediately, by the town doctor, who was also the mayor and postman and dogcatcher. *Emergency surgery?* I knew I had overplayed this, but really?

Act Two was in full swing. I had to go through with it. My parents had rediscovered their vows and I fully believed the gassy truth would separate them again, like the flatulent fumes dissipating into nothingness. We drove to the hospital, where I was promptly admitted and placed on a gurney. And from then on I remained present in body only: I pictured a camera above me, like I was on an episode of *Medical Center*. Chad Everett was my personal physician. I groaned and cried, holding out my hand, imagining the close-up of my trembling fingers tearing away from my weeping mother's as they rolled me away to surgery.

Chad would take care of me. And then he would be with me in recovery. And then spoon-feed me applesauce and ice cream. And then we would live together and I would be his receptionist.

After I recovered from an unnecessary appendectomy, and for the next several years, a succession of less dramatic incidents occurred that served as temporary epoxy for my disconnected family. I broke an arm. I sprained ankles and jammed fingers and developed an astigmatism that required eye exercises with thick glass prisms.

My father left his teaching position and partnered with another ex–band director to start a new business: a music store, cleverly named The Music Store. It was an industrially bland building, located "on the line," a four-lane service road that paralleled the freight train tracks leading out of town. They sold pianos and organs and sheet music, but their primary income came from selling band instruments to schools, which entailed traveling statewide to chum with band directors and principals and superintendents. My dad was a natural salesman with magnetic social skills and a good ol' boy charm coupled with a gift for telling dirty jokes. Everybody loved him.

The Music Store flourished, so much so that they opened a second store in Tulsa—practically a chain! My father had become a successful businessman, full-tilt, and at long last, our family had some money. By the time I turned fifteen, there were better clothes, impromptu trips to Vegas, smoky poker nights, and, best of all—a new house! The Jeffersons were saying it perfectly in their theme song every week on TV: "*Well, we're movin' on up!*" Indeed, we were. With three times the square footage, three levels, two fireplaces, and an enormous pine tree–spattered yard atop a hill with a view of Tulsa, featuring towering smokestacks of oil refineries in the day and twinkling city lights at night. My father was so proud, and deservedly so. He had broken out of the confines of his undereducated blue-collar family and was his own boss. And everyone else's.

If he had been a star before, he was now a superstar, and the title required his everything. Home was sort of a backstage, where he could shut down and regroup and didn't have to be "on." Even rare social occasions when friends and neighbors got together at our house were now considered depleting, debilitating. As soon as the last guest left, the other Bill emerged and retreated to his personal chair and television set without a word.

Click.

Something bigger than a sprained ankle was going to be necessary for family harmony and I prayed for the blessing of disaster.

We'd only been in the new house about a month and there was still furniture to buy, boxes to unpack, others in storage at my grandmother's, and decisions to make about exactly where the clown paintings would best be featured.

My mother took me to an eye appointment in Tulsa and we stopped by the new location of The Music Store to say hello to my father, who wasn't there. We were told we'd better get back home. They'd just gotten the call and my dad had already left:

Our new house was on fire.

Neither my mother nor I could really take in the news. How could this be true? We'd already lost one house to fire and we'd just moved into this one a few weeks ago—our new life, the dream house, the achievement of my father's success. We drove home silently, our gazes fixed ahead, our hearts pounding and our minds racing about the possible extent of the damage. Maybe it was small. Maybe it was contained. Maybe it would be over by the time we got there and everyone would say "It was nothing." Or maybe it wasn't even true.

But I knew, deep down, that if it was true, it was my fault. A punishment for asking God for a catastrophe to put our family in league. *Ask and ye shall receive.*

We could see the billowing smoke miles before we arrived. It was true. Déjà vu, except with better real estate. We exited the highway and sped through the town, past our last house, which had burned down five years earlier, and up the hill. Fire trucks lined the street, and neighbors and close friends stood in the yard as if attending a bluegrass festival. We got out of the car and my mother raced to my father. They held each other as the firefighters drenched what was left of our house and a few brave volunteers dragged out scorched evidence of our existence. My brother was playing with a friend from our old neighborhood and was kept there to shield him from the panic.

A neighbor my age, befittingly named Malea Stoner, walked up slowly and intently, throwing her waist-length blond hair over her shoulder, and attempted to embrace me too intimately, almost sexually. I didn't know what to do with her presumption—as if she could possibly understand or know that this tragedy was my doing. Her touch released some tiny increment of the poison and guilt bound up in me that would, in days to come, ripen into sorrow. I rudely shrugged her off and floated through the crowd, desperate for perspective, for salvation, some action to delude or take it all back.

It would have been inappropriate to sing, so instead, I saw it all play out from a crane shot, cut with close-ups of the ash-stained firemen, the silhouette of my father's arm around my crumpled mother, the slow pan of thunder-struck onlookers' faces, and that particular quiet when something is lost. Then the underscoring began and swelled with tragic poignancy. I had to remember this feeling for later, when I could use it onstage.

I learned that my father had brought my grandmother's used stereo console to my bedroom as a gift, and had put a favorite record of mine on the turntable and blasted the volume to surprise me when I got home. The stereo shorted out and my only possessions were literally the clothes on my back.

Neighbors packed us up with comfort food—country ham, mashed potatoes, and corn bread—and we drove to a motel just outside of town. I don't recall where. After you've stayed in a pink castle you don't remember anything else. I went to school the next morning, as usual, and everyone knew what had happened. Well, everyone except my ninth-grade algebra teacher.

Mrs. Sparks was the most meticulous, by-the-book taskmaster of the entire school. She had pencil-thin suggestions of lips and a beanie of solidly sprayed, sepia-dyed brown curls, and she wore a different pantsuit or, rather, uniform, for each day of the week. White for Mondays, brown for Tuesdays . . . If you were unsure of the day, you could just look at what she was wearing. She was also an amazing teacher and I truly liked her and I knew, or rather I thought, that she liked me.

I was underrested and overwrought as I walked to my desk and sat for her class. She asked us to pass our homework forward and open our algebra books. I raised my hand.

"Mrs. Sparks, I don't have my homework or book. Yesterday—"

"Dummy row!" she demanded. And pointed to the far left row of desks reserved for those she considered lazy or stupid.

"But you don't understand—"

"Mr. Harris, you'll be receiving an F for this assignment and there are no new books issued for free without turning in the old one," she rattled.

"But I don't have the old one," I said. "Yesterday—"

"Then no new book unless you have the money!" she clipped.

"I don't have any money," I stammered, beginning to break.

"Then you don't get a new book! Dummy row. Now."

I started to get up, unable to argue anymore. I knew I was to blame for everything and the dummy row was an exile much more lenient than I deserved.

"Mrs. Sparks," came a voice from the back of the room. It was Teri Mullins. "Sam's house burned down yesterday and his homework and book were in it."

Everyone waited to see if Mrs. Sparks would back down. She was famous for not doing so. After a moment, she pulled a ring of skeleton keys from her desk drawer and unlocked an ancient cabinet, snatching out a new book. She practically slammed it on my desk without a word and started the day's equation. It was as close to an act of compassion as anyone had ever witnessed her commit.

That afternoon I joined my family at what was left of our house. Friends with shovels were digging through the wreckage, piling it to be hauled away. There was nothing whole left of my stuff. A fragment of furniture here, a melted cup there. Then I saw the strangest thing: a blue spiral notebook, charred on one edge but intact, glossy, peering from the wet black ash. I plucked it out and opened it. It was a report I'd written five years ago titled "What I Did This Summer" in which I told the story of our *first* house burning down. I couldn't believe it was true. The only thing of mine that had survived this fire was my schoolboy's account of the first one.

I flashed on a story my Memo had told me: In the early 1920s, she, her husband, Sam, and baby boy, Darrell, lived in a tiny wooden house on the plains of Texas. A tornado came and they took refuge in the cellar. Upon emerging, they found their house was completely gone, with no sign of it having ever stood. The small leather-stringed purse that contained all of their savings, fifty dollars, had flown away with the rest of their possessions.

They walked during the day and camped out at night, receiving blankets and food from generous but poverty-stricken residents as they traveled on their way to a new life with no real destination. On the third day, in the middle of a vast field, my grandmother happened to look down, and before her lay the tiny leather purse. It was the kind of miracle that seemed impossible, not even fictionally believable, and though my Memo had never told a lie, I'd questioned her honesty.

As I stared at the fourth-grade report on the first fire, the only surviving remnant of my room, I knew that my grandmother's story was true. And I knew I wasn't to blame for this fire any more than I was for the first. Bad things happen to good people sometimes. I tucked the singed pages into my jeans and filled a small plastic bag with ashes that had once been my house.

The next day I walked into Mrs. Sparks's room and placed the bag of ashes on her desk in front of the entire class.

"Here's my old book," I said, matter-of-factly, "for your records."

And I took my seat for class.

11. Comfort Food

"They're blowing up New York!" shouted the voice, screened on the answering machine. "Pick up! Pick up!"

This was the third time the phone had rung, unanswered, at the ungodly hour of 6:00 a.m. I'd slept on an inflatable mattress, the only piece of furniture, not even really furniture, in our new house in Los Angeles, where I'd flown the day before after eight years of living in my beloved New York City.

I dragged myself up the stairs, certain that if anyone had called three times at that hour, someone must be dead. That was more true than I could have possibly imagined.

It was Liza, hysterically sobbing, and I grabbed the phone in a daze.

"What's wrong?"

"Turn on the TV. They're blowing up New York!"

It was just after 9:00 in New York, an ungodly hour for Liza, and I tried to make sense of the confusion. Liza kept her bedroom television on twenty-four hours a day and I thought perhaps she woke up to *The Towering Inferno* on Turner Classic Movies and thought it was real.

"Calm down. Take a breath. What are you talking about?" I muttered, switching on the tiny kitchen television, which, in partnership with a few pots and pans and some paper plates, were the only articles in my possession before the moving trucks were to arrive in the next few days.

And I saw it: the Twin Towers were both hemorrhaging fire and smoke and Liza screamed that two planes had rocketed into the buildings and it was an attack and the end of the world. We watched in silence forever and when the first building crumbled in a cloud of gray dust, done, gone, we joined hundreds of millions of others in a collective unspeakable gasp that shattered everything we ever knew.

A few months prior, Danny and I had decided to move to Los Angeles. For some time, Danny had expressed a desire to try the West Coast, but I hadn't been interested. Now, after doing eight shows a week for eight years with barely a break, I needed a change, maybe explore more TV and film, something new. Plus I was turning forty. I'd become depressed and isolated, and when we had both been cast in a Los Angeles production of *Hair* in June, it had become a beacon of possibilities—and a temporary respite from my alcohol intake, which was accelerating by the bottle. I was certain a move across the country would change my course and, subconsciously, my drinking. Having sung the Act One closer in *Hair* while fully frontally nude in a spotlight for three minutes, anything was possible.

We'd given up our fancy brownstone apartment on the Upper West Side two weeks before. Danny had driven with the dogs, Zach and Emma, and dashed to a corporate gig in Las Vegas while I remained in New York, staying at Liza's Upper East Side apartment, to musically supervise her appearance on *Michael Jackson: 30th Anniversary Celebration* at Madison Square Garden.

She'd been asked to sing Jackson's "You Are Not Alone" for two performances, each to be filmed and then edited into one special. The first was set for September 7 and the second, September 10. I was scheduled to fly to Los Angeles the next day at 9:00 a.m. on September 11.

The night of the first performance, backstage was aglitter with superstars who'd been invited to sing—an ever-joyous Luther Vandross, a skeletally thin Whitney Houston, Usher, Gloria Estefan, Marc Anthony, Britney Spears, and a host of others who were there to honor Michael, all leading to a performance by the legend himself.

Michael Jackson was forever pushing Elizabeth Taylor in a wheelchair throughout the bowels of the forum, as if they were kids at Coney Island. "Here we go," he would squeal in his high-pitched breathy voice, pushing and then releasing Elizabeth's chair as she whizzed down the hall, raising her arms in the air and squealing in delight.

When it was time, a stage manager knocked on Liza's dressing room door and led us to the wings, where I kissed her on the cheek and whispered our traditional good-luck phrase, "Take no prisoners!" I started off and she grabbed my arm and said, "Really listen. I'm singing this for you." And then I hurried to the director's trailer to watch her camera coverage.

Despite the lineup of young hip-hop and pop stars, the reaction to Liza's introduction was thunderous. She took the stage uncharacteristically timidly, as if not in the element she typically thrived. The music began and my heart pounded, as unsure of her vocal entrance as she seemed to be. Then she sang, low and slow. She applied the lesson she'd taught to me whenever I go outside myself: *Listen to the lyric. The words will always give you a point of view and tell you what to do.* Then I remembered she'd said "I'm singing this for you," and though I'd been listening to the lyrics for weeks, I heard them in a new way.

> *Another day has gone and I'm still all alone*
> *How could this be, you're not here with me*
> *Someone tell me why did you have to go*
> *And leave my world so cold.*

At first it was fragile and introspective, but as the song gained in strength, so did she. It suddenly hit me that this chapter of my life with Liza would be ending soon with my move to California. A gospel choir entered and supported her as she promised:

> *You are not alone, I am here with you.*
> *Though you're far away, I am here to stay.*

I realized that I was getting a very private good-bye at Madison Square Garden, witnessed by an audience of thousands.

She brought down the house, and it was clear that Michael was emotionally destroyed, even behind sunglasses that covered most of his kabuki-made-up face.

Instead of attending the after-party, Liza and I went back to her apartment, exhausted but triumphant. She got in her Luigi-logoed nightshirt and worn red fluffy slippers, and I stepped into a cozy pair of sweatpants that predated the Clinton administration. I thought about all the times Liza and I had come from some event, some show, some backstage where, moments before, people had been clamoring for one of us, and instead of swimming in the adulation, we'd gotten a burger or gone to a midnight movie and gobbled popcorn and Raisinets until we were sated.

Somewhere in the middle of the late-night airing of *From Here to Eternity*, I pushed mute on the remote and turned to her and said, "You were great tonight. You did it. And you don't need me for the second show. I really want to go to Los Angeles and start my new life and I love you but it's time for me to go."

It was now after midnight, on September 8.

We'd seen each other nearly every day for years, and the depth and complexity of our friendship had even at times become a threat to my relationship with Danny. He was my partner, my best friend, the person I'd committed to spending my life with. But the connection between Liza and me was like a private refuge to which no one gained entry and would take its toll on anyone.

I'd kept our moving to Los Angeles a secret from Liza until just a month before, not wanting to ignite any more emotion than was necessary and knowing that we would both deal better with less time to talk about it. But my saying I wanted to leave early suddenly made the move real. We'd had our two-week, live-in bon voyage party and now it was all ending.

"I understand. You need to go," she said.

I changed my flight to September 10 and as I boarded the plane early that morning, I checked my last e-mail as an official New Yorker and saw that Patti LuPone had written me a send-off message:

```
Sam — You are making a mistake. You don't belong in
Los Angeles. It is a horrible awful place and your
home and heart are New York. You are a traitor and
I am not speaking to you ever again.
```

I knew she was only joking about not speaking to me, but the rest of her e-mail was dead serious.

• • •

Only twenty-four hours later, New York was burning and I had deserted her. Danny was stuck, imprisoned in Las Vegas, because all planes were grounded indefinitely. No rental cars were available and buses were completely booked. I knew he would find a way to our new home even if he had to hitchhike.

Phone reception was sporadic but I was able to learn that everyone I knew was safe, except for a neighbor friend, Laura Rockefeller, who'd never been to the Twin Towers until that morning, for a meeting at Windows on the World. Her absence was discovered when her dog, JT (named for James Taylor), was heard barking incessantly after his mistress did not return home.

I told my mother that my friend Diann Duthie had watched the second plane crash into the building, and she replied, "So did your father." Suddenly I found myself screaming at my mother, "Not on TV! She watched it plunge into the tower from her window at 30 Rock! She saw it for real!"

The news played an endless loop of the planes, the collapse, the thousands of ash-covered citizens catatonically ambling north like tie-clad, high-heel-wearing zombies. My New York was unrecognizable. No horns honking. No natives shrieking. No trains rumbling. All oddly set against an untroubled, powder-blue sky, except for the impertinent interruption of tentacled, murky smoke that hovered over the south end of the island like a memory and a prophecy.

Three thousand miles away, I was desperate for community. That night I went to the house of my old friend Kelley Baker, where a group of mostly showbiz college cohorts were ostensibly meeting to find the same sense of community. When I arrived, they were sipping wine and noshing from a platter of cheeses and carpaccio and flaxseed crackers, bemoaning that the world was forever changed and nothing would ever be the same.

"Well, Disneyland will be next," said one. "It symbolizes the American dream."

"I think it will be the studios," said another. "The Hollywood factory is seen as the center of American propaganda."

"Los Angeles is such a target. It's the center of how the world sees the United States and it's everything fanatical Muslims hate."

Suddenly a voice fired from inside my throat that surprised even me. "Los Angeles is the center of *nothing*!" I screamed. "It's not a financial center, it's not a military center, it's not even a fucking fashion center! It's like you all just watched a screener of a really scary movie and you're discussing the sequel! You're drinking your pinot and wiping Brie from the corners of your mouth, moaning about nothing being the same. Nothing has changed for you *at all*! You live in a fucking vacuum and you have no idea what's going on! Yes, this happened to Americans, but it happened *more* to New Yorkers."

Much to my surprise, my college friends did not take offense. They sat mute, some even understanding, and the only sound was my quickened breath, as if I'd just run a race. Kelley put her arm around me and led me outside, where I could escape for fresh air, fresh anything. I sobbed in her arms for a while and then drove back to my new house and slept, didn't sleep, on the inflated mattress with our dogs, who seemed to understand that something very sad was happening.

They were New Yorkers too.

Danny got home by sneaking on a Greyhound bus and I picked him up at the downtown station. The passengers filed off in a single line, respectfully, kindly, hollow. I began to realize

I was wrong. In ways beyond the smallness of my judgment, something, indeed, had changed for everyone.

Danny and I talked. We cried. The click-clack of Zach's and Emma's toenails on the wooden floor echoed against the blank white Spanish stucco walls. We knew that it would be weeks before the moving vans would make it through state-by-state security checkpoints. Instead of our home in the hills being a clean slate for a new life, it just seemed barren. I couldn't even muster a real grocery shop. That would mean planning ahead. We couldn't delight in or even imagine a future. Where would we put the sofa? Who gave a fuck? What color should the kitchen be? How about black?

On the first Sunday after 9/11, Danny and I wanted to find someplace of worship where we could mourn with others who needed the comfort of collective citizenry. With no criteria for religion or denomination, we drove until we spotted a small, storefront chapel, crowded with polite and shell-shocked strangers—brethren of a common heart, silently engrossed in the solace of free donuts and coffee. We squeezed into a pew as the robed preacher entered and solemnly acknowledged the congregation with a nod. He would hold the staff to guide us. I took Danny's hand and we breathed deeply, desperate for a shred of relief.

"Welcome," he said, and took a sip of water. "This is a time when we are asking many questions. Why? How? Is it over? What does it mean?" He took another sip of water. "Last night when I was preparing today's sermon, I knew there were feelings that needed to be addressed and answers that needed to be provided. But then I thought"—he paused for another drink of water—"the best thing we can do at a time like this is move on with as much normalcy as possible. So I've chosen to do the sermon that I had already scheduled for this Sunday . . . Please open your Bibles to—"

I turned to Danny. "I can't do this. Let's get out of—" And he was already gone.

In the next days, our lives were as unchanging as the footage that played on every channel at every hour. Danny was glued to the television, somehow thinking something might make sense if he saw the buildings fall one more time. I couldn't watch anymore, or ever again. We both knew that if our move had been scheduled for after September 11, we never would have left. We would have stayed in New York to be New Yorkers. Danny would have been one of those Samaritans who went to Ground Zero to dig and search only to be turned away.

Across the country, that impulse just made him feel impotent and purposeless. Our hands and hearts were tied and we were of no use to anyone. Any attempt to curb, moderate, or control alcohol intake would have been a futile and stupid choice.

Bill Wilson himself would have poured me a drink.

A haunting, cloying voice in my head suggested that if we hadn't deserted our city, none of this would have happened. It was my fault—guilt and ego on a monumental level.

Patti LuPone e-mailed me: "I guess you were right," and it cut through me like a knife.

Then Oprah Winfrey's office called. She was doing a show called "Music to Heal Our Hearts" and would I please fly to Chicago the next day to sing? I'd performed on her show a few years before and she'd been everything I had wanted her to be. It was no surprise that, as perhaps the single most visibly powerful and reliable moral leader in our country at that moment, of course she was taking action. Of course she wanted to begin the healing. The surprise was that she would call me. Surely there were much bigger stars who would lend their voices to her aim.

My usual thoughts that analyze the career advantages of this kind of exposure were nowhere to be found. I was getting a chance to do something. Something that would give me a sense of service, of being a part of a solution, of using my gifts to make others feel better. Make *me* feel better.

The next morning my pianist, Todd Schroeder, came to my house and a taxi arrived to take us to the airport.

"What are you thinking of singing?" Todd asked.

"I have no idea," I said. "We'll talk about it on the plane."

The plane.

It was the first time either of us had flown since the tragedy only days ago, and though we didn't discuss it, we were both afraid. I'd narrowly escaped flying on September 11 itself and who knew if this was over? When I saw the turban of the taxi driver my fear was exacerbated. For the first time in my life I understood true bigotry and a hate born of fear.

Get in the car, I told myself. *You are not one of those people.*

As we pulled away, the driver offered Todd and me a stick of gum. Against everything I knew to be right and good, I couldn't help but worry that it was poisoned with anthrax. I accepted the gesture of goodwill and forced myself to chew it. I caught him watching me in the rearview mirror. I told myself that if I was scared, just imagine: this Muslim driver was probably even more afraid than I was. He could be the target of nationalistic violence, and yet he bravely still wore a traditional turban and beard, and a laminated prayer card hung from his rearview mirror. He must have told himself *You are not one of those people* as well.

After initial pleasantries, our ride was silent for most of the way. Then our driver spoke in his thick Middle Eastern accent: "What do you think they should build in the place of the towers?"

I thought for a moment. "I don't know. A memorial? A park like in Oklahoma City."

"Do you know what I think?" he continued. "I think they should build two more towers . . . each of them one story higher!"

Airport security was heavy and methodical and we were grateful. The flight was quiet. Passengers were more compatible, less rushed. Anytime anyone rose to go to the lavatory, all eyes darted in their direction. Flight attendants were elevated from waitstaff to trusted heroes. Our first-class breakfast was served with plastic utensils for security purposes. We landed in Chicago without incident and it felt good to be somewhere else.

Todd and I were rushed to the studio for rehearsal. When I'd done Oprah's show before, the machine of her production company, Harpo, had been a sight to behold. It was a self-contained city that resembled the strange combination of a five-star resort and a municipality. Her Majesty had been nowhere to be seen and I met her only seconds before the floor manager counted us down to airtime.

This time was different. While the same machine was in full play, it more resembled Oz, with *Buzz buzz here, buzz buzz there, and a couple of tra-la-las* nearly audible. In the midst of the tragedy there was a joyous, dogged purpose in what Oprah herself had proclaimed was necessary for the healing of the country. A grand piano was rolled into a studio hallway and we were asked to explore songs. Oprah appeared in a gray sweat suit without a stitch of makeup, her hair stuffed under a baseball cap, and she hugged me and thanked me for coming. I introduced her to Todd and she told us she had an idea.

"Do you know 'Precious Lord'?" she asked.

"Kinda sorta not completely," I admitted.

"It's my favorite hymn and it was Martin Luther King's favorite hymn and I think you would really sing it beautifully."

"Okay, perfect, we'll try it. I had another idea on the plane and maybe we can combine the two songs," I told her.

Within ten minutes, five different CDs of artists singing "Precious Lord" were delivered to my hands along with lyric sheets, a CD player, and headphones. I suspected Oprah's kingdom must have a record shop, somewhere between the gym and the post office. Todd and I learned the song within a few minutes and set a key, then combined it with the idea I had on the plane.

Half an hour later, Oprah returned and said, "Whatcha got?"

She gathered several production assistants around the piano and asked for quiet. "Sam Harris is going to sing!" Todd and I tried out the new arrangement and when we finished, Oprah sensed my volatile state, held me by the shoulders, and zeroed in, saying, "You can do this."

It was all surreal—all of us trying to find a scrap of faith in the rubble.

"Will you come to my place for dinner tonight?" she asked.

"Of course," I said. I knew that Oprah didn't typically fraternize with the guests, but this was a different situation and rules were being bent and broken every which way.

An assistant placed a proper calligraphied invitation in my hand with Oprah's home address and the time notated.

I guessed they knew I would accept.

Todd and I were the first guests to arrive at the high-rise on Lake Shore Drive and were greeted by a houseman. The vast apartment was all very French. Brocade and tassels were everywhere. It reflected a gracious and refined taste that had been learned and earned since Oprah's meager beginnings. Like everything else she did, it was the best of the best.

Oprah entered the living room, followed by her two cocker spaniels and her right-hand person, Lisa Halliday, whom I took to immediately. Oprah said that music had always been the conduit for healing for her and it was the tool we needed to start mending. I sat on the floor with the dogs and found myself singing a song that I loved and had recorded: "The Rescue."

Oh come, you've been down so long
The current pulls so strong, this life that you've been leading
Oh please take this love from me
It's stronger than the sea, this love that you've been needing.
Have I reached your heart in time to stop the bleeding?

Oprah wiped away a tear and rose, as if shaking off the despair, and called to her chef to ask how dinner was coming. She seemed to be, at once, completely emotionally available and equally skilled at moving on.

The other guests who were to perform on the show arrived: gospel icons, BeBe and CeCe Winans, Donnie McClurkin, and the opera diva Denyce Graves. It struck me that I was the only Caucasian in this group of gospel and opera royalty who had been asked to "heal our hearts." I was honored and intimidated, and Todd and I shared many a "can-you-believe-we-were-invited-to-this-party?" glance throughout the evening.

I kept waiting for someone to tell me that I was just there to sing backup.

Oprah sat at the head of the dining table and a place card designated my spot immediately to her right. Dinner was comfort food: pork chops and collard greens and fried green tomatoes. I realized it was the first real meal I'd had since *the day* and it reminded me of my Memo.

We were a fellowship of artists, bound in search of respite.

Everyone shared their most personal stories and their attempts to pull themselves from the black hole of helplessness. Donnie had been on the 9:00 a.m. flight from JFK that I had canceled, and he had witnessed the second plane crash into the tower from the air. His plane was diverted to St. Louis for several days.

Oprah engaged with fierce investment and I realized that what made her so singular was her authentic, intense curiosity. Though she is regaled as a woman of great wisdom, it is her vigorous need to know, to learn, to explore and examine that keeps her going. I felt that if she ever actually found the answers to her quest, she would deflate and become purposeless. It is her aggressive search for her own healing that keeps her in service to others. Her integrity was astonishing.

Wine was poured freely, and between my emotional exhaustion from the past week, moving, fear of flying, and nervousness about my upcoming performance, I chugged even more than my regular two-bottles-a-night custom. The evening ended much later than it should have for a group of people who had an uncivilized 6:00 a.m. call for a live national television show. But we had prepared in a less disciplined but more important way.

By the time I got back to my hotel and in bed I was afraid my vocal cords would atrophy if I slept, so I lay in the dark and tried to meditate.

A few hours later we were driven to the studio. Makeup, sound check, lighting, bagels. We'd each been given private dressing rooms but we all chose to cram into the greenroom, nervously trilling and humming and pacing—together.

We were asked to say something before we sang and I was terrified that I might not be able to keep it together. I was on the emotional brink, sleepless and slightly hungover. At the commercial break before my performance, the producer, Kandi

Amelon, took me by the hand and led me to my mark on the set. Somber blue light bathed the stage like a mist and an American flag waved on a screen to my left. Oprah introduced me from her seat in the studio audience. She was there to be healed too. She spoke in a matter-of-fact, time-to-deal-with-it manner, but when she threw her first question to me, I was momentarily breathless, as if a heavy hand was pressing against my chest. Then I spoke, slightly trembling, about everyone feeling helpless, not knowing what to do, but that all of us had different gifts we could contribute. Mine was music.

Todd gave me a single note and I began, slowly, a cappella.

Precious Lord, take my hand
Lead me on, help me stand.

I choked up and, for a brief moment, doubted if I would get another note out.

I'm so tired—

Todd's hands answered my prayer with a gospel phrase.

I'm so weak, I'm so worn.

Todd began to play with strength and I took it from him.

Through the storm, through the night
Lead me on to your light.
Take my hand, Precious Lord, lead me . . . lead me home.

Then tempo commenced, a new key emerged like a ray of light, and I sang "You'll Never Walk Alone." I summoned all of the hope and trust that I had been seeking. I demanded that we would survive. I demanded that we would unite. I demanded that we would triumph. Near the end, I repeated the line "You'll never walk . . . you'll never walk" and led a bolt-from-the-blue key change that promised a tenacious, you-won't-tear-me-down conviction that I knew I needed to feel and hear and believe was possible.

When I released the last note, Oprah joined the audience in jumping to their feet and she ran to me, yelling, "Yes! Yes! Yes! Hit that note at nine in the morning!" She embraced me hard and sure. This was not a funeral—it was a declaration.

BeBe and CeCe dueted on "Bridge over Troubled Water," Denyce performed "American Anthem," and Donnie McClurkin blew the roof off the studio with "Stand." At the end of the show, we all gathered to sing "God Bless America." Oprah and I clung to each other throughout the anthem and she sang in a proud, lusty voice with the same fervor as her soulful guests.

When the show came down, I went to Oprah to thank her and say good-bye. She said, "I'm flying to the West Coast. Do you want to come with me?"

"I already have my flight," I responded. "Your staff took care of everything."

She looked at me like I was an idiot. I was.

"I mean on *my* plane," she clarified. "Do you want to fly with me on *my* plane? I can drop you off in Los Angeles before I go up to Santa Barbara."

"Oh! Yes. Of course I do. Sorry."

She was going to "drop us off" in Los Angeles. I'd never heard that phrase used when a plane was involved.

I wondered if I would be parachuted directly to my house.

Todd and I boarded the private jet with Oprah, her longtime

partner, Stedman, her friend and hairdresser, Andre Walker, and BeBe. We didn't have to show IDs or remove our belts.

After takeoff, we alternated between conversation and contemplation. The sum of the past days fell upon me and the soft rumble of the engine invited sleep, but I willed myself to stay awake. It wasn't every day I was on Oprah's private jet. I thought about the circumstances that got me here: Liza's call the morning after I left the only city I'd ever felt was home. The endless footage of the buildings falling. My endless search for a sense of community. I gazed out the window and thought about all the cities I'd played and all the people I'd played to and all their disparate races and religions and economics and how this tragedy had united us all.

I wondered how long it would last.

Oprah had brought Tupperware containers of leftovers from the previous night's dinner party, and as we filled our plates, she pulled out a tape of the show we'd performed live only a few hours before and put it on.

"She never does this," whispered Andre. "When the show is done, the show is done."

Today was different.

We gathered, unbuckled, clustered on chairs and draped across sofas and sprawled on the floor like a family in their den on movie night, and watched each performance, cheering, like thankful air gushing from our lungs. We used real silverware to stuff our bellies and I dug into the reliable comfort of fried green tomatoes.

They were a little soggy, like us. But they held up just fine. Like us.

When the show was over, Oprah said, quietly, "Let's watch it again."

And we did.

12. Crossing the Line

In the last, scattershot days of summer before the mythical world of high school was about to begin, Curtis Davis hosted a backyard party.

It was a rite of passage of sorts, celebrating an impetuous silly freedom that we presumed we must shed with the expectations of maturity. Everyone was frolicking about, tossing balls and Frisbees and bouncing on the trampoline. I was always uncomfortable in these situations and somehow managed to bow out or have an excuse or be engrossed in something else when sporty activities began.

It was baffling to me how I could be so coordinated when it came to choreography but a complete klutz when it came to anything remotely athletic. I could run, sure, but only when being chased or sidestepping a battery of dodge balls in PE class.

I'd found an exercise-free corner of the yard and had immersed myself in conversation with Devena Stevenson when a Frisbee landed at my feet.

I was paralyzed with fear. I was also paralyzed by my shoes. My Thom McAn Earth Shoes. I loved them. They were the biggest thing to hit the footwear industry since mankind evolved from woven grass tied to wood. I had owned a half dozen pairs in succession since the previous year in eighth grade, simply replacing them with a new, identical pair when the negative heel got too negative and I began to fall backward while walking forward. They added an extra two inches to my compact five-foot-seven frame and gave me an air of buoyant confidence . . . as long as I was indoors or standing still.

I stared at the Frisbee lying mere inches from the tawny duckbill toe peeking from under my faded denim bell-bottoms. Between my unsteady footwear and unstable agility, I was terrified. I knew it was simple. All I had to do was pick up the Frisbee and fling it back to the thrower. I glanced at the faces of expectant players and the pressure was on. I had no choice. I listed forward on my waffled sole and grabbed it. So far so good. I aimed as carefully as I could—and threw.

It spun through the air in slow motion and I breathed a sigh of relief that I was actually able to achieve liftoff rather than some lame, haphazard roll into a nearby hydrangea. But it wasn't over. Suddenly the Frisbee soared off its intended course, and just as Mark Pogue sprang high into the air from the trampoline, it met with his face at the exact wrong moment and smacked him straight in the mouth, busting his lip. He yelled out and came down with a painful *boing*.

His teeth glistened with blood.

I had crossed the line, entered No-Sam-Land, and hurt someone—with a Frisbee—the single most innocuous form of sports equipment known to man. Mark's lip was swollen and purple as a ripe plum, and though he didn't blame me, I knew I could never again attempt anything remotely jocklike in the future. If this was the result of a simple Frisbee toss, a game of Ping-Pong might result in quadriplegia and anything with a ball or a bat would undoubtedly mean certain death. I swore in my heart that I would stick to things at which I was completely proficient, natural, superior, the best. Which was a bit limiting, since it meant not trying anything new, ever, when the world was full of literal and figurative Frisbees landing at feet left and right.

I justified my oath in knowing I was an artist, and persons as unique as myself didn't have time for kids' games. As my "uniqueness" grew more evident, I decided to take the bull by the horns—and decorate them! I began wearing 1950s pleated and cuffed gabardine pants and knit pullover sweater vests, tweed-twilled two-button suits, wing-tip shoes, and skinny belts and ties, all of which I'd found stuffed in mildewy barrels at my Memo's storage garage. They'd all belonged to my uncle Darrell, who died before I was born but left a treasure trove of fashion.

Still, something was missing.

What could be better than Sun-In, a spray-on hair lightening product that could give me a natural, summer-streaked appearance, and at under three dollars?! I couldn't resist. I bought a bottle and read the directions carefully: *Apply sparingly and test on a strand of hair before using.*

Kind of like testing a carpet before applying cleaning fluid. It went on: *Highlights are permanent.*

Well, why shouldn't they be?

Subscribing to my typical now-quicker-more philosophy, I saturated my hair with the stuff and used a blow-dryer to hasten the process. Within minutes I had a new look. And that look was bright orange-blond hair.

Highlights are permanent . . .

There were no highlights . . . just a head of orange-blond hair.

I hoped that my locks would grow out before my new life in high school, which was only a few weeks away, but that seemed unlikely unless I shaved my head and started from scratch.

On the first day of high school, I entered the double glass doors in a stylish fedora but was told to remove it immediately, as no hats were allowed in the building—even a fashionable chapeau that matched my retro outfit. No one commented on my clothes. Everyone commented on my hair. Actually, they asked what had happened to me. I told them, matter-of-factly, that I'd "spent a lot of time at the public pool and it was totally natural." Forget that the *natural* color of my hair could not be found anywhere in nature, except perhaps in those creepy bioluminescent jellyfish skulking miles beneath the sea. And never mind that I sported the same pallid, sunless skin. And that everyone knew I couldn't swim.

But bigger things were at hand. Prior to high school, there had only been Christmas shows and band or choir recitals, but no real musicals or plays. At lunchtime, a sign-up sheet for tryouts was posted for the fall musical: *The Music Man*. I hoped the starring role of Harold Hill could be seen as an apricot blond.

I learned the complicated and wordy song "Ya Got Trouble" for the audition, thinking that already knowing it would give me an advantage and save them the agony of teaching it to someone else. Seniors were usually awarded the lead roles and I couldn't take any chances.

I sang both Harold Hill's part and the townsfolk's echoed melody in the chorus with gusto, and immediately knew I'd won the part from the relieved sparkle in the eyes of the drama teacher, Mr. White.

What a coup! We began rehearsals the next week and I was so excited about a full cast and costumes and a real band. However, since I was used to directing my own extracurricular shows, being in a production that I wasn't overseeing proved a bit of a challenge. The keys were too low for my first tenor voice and I sounded terrible on most of the songs. Transposing the music for the entire orchestra was out of the question, so I struggled, unsuccessfully, to hit the long, low notes in "Marian the Librarian," which mostly resembled an elongated burp. But I figured I could act my way out of it. There were other matters of concern. My little brother, Matt, was cast as Winthrop, the lisping trumpet enthusiast, and I knew he'd deliver. But the rest of the cast was suspect.

The Music Man must be performed with energy and zeal and rhythm, especially in the opening number, "Rock Island," which is basically a fast-paced rap between traveling salesmen in a train car. However, most people in Oklahoma talk slow. Really slow. No matter how much we rehearsed, my fellow cast mate David couldn't wrap his mouth around "Whadda-ya-talk, whadda-ya-talk, whadda-ya-talk, whadda-ya-talk?" and the song would plunge from the cadence of a quickening train to a dreadful dirge every time he spoke. It gave you the feeling the train had hit a deer or a small bear, and then it would rev up again with the next salesman.

David was a handsome boy and one of my first teenage crushes. He'd lived next door to us on Washington Street and we'd been lab partners on a biology project where we made a life-size human body out of papier-mâché with the vascular system painted on. We'd named it after our social studies teacher, Miss Liptack, and gave the dummy ample breasts to solidify the likeness. David had one silver-capped tooth right in front. It gave him a pirate kind of look that I found very manly and slightly glamorous. Even with our history, my crush, the Liptack bond, and his shiny tooth, I couldn't forgive his tardy tongue. It was exasperating.

But I wasn't directing so I just kept my mouth shut.

The role of the mayor was played by someone very tall whose name I have blocked from memory but is forever etched as the Guy Who Never Made a Cue. Ever. If there was a lull, it was because the mayor had dropped a line or failed to make his entrance.

But I wasn't directing so I just kept my mouth shut.

I began to attend all rehearsals, including scenes I wasn't in, simply as an observer. One day, when they were rehearsing "The Wells Fargo Wagon" number, a boy in the ensemble who sang the line "I got some salmon from Seattle last September" pronounced the *l* in the word "salmon." After the song, I privately and politely pointed out that the *l* is silent and the word is pronounced *SAM-on*.

The next time they did the song, he blurted out "I got some saLmon from Seattle last September." I waited until the song was finished and tactfully corrected him again, but this time in front of the company. "*Sam*-on," I said. And then enunciating, ever so slowly, "Saaam-ooonnn."

The next time they ran the song, I had my eye on him and he knew it. Just before his line he saw me arch an eyebrow nearly up to my bicolored hairline (my orange-blond mop was growing out), but he buckled under my glowering intimidation and sang "I got some saLmon from Seattle last September."

I jumped up onto the stage in one furious leap and threw my hands in the air, yelling, "*Hold it!! Hooold iiittt! It's sam-on! Sam-on!*" The music stopped. "Have you never heard the word *sam-on*? It's a fish. A fish called *sam-on*. It swims upstream! Like me! *Saaam-on*! Now do it again and get it right this time!"

Mr. White stared at me, flabbergasted. He said nothing. I was back on my game—back in the director's seat. No one dared stop me. Having thus far only been in shows of my own design or productions with real adults, and now working with these amateurs who looked at the show as something "fun to do," I was a living, breathing terror. The Jerome Robbins of Charles

Page High School. But we would never hear the word "salmon" pronounced incorrectly again.

I suspect that, to this day, the saLmon culprit has not so much as ordered the fish at a restaurant for fear that I would creep up from behind his booth at Red Lobster and strangle him.

As the school year progressed, Mr. White was becoming somewhat of a Jesus freak. I'd heard it had begun the previous year when he'd chosen *Godspell* as the musical, but now his devotion had accelerated as he grew longish, scruffy blond hair and his lenient blue eyes took on a tranquillity that reflected either redemption or quaaludes, I couldn't know. He started wearing baggy linen pants and leather sandals and walked with a staff. In drama class, he insisted we cut all curse words in all monologues we performed, and even the word "damn" was replaced with "dern" when we did Neil Simon's *Plaza Suite*.

New Yorkers don't say "dern." Ever.

Mr. White started hosting prayer circles and Bible study meetings and Jesus hayride retreats with bonfires. One step away from sacrificing a goat. He painted JESUS LIVES! in giant, bold letters on his teal-trimmed garage door. At the end of the term, rumor had it that he would not be returning. "He was let go," it was whispered, "for being too religious." Being *too* religious in Sand Springs was hard to do. One would have to be medically diagnosed with OCJD—obsessive-compulsive Jesus disorder—to be considered too religious. Unlike regular OCDers, who can't wash enough or clean enough or turn off lights/stoves/toasters too much, Jesus OCDers can't testify enough or get God-fearing enough or morally good enough. But even in the nucleus of unquestionable religious zealotry, Mr. White's devoutness rode the fine line between sainthood and crazy. And crazy won. If Joan of Arc had lived in Sand

Springs, she might not have been burned at the stake, but she would definitely have been labeled a lesbian and her house would have been egged. But then, she probably would have had the good sense not to paint VIVE JÉSUS! in giant, bold letters on her garage door.

Sand Springs was feeling more and more beneath my professional and sanity standard. It was clear that if I was going to pursue my dream of acting and singing and dancing, I needed to cross its borders. While visiting relatives in Dallas, my family had been to Six Flags Over Texas, a theme park which featured multiple live shows that played several performances a day. I begged to audition. Sure, I was a hotshot in Sand Springs, but who knew if I was even qualified for the next step outside our little world? There was only one way to find out, and since my parents had no knowledge of legitimate acting programs or any real theatrical opportunities, Six Flags seemed the most accessible option. I was only fifteen and the minimum age was sixteen, but my parents recognized that my lust for a real stage could not be restrained, so my father agreed to back me in lying about my age and make the five-hour drive to Dallas for the cattle call.

Three days before the audition I came down with mononucleosis: the kissing disease. If only. My throat was practically swollen shut and I was feverish and weak and couldn't sing a note. But nothing was going to keep me from my big chance and, as usual, my parents let me forge ahead like King Henry V unto the breach, Teddy Roosevelt at San Juan Hill, or Barbra Streisand on the bow of a tugboat.

My father and I began our trek before sunrise and arrived midmorning at the hotel where the auditions were being held. We entered the enormous ballroom, an entirely new, breathtaking world, where hundreds of hopefuls were humming and bleating, stretching like Gumbys on row after row of stackable burgundy banquet chairs. At the front of the room was a long production table, behind which sat a dozen directors, choreographers, and staff. I signed up and got a number and my father and I found a place among the throngs to wait my turn. In the back of the room were camera crews from local news stations covering the event, as this was the largest turnout in their audition history.

The auditions began. One after another, names were called and singers and dancers, ages sixteen to twenty-five, dashed to the front of the ballroom to sell their wares, often barely heard over the distracting chatter of the crowd. Regular warnings to be respectful were ignored.

After several hours, my name was called. The antibiotics had kicked in somewhat, but I could still barely swallow. I wondered what would come out. My father gave me a nervous pat on the back and I walked to the pianist and handed him my music: a medley I'd constructed specifically for this audition of "Be a Clown" and "The Hungry Years."

"Be a Clown" is a zippy Cole Porter song written in the 1940s about the foolish jubilation of show business. "The Hungry Years" is a dirgy but catchy Neil Sedaka ballad written in the 1970s about looking back on one's salad days and missing the struggle after having made it. I was fifteen. I'd neither accomplished anything nor suffered salad days. In fact, I'd probably never even eaten a salad. (Iceberg on a burger was as close as was legally allowed in Oklahoma.) And—I was a little fat.

I was singing "I miss the hungry years" and I was a little fat.

Sensing I had to change things up or I'd be just another drowned-out wannabe in this mass of competition, I told the pianist to forgo the introduction on the page and just give me a low bass roll, after which I would come in on two high notes, long and out of tempo, to get their attention, and then go into the song.

I found my spot and introduced myself, though I was uncertain I could be heard above the commotion. The pianist rolled the low note for my pitch. I planted my feet and took a deep breath and belted, at the top of my lungs. "Be-e-e-e- a-a-a-a clown, be a clown . . ."

My out-of-the-gate, powerhouse notes quieted the room like a gunshot. I had 'em. Who was this short, fat kid and where did that come from? I made my way through "Be a Clown" for sixteen bars and then moved into the tearjerker:

I miss the hungry years, the once upon a time
The lovely long ago, we didn't have a dime
Those days of me and you, we lost along the way

I held out the last vowel and slid into a key change, tears welling in my eyes.

Oooh, how could I be so blind not to see the door
Closing on the world I now hunger for
Looking through my tears . . . I miss the hungry years

I finished the song and lowered my head as though I'd divulged my deepest truth. Actually, I had. All of the depth and drama of my life was laid out, messy, for all to see.

For a brief moment, it was pin-drop quiet. Maybe they thought I was dead. Then it happened. Applause erupted from the crowd of auditioners. The production staff rose from their long tables and came to where I was standing, beaming, shaking my hand. One man hugged me. A woman cupped my face in her palms and just stared into my eyes. The local news crews ran to the front of the ballroom. Camera lights switched on. Photos were snapped. Flashes flashed. I was asked to do television interviews. But not until I'd finished my paperwork and my contact information had been verified.

My father watched.

That summer, I left home at fifteen to perform at Six Flags Over Mid-America in St. Louis. Whatever trepidation my parents felt about their little boy going off to a new city with no supervision, to live in an apartment and have a job, was masked by enthusiasm. I was free at last—the canary flying cheerfully into the mine shaft, oblivious to the prospect of gas.

The show was called *Ramblin' thru Missou!*, a hand-clapping, foot-stomping revue that I performed five times a day at an outdoor amphitheater in the prickly Missouri heat, costumed in a red checkered shirt and denim overalls. I'd escaped Oklahoma but I was still wearing its uniform. None of it was remotely glamorous in the way I'd hoped, but I was doing what I loved and I thought of myself as a seasoned pro.

When I returned to Charles Page High the following fall, I was thrilled to find that our new drama teacher, Mr. Briscoe, was not religious. Given a choice, he would have preferred the label "anti-Christ." He was a Vietnam vet with a salty tongue that wagged nonstop about brutal battles, blown-up body parts, blookers and big boys and boom boom—but not much about acting.

"Briscoe," as we were asked to call him (perhaps to reinforce his military station), had a handsome, broad, slap-cheeked Irish face with sandy, floppy hair that he pushed away from his expressive eyes at the end of every heated sentence. He stood in a perpetual slump that accentuated the beginnings of a deserved postwar belly and planted his duck-footed heels at shoulder width, but was forever in a state of motion—slightly pitching left and right, as if he were at sea.

Briscoe saw me as a kindred spirit, out there in my own trenches fighting for what I loved. The fall musical was *The Fantasticks* and was perfect for me to play young Matt, who hankers for something outside his village.

It was also perfect for Briscoe and his choir director colleague, Mr. McConnell, who decided they would actually play parts in the show. Briscoe thought that since he was going to make his teaching debut, he may as well be front and center to really display his thespian qualifications. However, there are only eight characters in *The Fantasticks*—a small show for a high school of twelve hundred students—and Henry and Mortimer, two of the showier roles, were taken by teachers.

As the school year progressed, the differences between Briscoe and his predecessor became more and more evident. Whereas Mr. White had substituted profanity in all material, even classroom monologues, Briscoe encouraged expletives and obscenities and suggested scenes from *American Buffalo, For Colored Girls Who Have Considered Suicide When the Rainbow Is Enuf* (though there was not a single black girl in class), and my favorite: *Who's Afraid of Virginia Woolf?* There is nothing quite like the sound of Edward Albee's dialogue coming from the lips of sixteen- and seventeen-year-old Georges and Marthas with thick Oklahoma accents:

"Don't shoot yer may-outh off about yew-know-whut."

"I'll talk about any goddamn thang I wanna! Any goddamn thang!"

"What'll it be?"

"I'm gunna stick to bourbon."

George and Martha. Sad, sad, sadder than Mr. Albee could ever have imagined.

I loved everything about Briscoe's sensibilities. He was a rebel, if not so much an acting teacher; more Kerouac than Stanislavski. But he knew to play it safe for proper school productions. *The Fantasticks* had been a big success and I was feeling my oats. So was Briscoe. The next production was *Bye Bye Birdie* and I was set to play Albert Peterson, the English teacher/manager of the Elvislike Conrad Birdie. I asked Briscoe if he intended to be in the show this time. He said there were certainly several parts he could play and it would really be a chance to show the students and parents that plays are fun for everyone. "Oh," I said, looking at him blankly, and let my silence hang like a mirror.

Briscoe did not appear in *Bye Bye Birdie*.

Though not my intention, it seemed a turning point for him, and me: the moment when the fire that had, long ago, inspired him to make the theater his life was officially and permanently snuffed out, enlisting him to fully embrace the significance of his role *offstage* as a teacher, mentor, pathway to a generation that might go further than he had. And from that day on, he gave me free reign to do anything, try anything, and fully embrace the significance of *my* role as the incessantly curious, ferociously driven student.

He allowed me to have all my song keys reorchestrated to fit my register. He let me choreograph, supervise costumes, and throw in my two cents on direction and set design. And of course I would need my own dressing room.

There were only two changing rooms—one for boys and one for girls, but between them was a five-by-eight storage closet with costumes hung from floor to ceiling. The space was windowless and claustrophobic, like a moldy locker that reeked of decades of greasepaint and unventilated flop sweat. But with a little redecorating and some Glade Rose Garden air freshener, I knew it would be perfect.

I cleared racks of wardrobe from one wall and set up a makeup station and mirror against a bank of unpainted, chalky cinder blocks. A small side table sat empty to receive flowers and telegrams from opening night well-wishers. There was no one in my world who would possibly send a telegram, but it wasn't beyond the realm of possibility that Michael Bennett or Mike Nichols or Bob Fosse would hear of my performance and wire:

```
SAM STOP  COME TO BROADWAY IMMEDIATELY STOP
STARDOM IS WAITING STOP
```

I taped my name to the outside of the door, but not in the shape of a star, so as not to appear pompous.

Briscoe had given me a playing field with no rules and had stomached and even rallied my puffed-up teenage attitude, so twenty-odd years later, as a *real* seasoned but hopefully less pretentious veteran, I was beyond thrilled when I got a call saying he was coming to New York with his wife, Marva, for a jam-packed week of Broadway.

I was appearing in Mel Brooks's *The Producers* at the time, which had become one of the biggest hits in musical theater history. I had replaced Roger Bart in the role of Carmen Ghia, the swishiest, most outlandish gay part ever written for the stage and, terrified of stepping into another actor's calf-skinned pointy-toed boots, had taken the advice of my onstage counterpart, the wonderful actor Gary Beach, who told me, "Just go out there and scare them!" One can't really be too scary or go too far in *The Producers,* where nothing says musical like a human-formed swastika reflected in an overhead mirror like a shot from a Busby Berkeley movie. The audacity of mincing and prancing and long sibilant *s*'s was oddly freeing for me. I was a *professional sissy!*—on *Broadway!*—paid and applauded for the very blemishes I'd desperately sought to cover for an entire childhood.

The Briscoes set a date, and I arranged for excellent seats at the show and dinner at a popular actors' hangout for after. I was excited. "Hometown boy does good" is, after all, the ultimate showbiz story.

It was the musical's second season, and patrons previously unable to secure tickets were now coming in droves. On the night that the Briscoes attended, the audience was, thankfully, low on the Japanese tourists who would sometimes fill nearly every seat and mostly just gape, smiling fixedly and hunching forward as if they were expecting something *really* funny to happen . . . that never seemed to happen. They didn't get any of the brilliant Mel Brooks inside jokes, and it was like playing high comedy to an oil painting of an audience. An anime oil painting of an audience. But on this night the house had been exceptional, laughing at every ridiculous gag, and I felt particularly *on*. As soon as the curtain rang down, I dashed up the stairs to my dressing room and haphazardly removed my makeup, changed into street clothes, and rushed back down to the stage door of the St. James to meet the Briscoes.

There they were. Briscoe looked exactly the same—maybe a few more pounds around the gut, but the same roseate face and swiped hair and that odd sea-leaning thing. Marva looked the same too. Squat and round and happy-happy-happy, with her uncommonly turned-up nose, bright green eye shadow from lashes to brow, and a vibrantly red-framed open mouth, wide as a yawning cat. They just stood there, smiling from ear to ear, like the Japanese audience I thought I'd avoided. They could have been a photograph but for Briscoe's oscillation, and

I found myself swaying with him, slightly, slowly, side to side, just to keep eye contact. In the silence, I could already imagine the kudos and prepared myself for humility.

"How ya doin'?" they both finally said, practically in unison.

"Uh, fine . . . I'm so happy to see you," I said, as I wiped my face with a towel, still a bit sweaty from the heat of the show.

"Ya look great," said Briscoe.

"Thin," Marva added, as if this was a bad thing.

I suppressed my need to ask, *So did you enjoy the show? . . . And how about me?*

Instead, I brought them into the magic land of backstage, where anyone, particularly anyone with any theatre in their blood, gets that undeniable euphoria of the inner sanctum where civilians are rarely admitted.

I waited for a response as they entered the hallowed vestibule, where the walls and pipes had been painted layer over layer in backstage beige, like rings on an ancient oak, marking the seasons of George M. Cohan, Beatrice Lillie, John Gielgud, Laurence Olivier, Gertrude Lawrence, and landmark shows including *Oklahoma!*, *The King and I,* and *Hello, Dolly!*

"Hmm . . ." was all I got.

I was sure their silence was evidence of their starry-eyed state. I took them on a tour, showed them the set.

"The wings are smaller than I thought they'd be," Briscoe observed.

I walked them onto the stage where the ghost light had just been set and they could view the ornate house from the actor's perspective.

"I can't believe you have to walk up stairs to get to your dressing room? What a pain in the ass," was all Briscoe could muster. "When I was at Oklahoma University, it was much better than this. Bigger. More up to date. This place is O-L-D-E."

Marva nodded in agreement. They were clearly disappointed. Neither of them ever mentioned my performance. They never even acknowledged I'd been in the show. Or that there *was* a show, for that matter.

I found myself seeking, no, *begging*, for Briscoe's approval. I introduced him to the cast and crew, all of whom said lovely things about me. The praise prompted nothing. Nada. Ignored. We walked out of the stage door, where Marva commented on a chorus boy's ass. I signed a few autographs, apparently nothing unusual for them. We went into the restaurant where the owner, Angus, greeted me with a hug and walked us to a primo table I'd reserved. Zero. We ran into recognizable stars of other shows. Zip. I dropped so many names we were lucky the floor didn't give way. I tried everything. Every desperate trick from my *Actor's Kama Sutra Multi-Positions to Pleasure and Dazzle Relatives and Hometown Visitors* handbook. Zilch.

Throughout dinner, the Briscoes talked nonstop about their trip, including several incredible shows and performances they'd seen on Broadway, and details of their lives at the shoe store they now owned in Tennessee.

"The Earth Shoe is going to make a comeback. Mark my words!"

I finally stopped digging and sat back and noshed on seared tuna, attentively nodding and being a good host.

But my mind darted and fished for some possible explanation: maybe my flamboyance as Carmen Ghia really *had* scared them. Or perhaps Briscoe felt jealous, or somehow mocked, or completely outside the very profession he was supposed to have represented to me as a student, and his wife just followed suit to protect him. Or maybe they were just overwhelmed by my whole world and didn't know what to say.

I flashed back to the day I'd been so unsupportive of Briscoe performing in our high school production of *Bye Bye Birdie* twentysomething years prior—the day I'd snatched the last remains of his original identity and morally relegated him to the sentimental but inferior role of the wind beneath my wings.

It occurred to me that if I had been more aware, less brutal, perhaps Briscoe would have heaped on the accolades and shown the pride that every student, no matter how old, seeks from past teachers. But I hadn't been. I'd cheated him out of much more than a performance—and now, unconsciously or otherwise, he was cheating me out of much more than mine.

I never learned the real reason. I never asked. At first I was too hurt. Then too angry. Ultimately, impervious. But one thing I know for sure: old actors never die—we just teeter a bit and wait for our comeback.

Like Earth Shoes.

13. "I Know, Baby. I Know."

I am eight years old, playing tag in the searing, gummy heat of summer. One of the older kids from the next block interrupts to introduce us to another kind of game, "only a lot more fun," he swears. He asks who wants to be first and I volunteer. He hands me a brown paper bag and tells me to put it over my mouth and breathe in and out as deeply as I can. After half a minute or so, he tells me to spin around as I continue to breathe into the paper bag.

I go faster and faster and I start to get light-headed. My lips tingle. I can feel the blood drain from my cheeks as rapture engulfs me. I am released from the bondage of my eight years on earth. I am free.

The next thing I remember is opening my eyes to find a circle of my friends' spinning, concerned faces staring down at me. Something wet trickles from my forehead and down the side of my face. I touch it and see that it is blood. I had passed out and hit my head on a rock.

The older kid leans in. "Hey, Sam, are you okay?"

"Let's do it again!" I say.

Five years later, summers remained thick and sticky but the games had changed. My second cousin Jay was coming to visit for a week, taking a bus from Texas, and I was elated. I'd only met him a few times, and even as a small child he'd possessed an air of enviable danger—my polar opposite. He was only nine months older than I, but when he arrived, his shoulder-length hair, worn jeans, and weathered backpack suggested he was much older, maybe a ripe fifteen. And after a thirteen-hour bus ride, "ripe" was the accurate word. The pungent consequence of his travel would have disgusted me coming from almost anyone else, but it just made him more fascinating. Once we were alone in my room, he impressed me by puffing his cheeks out, forcing air up into his closed mouth, then opening it to emit a trace of cigarette smoke still left in his lungs. I hated smoking, I hated that my parents smoked, but on Jay it was meritorious.

On Friday night, my parents went out for a rare date-night and Jay and I put my eight-year-old brother to bed. I antici- pated the excitement of staying up late to watch *Love, American Style* and watch Jay smoke. But as soon as we were alone, he asked, "What kind of likker do your folks have?" Clearly, he had a different plan in mind. Jay had the supercool distinction of being the son of a man who worked at Seagram's, which quali- fied him as an expert in all things alcohol. With equal parts fear and excitement, I led him to our newly transformed basement, which now boasted bright red shag carpeting, veneer panel- ing on every wall, a yellow distressed-brick fireplace, and an ornately framed painting of Parisians in the rain. Tucked in the corner was a wet bar and an unlocked liquor cabinet. Jay's eyes twinkled at the prospects.

Something was going to happen.

He pulled out bottles of all varieties: whiskey, bourbon, vodka, rum. He mixed a bit of each of them into a large plastic tumbler, added ice, and, after a quick jaunt upstairs to the refrigerator, a mixer of cherry Kool-Aid. "Try it," he said, thrusting the tall glass toward me like Eve with an apple.

"Are you really supposed to mix all those different kinds together?" I questioned. Jay looked at me, head cocked to the side, an eyebrow raised.

"My dad works at Seagram's," he pointedly reminded me.

Who could argue with that? I took a sip. The sweetness of the Kool-Aid cut the burning bite of the concoction, but the feeling was hot and hard, abrupt and arresting. Jay looked at me with wide-eyed promise, as if a key had been turned and an instant change was going to occur. It did. I took another sip and it trilled through my body like summer rain. Then another sip. Then a gulp.

Within minutes, I was happier than I'd ever been. I was as cool as Jay. I acquired an ease and access to a Sam I'd only fantasized about. I grew courage and teeth and said "shit" and "damn" and wanted to say "fuck," but that probably would have required heroin.

Jay mixed another drink for me and one for him. And then another for me. He talked about girls and I nodded in agreement. The alcohol somehow allowed the freedom of my true self and the guise of my false self to coexist—like a magic elixir.

I asked for another Kool-Aid cocktail and he suggested I hold off. *Hold off?* I knew from experience that if one of anything was good, two would be twice as good. And if two were twice as good . . .

I made myself another. Jay declined.

I walked to the front porch and placed my hands on the iron railing. The moon peered through tendrils of clouds, punctuated by stars. I stared out from the tiny hill on which our house was perched and found an introspection and perspective that

I'd never known—so obvious but unavailable to me until this moment: my whole, giant, tiny world lay before me like a map of my life.

Across the street were "The Woods," where, the summer before, the neighborhood boys and I had found the wreckage of a car and placed its severed roof over a five-foot-deep hole we'd dug in the ground. We camouflaged it with leafy branches and made an entrance slide from an old pine tabletop. It was the perfect fort. On my own and as a surprise, I'd been inspired to drag a bag of cement through the brush on a piece of cardboard, mix it with water from the creek, which ran from nowhere to nowhere, and pour a paved patio just outside the entrance. After it hardened, I landscaped with manicured wildflowers indigenous to the area. The other boys hated it, but I was bossy and relentless, so it stood. They did, however, draw the line when I suggested running curtains around the perimeter of the car top.

I gripped the porch railing and scanned the grove of snarled blackjack oaks, festooned with gingerbread cookie–shaped leaves. Other secrets were hidden within. The Woods was also the setting of my first sexual experiences with a boy, in that inaugural bloom of our youth: playful at first, mostly friction, then mutual masturbation, then more. After each time we vowed never to do it again, the dialogue always being the same: "It is wrong." "It is sinful." "We should not do this." Until one of us would call the other and say, "My parents are gone for a couple of hours," and we understood the code.

Once, my accomplice had some sort of pimple on his penis and came to me, convinced that we must have syphilis or gonorrhea, which we'd learned about in a graphic, gruesome film shown in gym class. Somehow, we missed the part explaining that venereal diseases could only be acquired by having sex with someone who had one, and thought that it might just materialize from contact—especially sinful contact. The film's lesson had been abstinence, not safe sex, so we were certain we would end up wandering pell-mell through the streets of Sand Springs, demented and blind, finally dying in an alley behind Dean's Coney Island, where we'd survived on scraps of discarded chili dogs. This would be better than confessing our damnable tryst in exchange for antibiotics.

After a few days, the pimple disappeared and we carried on.

Having entered our teenage years, our encounters took on a different meaning; a different, prickling guilt. Especially for him, because he was definitely and completely into girls. It was confusing. All influences of authority—parents, teachers, God—said that premarital sex with a girl was a sin. But teenage hormones were raging and my partner in crime's justification was that, with a guy, the perimeters seemed to be a little more vague. We knew it was wrong to be a fag, but we *certainly* weren't fags! After all, there was no kissing allowed, though I attempted it many times. He would graciously pull away. He knew. And he was kind.

Contemplatively drunk, I knew I had to get out of this place.

I gazed farther beyond the woods to the lights of the baseball field and I flashed on my failed Little League tryouts.

I had to get out of this place.

My eyes wandered to the top of the hill beyond the woods, taking in the steeple of Broadway Baptist Church, and recalled the Sunday school teacher who told me the Holocaust was a myth.

I had to get out of this place.

Across and to the right was the practice field for the high school marching band, where I'd heard E. E. Bagley's march "National Emblem" echo over the town nearly every morning of my life at 6:30 a.m. when my father was the band director, reminding me that he was in charge—and he had a theme song to prove it.

I had to get out.

I'd not yet heard the phrase "never mix, never worry" and apparently neither had cousin Jay. The map of my life was starting to spin and my stomach began to cry mutiny. I fixed my focus behind the practice field to the home of my best girlfriend, Teri Mullins, who was my accompanist every time I sang at anything for school.

I staggered into the house and found the phone, stretching its long cord to the middle of the living room floor where I could sprawl. As I began to dial, each revolution of the rotary wheel spiraled in an infinite whirlpool . . . 2 . . . 4 . . . 5 . . . *What was Teri's number?* I'd dialed it a thousand times. Finally, I was able to complete the call and, thankfully, it was Teri who picked up.

"I'm going to die," I slurred calmly. "I am going to die in the next few minutes and I wanted to tell you I love you and you're my best friend."

Teri immediately recognized my condition and I detected a slight titter of congratulations. She'd already tried alcohol, pot, and boys. Until now, we had only one of those things in common. "You're not going to die," she assured me.

"But I want to," I retorted, not sure if I was speaking as a result of my current emergency or in a more honest, general way.

"You're not going to die. And I love you too. Now go outside and get some air and I promise it will get better."

Jay helped me to my feet, as precarious as a newborn calf's, and back out to the porch. I steadied myself on the railing overlooking the garden and did what I always did for clarity or escape:

I sang.

I slowly lifted my hands, acquired balance, and I sang.

"The Star Spangled Banner."

At the top of my lungs.

Jay warned that someone was going to call the police, but I was resolved to a big finish.

O'er the land of the free!
And the home of the brave!

I waited for the applause in my head to reach its peak and then promptly threw up into the vincas. And then I threw up again. And again. Acidic to what I prayed was the last drop. Weakly, I lowered myself to the cool cement porch and closed my eyes, commanding the wretched sickness to disappear while clinging to the euphoria. I forced my heavy lids open to find june bugs dizzily penciling their shadows around the porch light, seemingly drunk as well. Suddenly, several blurry Jays entered the frame, looking down with more than a tinge of concern.

"Hey, man, are you all right?"

"Am I dead yet?" I replied.

He undressed me and gently put me to bed, offering a trash can into which I would puke over the next hours, while he lay snoring in the twin bed a few feet away.

The next morning I woke, my eyes poisoned and my head pounding out of rhythm with my throbbing pulse, like a drummer with a bum arm. My breath was raspy and rank and a thought worse than death pushed its way through my swollen brain: it was Saturday and I had flag girl practice.

I was the drum major in our junior high band and had taken on the responsibility to choreograph the squad through the summer in preparation for the fall. Our latest routine was set to

"Black Magic Woman," and I had some seriously complicated, crowd-pleasing moves to teach. But I could hardly move myself.

Rather than walk the endless mile to Squirrel Hollow Park for practice, I decided I would tell my mother the awful truth and she would let me go back to bed. It would be worth it. My father was gone for the day and I was grateful, certain my mom would be more sympathetic. Though the half-empty liquor bottles and vomit-covered vincas had already tipped her off, she let me go through the grueling act of confession, and then finally said, "Sam. I know."

I cried to her, swearing I would never drink again. She insisted I walk to practice anyway, reminding me that it was my responsibility and not the flag girls' fault that I was a hopeless drunk. Then she tortured me. "And when you get back, I'll make some chili hot dogs for you and Jay for lunch. Really spicy, meaty chili with beans. How does that sound?"

I ran to the bathroom and vomited again. Then I showered to remove the stench of my transgression and went to twirl deliriously spinning, nausea-inducing flags.

Black Magic Woman, indeed.

"Let's do it again," I had begged at age eight.

I wouldn't have my next drink for two whole years. But that one would last for the next twenty-nine.

It was 2:58 a.m. in Los Angeles. I screened.

"Baby, it's me. Are you awake?"

What kind of a question is that? It's three o'clock in the fucking morning! Is she kidding?

But yes, I was awake. In fact I was in the kitchen, noshing from a peanut butter jar while I held my arm over the stove flame, thinking it would be interesting to see if I could find the perfect distance between the gas fire and my arms to singe the hair without burning the skin. The smell of burning hair was acrid as I continued to singe and nosh. I got too close to the flame and dropped the peanut butter jar, which shattered on the iron burner. In an effort to collect the pieces, I cut my finger, which then led me to the experiment of sprinkling Sweet'N Low on the blood and sucking it off my finger to see how it would taste. Then I chased it with another swift gulp of vodka, finishing off the bottle.

It was 6:00 a.m. on the East Coast—way early for Liza to be up.

I picked up the phone. "Hey there. Yes, I'm awake. Are you okay? I've left a dozen messages over the past couple of weeks."

There was a pause as she drew deeply on a cigarette and then exhaled. Finally she said, "Baby, I'm in rehab."

My heart sank. No one had worked harder for their sobriety than Liza. No one.

She continued. "I'm sitting here with my counselor and Family Week is coming and I want you to come. You're my family. And I really need you. Can you come?"

I wrapped my finger with a wet paper towel to stop the bleeding. "Yes. Sure, I can come. Of course. Where am I going?"

"I'm gonna hand over the phone to Carol and she can give you the details. I love you so much. You're my family. Thank you. Dress warm." And she was gone.

The next morning, I headed to LAX for a 7:00 a.m. flight to somewhere in Pennsylvania and found a days-old tabloid rag stuffed in the car service seat pocket that reported my friend was in rehab. I was so out of the loop.

Six hours later, I was met at the airport by a seventyish, doughy man in blue slacks and white socks, holding a sign bearing my first name only. As I approached him, I took in his kind eyes and noticed he'd missed the same spots when shaving enough times to leave patches of gray whiskers sprigging haphazardly from his full cheeks and neck. He insisted on loading my oversize suitcase into a van and we headed through the snow-covered countryside in the middle of nowhere.

"For just tonight you'll be staying at a hotel. I'll pick you up first thing in the morning to drive you to the facility." *The facility.* After several attempts at conversation during which I grunted single-syllable responses, he finally surrendered to silence. Then he said, "You're going to like this place. It really works." I slowly lowered my sunglasses on my nose and looked at him in the reflection of the rearview mirror. "I am here," I corrected him, "for a friend." I pushed my sunglasses back up and hunkered into the worn vinyl seat.

He dropped me at a Days Inn or a Ramada Inn or a Something-or-Other Inn and said he'd be by to pick me up the next day at 6:00 a.m.

"Six a.m.? In the *morning*?"

What had I gotten myself into? I was tired and edgy, but glad to be there for my dear friend and grateful that she was getting the help she needed.

The woman at the reception desk was perky. She welcomed me, pointing out the restaurant and gift shop across the lobby, and wished me a great night. As soon as I entered my room, it occurred to me that I should get to bed early since I was on West Coast time and the old man was picking me up at what I considered 3:00 a.m. I called room service. "This is Sam Harris. Could I please get a cheeseburger and a glass of wine."

"Yes sir, Mr. Harris. That'll be about forty-five minutes."

"Really?"

"We're backed up."

"Then cancel the hamburger and just bring the wine. Could you possibly bring *that* faster than forty-five minutes?"

I showered and put on boxer shorts and a tank in time for a knock at the door. A girl in her early twenties was on the other side. Her skin was superwhite and starchy, and she would have been almost pretty if not for the bad bleach job and overly applied eye makeup, smudged by a long shift. She was quite bosomatious, and her faded black T-shirt pressed against her polyester pea-green vest bearing the logo "Days Inn" or "Ramada Inn" or "Something-or-Other Inn."

She held a tray bearing the tiniest glass of wine that I had ever seen. Impossibly small. Tragically minute. Barely more than vapor. I asked where the rest of the glass of wine might be. She chomped her gum and laughed, acknowledging it was small. I signed the check, threw back the glass, and replaced it on the tray with a sturdy whack. "Could you bring another or do I have to call room service again?"

"I can do that," she said, slightly kittenish in a gum-smacking sort of way.

"Make that two. They're small."

"No prob."

A few minutes later, she returned with two of the tiny glasses, filled to the brim. "Better?" she asked with a smile. "I dig your tattoos. Where'd you get 'em?"

"One in Los Angeles and the other I have no idea."

I signed the check and bid her good night.

Twenty minutes later I was not sleepy and was nervous about the next day. I didn't want to drink too much because I needed to be fresh. But a little more wine couldn't hurt. It was just wine. Ordering by the glass seemed uneconomical, so I called room service for a bottle. I'd throw out what I didn't drink.

While waiting, I realized I was starving, but I'd already

made such an issue of the forty-five-minute burger that it would be humiliating to call back and order food. I decided to see if anyone had left anything in the hall. Sometimes you can get practically a whole meal from people's leftovers. I carefully positioned the chain lock so that the door would remain lodged open and headed out to scavenge. Sure enough, someone had left part of a Philly cheesesteak and more than a handful of fries. I carefully cut off the chewed part, added a little mustard, and stuffed the remainder in my mouth.

Suddenly I heard the elevator *bing*. Someone was coming! I rushed back to my room and accidentally hit the door so that the chain slid down and the door locked. I stood in the hallway in my boxers and tank with cheesesteak Cheez Whiz and mustard running down my chin. The same room service girl rounded the corner with her tray. She gave me a flirtatious once-over.

"I locked myself out," I said, mouth full, stating the obvious.

"Good thing I came along first, huh?" she replied, and used her pass-card key to open the door.

"I was looking for the ice machine," I floundered, finally swallowing.

"It's by the elevator. But next time you might want to take an ice bucket."

I realized she'd put her hair up and reapplied her makeup since her last visit.

"You're not from around here, are you?" she continued.

"No. That's why I'm staying at a hotel . . ."

"Do you need any help with that bottle of wine? We're closing soon."

Seriously? The room service girl wanted to join me for a drink?

"I have to get up early so I'd better not," I said, and tipped her generously, thanked her for all her trouble, and bid her good night for the third time.

Once inside, I poured most of the bottle into a tall glass, plopped on the bed, and turned on the TV, hoping to find something dull. I soon got up for a refill and on my way back, I tripped on a shoe and spilled some of the wine on the polyester bedspread. I guessed the equivalent of a small glass had been lost, just sitting there, a reservoir of yellow floating on top of the heinous flowered print. I considered funneling it off the bed and into my glass like a little river, but I'd seen a *60 Minutes* where they'd shone a black light on hotel bedspreads, and the fluids that permeated them were epically grotesque. I had to draw the line somewhere.

"Goddamn it!!" I screamed, and I headed for the phone.

"This is Sam Harris and I just spilled the *entire* bottle of wine. Can you send up another?"

"I'm sorry, Mr. Harris, room service is closed."

"But the girl was just here ten minutes ago. I'm not asking you to cook anything. Just bring up a bottle of wine. I'll pay extra. I'll pay double."

"Truly sir, we're closed."

"What if I come down and get it myself?"

"We're locking up, Mr. Harris. We open for breakfast at five a.m."

"Oh goody. Breakfast at five a.m.," I spouted facetiously. "Should I put my order in now?"

I slammed down the phone and went to the bathroom, where I chewed an Ambien to make it work faster, then chased it with what was left of the wine.

I lay down on the fiber-filled wine-repelling comforter, leaving the pool intact in case I changed my mind about drinking it, and channel surfed to Tony Robbins's gargantuan mouth telling me that "*personal power equals action!*" It was only ten o'clock. Seven o'clock in Los Angeles. How was I going to fall asleep at this hour? It was ridiculous that they couldn't bring up a bottle of wine and I was furious. How dare they?! I watched Tony's teeth for another twenty minutes. *"Make decisions, take action, clarity is power!"* Having consumed nearly two bottles of wine and a sleeping pill, and inspired by Tony, I had a really good idea.

I carefully set the chain between the door and the frame again and crept down the hallway, into the stairwell and down the fire escape stairs, tiptoeing, barefoot in my boxers. When I got to the lobby floor, I cracked the door enough to see that the woman at the reception desk was reading a book. The coast was clear.

The tile floor was cold as I darted behind a column, then to another.

Scamper, scamper, scamper, hide. Scamper, scamper, scamper, hide.

I could see that the faux-iron gate at the restaurant's entrance was chained, but there were arch-shaped, faux-brick windows along the side of its wall. I scampered once more to another column, and when I was sure the woman at the desk was engrossed in her book, I hoisted myself up and through a window, into the dark restaurant.

I snuck around the cash register and counter and into the kitchen. The floor was syrupy and my feet made a sucking sound with each step. An ambient glow emitted from an industrial glass-doored refrigerator that housed milk and faux-cheese and gallon-size screw-top jugs of cheap wine. It was padlocked.

Apparently, I was not the first guest to get this idea.

Suddenly from nowhere, the bosomatious bleach-blond girl appeared.

"Looking for me?" she inquired, adding a provocative smack of her gum.

I nearly jumped out of my boxers.

"Uh, no, I was . . . uh . . . looking for . . . milk. I have this brownie in my room and you know how horrible it is when you don't have milk."

"You're drunk," she giggled.

"No, I'm just jet-lagged and I have to be up in a few hours and . . . yes, I'm a little drunk."

She cozied up to me, rubbing against my thigh.

I continued, "And a little . . ."

"What?" she said, coyly.

"Gay . . . a little drunk and a little gay."

"Cool," she said. "No prob. How'd you get in here?"

I pointed to the window and begged her not to tell anyone. She promised she wouldn't.

"I like your tattoos."

"You mentioned that."

"I have the key to the fridge, if you want some . . . *milk*."

She removed the padlock from the door and handed me one of the giant jugs of wine.

"You sure you're gay?" she whispered.

"Pretty sure," I replied.

"No prob."

The next morning, I managed to get up before dawn and prepared my head for Family Week at rehab, whatever that might be. I was there for Liza. She needed me. She was an alcoholic and I would do anything to help her.

At 6:00 a.m., it was colder and frostier and so was I. The same driver met me in the lobby. He'd shaved, but had missed the same spots. This time he didn't attempt conversation, for which I was grateful. We drove through the sterile, snowy landscape and arrived at the lodging area for guests. I was told

I would be staying at "the Villa." Things were looking up after the crappy hotel I'd barely slept in the night before.

The Villa was an old, masculine colonial building in need of fresh paint and some sprucing up. I pulled the collar of my coat closer around my neck and dragged my enormously oversize suitcase to join other family members who had just arrived at the steps of the columned, wooden porch. Their faces reflected the defeat and hope that had brought them here, and polite conversation was limited to only the essential.

A chipper attendant in her midfifties, with closely packed, overly permed Chia Pet hair, wearing high-waisted jeans and a "One Day at a Time" sweatshirt, carried a clipboard and shrieked in a cartoonishly high-pitched voice:

"Please form two lines. Those staying at the Villa, make a line on the left. Those at the Château, to the right. As you enter, please leave your bags on the porch and make sure they are labeled. They will be returned to you after checking for inappropriate contents."

I wasn't so concerned about inappropriate contents, but I was afraid that I'd be judged for the inappropriate clothes I'd brought. Clearly, I was not going to need my Ted Baker shirts or Hugo Boss suit.

I looked around at the silent line in their gray and black overcoats, shuffling forward, their breaths pluming in the bitter cold. They checked in, stacked their luggage, and disappeared into one of the side-by-side structures. They were following orders. They had nothing and everything in common. When I got to the chipper attendant, I couldn't help but ask, with all my charm, "Which is the line for the barracks and which is the line for the gas chambers?"

She stared at me vacantly and pointed to where I should deposit my luggage.

I entered the Villa and schlepped up three flights of stairs with other guests and finally found my room. It had no lock on the door. It was tiny. Grim. Like a 1930s dorm room that hadn't been painted since the 1930s, when apparently dull beige was all the rage. Two twin beds with transparently thin coverlets hugged opposing walls and a small table was squeezed between them. There was no phone. No TV. No clock. A door, which opened just enough so you could squeeze through before hitting a bed, led to a minuscule fluorescent-lit bathroom, shared with the adjoining room. I tried calling Danny but there was no signal. I imagined an invisible lead shield dome over the facility to restrain communication and undue influence.

I fell back onto one of the twin beds and it was so rock-hard that it stunned me. It had apparently petrified since the 1930s. The chipper attendant appeared in the doorway, clipboard in hand, and a young man brought in my suitcase. He was wearing a T-shirt that said "Quitting is for Quitters."

"Find everything okay?" she chirped.

"I don't suppose there's a terry cloth robe behind that door," I joked.

She stared back at me with a blank, overextended smile.

I tried again. "Or turndown service with a little Godiva chocolate on the pillow."

"Okay then," she clipped, and left the doorway.

"Or a minibar . . ." I muttered.

She reentered the doorframe in a flash, her eyes a little wider. "Beg pardon?"

"Nothing," I said.

"Okay then." And she was gone.

I lowered myself slowly onto the stone bed, tired and hungover. I closed my eyes. We'd been given no schedule and I could use a nap. Suddenly a bullhorn boomed, no, *blasted*, from just

Sam Harris

outside my door. I sat up in a start. The building must be on fire. The chipper attendant's voice blared, no, *trumpeted,* through the speaker: "Welcome, family members and loved ones. Please meet in the GRAND ROOM on the third floor. Please meet in the GRAND ROOM on the third floor."The bullhorn sounded again to signal the end of her announcement. The first one wasn't enough.

Where the hell am I? I pulled myself up from the slab and joined in the herd of slump-shouldered guests, shuffling down the stairs. No one spoke.

Like the misnamed Villa and Château, there was nothing grand about the Grand Room. It was a fake-paneled, stained-carpeted, forty-by-thirty room with a low cottage cheese ceiling and folding chairs facing a smallish TV on a metal stand. The lights were dim and I found a seat in the back row. An instructional video had begun, which featured a doctor, grimly facing the camera:

". . . to give you a better understanding of what your loved ones are going through. Alcoholism is the great leveler. Rich, poor, young, old, presidents, and paupers. You are not alone."

The woman next to me seemed exhausted, spent, barely functional. "Who are you in for?" I cleverly whispered.

"My son."

"I'm here for a friend."

I felt a tapping on my shoulder. It was a man in his midfifties, with closely packed, overly permed hair, wearing high-waisted jeans and a "It's alcohol-ISM, not alcohol-WASM" T-shirt.

"Could we please have quiet?" he said. "What we don't know *can* hurt us." I smiled and nodded. Oh, brother. As soon as he was gone, I leaned in to the woman and spoke in a hush, barely moving my lips, like a ventriloquist. "I know all this stuff. My mother and my brother both went to Betty Ford . . .

which is a hell of a lot nicer than this, by the way. They have swans."

The woman politely smiled, but her eyes were empty. "We should probably watch this."

Okay then. The video used animation to explain the way the brain responds to alcohol: little dopamine characters, pleasure centers, the alcoholic's need to drink more and more to achieve the same effect, just to feel normal. It ended with the doctor, in a close-up this time, saying, "It is a vicious cycle. One that, unless broken, can end in incomprehensible demoralization and even death."

The screen went to black. Lights up. The Grand Room looked even less grand in fluorescent lighting.

I turned to my only acquaintance and said, "The ending could be a little cheerier, but I'm seeing Sundance."

Nothing.

No one here thought anything I said was funny. I couldn't wait to see Liza. *She'd* think I was funny!

The man who'd told me to shut up approached me and I was sure he was going to slap my wrist again.

I hated this guy.

"I'm Bob. You're Sam Harris, aren't you? I recognize you. Big fan."

I loved this guy.

"We're going to take a van to the cafeteria and you can join Clara for lunch."

"Clara? I'm here for Liza," I said.

"She's registered as Clara here. We didn't want it to get out to the tabloids."

"But it's already out."

"It would be confusing to change her name midway through treatment."

"For who?" I asked, a bit confused, then, "Never mind . . . How's she doing?"

I was more eager for information than Clara-fication.

"Great! I think we've made some real breakthroughs. It's all about honesty here."

"Except for the name thing . . ."

I entered the cafeteria. A dozen 10-top round tables were mostly occupied and a line of people with trays were being serviced by net-headed women with closely packed perms, doling out grub by the glutinous poundful. I suspected cream of mushroom soup was in every gummy dish. They wore white T-shirts, none of which bore slogans, but the stains on them spelled "inedible." I scoured the room for Liza and our eyes met. She screamed, "Schmoolie!" and ran across the room. Our embrace was longer than usual, solemn and warm as a fireside.

I took her face in my hands. "Are you okay?" I asked, looking deeply into her eyes for the truth.

"I'm really, *really* good. I'm so glad you're here."

"Me too," I replied. And, finally, I was.

She dragged me to her table of mostly younger residents.

"Everybody, this is my best friend, Sam."

A girl in her early twenties offered, "Clara's told us so much about you."

They were all in on the name thing. The food looked grotesque. Heavy-duty carbs, like what I imagined they served in prisons to keep the inmates lethargic and sedentary. I wasn't hungry. Liza and I walked around the room, hand in hand, toward a plate glass window overlooking immaculate powdery-white hills.

"Do you have a fake last name too?" I had to ask.

"Cobb," she replied. "As in corn-on-the. I was having dinner and it came to me."

"Clara Cobb. Awful."

It was one of the qualities I loved most about her—the ability to move through obstacles with ridiculous humor. I was with my friend. My hysterically funny, simpatico, brave, scary friend.

"Schmool, it's been really good. We have sessions all day. They call me on my stuff. I have chores. I make my bed. It's empowering. Everybody here is just like everybody else."

Suddenly the twentysomething girl screamed out, "Look!! Out there in the field. There's a guy with a camera!"

Liza dove under the closest table, taking me with her. We crouched low on our haunches and, through the yellow poly-cotton tablecloth, we could see a rush of shadows forming a human barricade to shield our hideout from view.

"Goddamn it! Those sons of bitches!" she yelled. After a minute, she poked her head out and asked the girl, "Are they still there?"

"I don't know," the girl reported. "I'm not even sure what I saw. Maybe it was a hunter."

Liza thought we should stay under the table for a while just in case. My legs were starting to cramp. We both settled. Dried chewing gum grazed our hair. Then she poked her head out again and asked the girl, "Baby, can you get me another piece of the banana cream pie? Schmooli, do you want one?"

"Sure, why not?"

"Make it two," she said, and pulled her head back inside the fort.

The girl returned a few moments later with our order.

And there we were: Liza and me, sitting together, cross-legged, eating banana cream pie, under a table. At rehab. In the middle of nowhere. Our own private sanctuary in a room brimming with alcoholics and addicts and overly permed counselors with cliché-emblazoned T-shirts, all gorging on too many carbohydrates.

Liza and I have always had a saying about our lives in show business: "The Glitter, the Glamour, the Gutter." This moment firmly fell into the latter category. But there was also something wonderful about it. The irony and the absurdity and the bond. We devoured our pie and she swiped whipped cream from my cheek and sucked it off her finger as she unfolded the details of her two weeks there. Her eyes were bright and clear. She was at her most present.

Our first rehab family class together was starting soon, so we finished our pie and Clara and I crawled out to begin the work.

My memory of the following week is a hodgepodge of images— like pieces from a dozen different puzzles, most of which don't fit anything:

Role-playing exercises—acting out the disease and each other.

Letters to the disease.

Not sleeping.

Lists of all the ways in which alcoholism affects loved ones.

Horror stories from other residents. Spouses who seemed more damaged than their alcoholic counterparts. Children who wanted their parents back. Parents of troubled children who couldn't face their part in the situation and stormed out.

Classes on detachment. "Do not prevent a crisis if it is the natural order of things."

Still not sleeping.

Tearing through my bags and realizing my sleeping pills had been confiscated. Those fuckers.

Needing a drink.

"Let Go and Let God."

Eat me.

Confusion.

A "Nothing Changes If Nothing Changes" T-shirt.

My disdain of stupid T-shirts.

More confrontational classes.

Salivating at the thought of a drink.

A desperate need for sugar.

Jumbled thoughts.

My inability to find or form words.

A growing interest in glutinous cream-of-mushroom-soup-based carbohydrates.

Itching.

Waking with my arms bloody from scratching in my sleep.

Stuffing the bloody sheets in a hallway trash can.

Shaking.

Confusion.

Really needing a drink.

Chicken fried steak with gravy.

Liza getting better.

Me getting worse.

The "Butt Hut," where we stood in the freezing cold between classes or meals and sucked down one cigarette after another.

Trying to put on a good face.

Trembling hands. Not from the cold.

"I'm sorry I'm putting you through this," she said, lighting another Marlboro and offering me one.

Taking it, I replied, "I thought we were going to have little lunches with finger sandwiches and take rowboats out on the lake."

"It's the dead of winter."

". . . go ice-skating out on the lake."

The fluorescent light of my tiny bathroom, making my face appear a pale green. Wondering if it really was.

Watching people change. Watching my friend open up.

Watching families reunite.

The closing ceremony at the end of the week, where residents and loved ones joined together in a church.

The middle-aged Irish New Yorker priest who spoke in the parlance of a black man. "Hey, ya'll, wassup? Halle-*lu*-jah!"

Listening to some of the younger residents recite poems or sing original songs.

Liza inspired to get up and sing "I Can See Clearly Now."

My horrifying fear that she was going to try to get me to sing.

Liza introducing me as her best friend and the greatest singer in the world.

Liza handing me a microphone.

Whispering "I'm gonna kill you" to her through gritted teeth.

"Just sing." Liza looking at me insistently.

"I can't."

"It's what we do."

"I'm exhausted. My throat is bad. Please, please don't make me do this."

Liza encouraging the crowd to applaud as if I am waiting to be coaxed.

Me taking the mic and standing up before the crowd.

The voice in my head telling me: *Never decline a request to sing.*

Knowing I just couldn't.

"Thank you, Liza. Clara . . . Everyone here is so amazing. I am overwhelmed by what goes on here. I'm just a visitor and I don't really . . . it's not really my place to . . . good luck to you all."

I sit.

Polite applause.

A young, fat girl with purple hair and lots of tattoos getting up and singing an operatic Italian aria with an overwhelmingly honest, clear, pristine, passionate voice. She is an angel. She is mesmerizing. The package doesn't fit the packaging.

Nothing makes sense.

Things are not what they seem.

The crowd explodes with applause and Liza takes the girl in her arms.

Everyone is crying.

Except me.

I cannot feel anything.

I had agreed to stay in New York a couple of days for Liza's transition back into real life, and on the drive there, her infectious optimism finally scratched through the surface of my numbness. She put the *Chicago* cast album on the CD player, blared the volume, and we sang at the top of our lungs: *"Me and my baby, my baby and me!"* The driver was either in horror or heaven, I couldn't tell which. At last we crossed the bridge and I was grateful to be in the city.

Upon arriving at her apartment, we were greeted by Bill, who worked in New York as an extension of the rehab center. Liza gave him a kiss of familiarity and he gave her a nod. He had gathered her assistant, housekeeper, houseman, and lawyer for a meeting and they sat in the living room, waiting, like the von Trapp children. A chair had been placed for Liza to face the group and I sat with the others. She was prepared.

"It's good to be home," she said. "I am strong and healthy and clear. We will be reorganizing work times, setting some boundaries . . ."

She talked on, straightforward, lucid, and indisputable.

Sam Harris

I noticed that Bill was watching me, not her. I realized my legs and feet were twitching and I thought he was asking me to stop being so distracting. Then I realized he was gesturing for me to meet him in the kitchen. Once we were alone, he asked if I wanted to go for a coffee, explaining that she'd be a while and it wasn't necessary for us to be there. We bundled up and walked two blocks to Neil's Coffee Shop. We settled in a window booth and ordered coffee and bagels from our unshaven Italian waiter. Bill knew how close Liza and I were and I presumed he wanted to get the inside scoop on her actual emotional state.

I happily obliged. "She seems good. I know she's been through this before, but I think it's different this time. I'm glad you're going to be here. It's hard for her to be alone right now and I'm leaving in a couple of days."

He asked how Family Week was. I told him tough, but she did really well. "She's dealing straight on."

I told him I was encouraged to lay a lot of things on the table and it was good for our relationship.

"How about you?" he asked.

"Me? I'm fine."

"I mean how was it for you?" he dug.

I sat for a moment. "Honestly, it brought up some stuff . . . I don't know if I never adjusted to the time change or I'm coming down with something or . . . I may have a drinking problem . . ."

What? What am I saying? How did that come out of my mouth?

Bill showed no signs of, well, anything. "Oh?" he said flatly.

And it was on.

Out of the blue.

"Well, I pretty much drink every day. I have since I was about sixteen."

"How much?" he asked.

226

"In the past ten years, two or three bottles of wine a night. And vodka. No drugs. Ambien. I don't sleep well."

Bill looked at me with knowing eyes. "For me using wasn't the problem. It was the solution. Until it wasn't. Until it stopped working."

I wondered if he was wearing an "Easy Does It" T-shirt under his sweater.

I focused on my coffee and stirred it with my finger.

I flashed on all the nights I had sat alone, drinking, surfing porn on the Internet, never making plans because I didn't know what condition I'd be in. Or because I did.

Lugging trash bags of empty bottles to neighbors' trash cans so garbagemen and homeless recyclers wouldn't judge me.

The isolation. The thoughts of suicide. The good-bye letters I'd written to loved ones.

The smallness.

I continued. "When my partner's out of town it's pretty much full-time. Blinds are drawn. I don't answer the phone. Sometimes I do things I don't remember. Or say things or . . . I've just been so . . . sad."

"Do you think you're an alcoholic?" he asked simply.

"I don't know. I've never used that word. I mean I know I drink a lot. But a lot of people are worse off than me."

I remembered packing for our move from New York to Los Angeles. I'd come across an old journal of Danny's and, naturally, had read it. It said: "Sam is such an alcoholic. I don't know how much longer I can take this."

I remembered carefully removing the page with a box cutter and tossing it away as if it didn't exist.

"I work," I continued. "I've never been drunk onstage. I haven't been arrested or lost my savings or my relationship or my car, so . . ."

Sam Harris

"When was your last drink?" he asked.

I flashed on sneaking down the fire escape stairwell in my boxer shorts and hoisting myself through a window and breaking into a restaurant. For a drink. *Was this a dream?* No. I had not given this episode a second thought until this moment, and it occurred to me that this behavior was . . . unusual . . . but not necessarily for me.

"Last week." I left it at that.

Bill handed me his card. "If you're an alcoholic, you'll find out. If you're not, well then, cheers." He dropped a ten-dollar bill on the table and we slipped into our coats and scarves and trod over the slushy sidewalk back to Liza's apartment building in silence.

Snowflakes the size of packing material wafted and floated down. There was a stillness. No breeze. It was quiet for New York. Considerate. Bill told me he would be back later that night but had some work to do. I politely shook hands with this stranger whom I'd practically vomited honesty to. He said our conversation was just between us. Then we parted as he started up toward Lexington and I toward the building. After three or four paces I stopped and turned around.

"Bill?"

He turned and we stood, staring at each other for a brief, endless moment.

". . . I'm an alcoholic."

As gently as the snow falling around us, he walked to me and gave me a short but dedicated hug. Then he walked away.

I took the elevator to Liza's apartment and let myself in. The staff meeting was over and everyone was gone. It was a Sunday after all. Liza yelled out from her bedroom, "Schmooli, is that you?"

I walked down the hall and to the doorframe of her room.

And the dam broke. All of the tension of the last week, the last years, the last life, had culminated in this single moment of release. I couldn't speak. Liza remained in her bed, knowing somehow to let the moment stand.

"What is it? What happened?"

I somehow managed to move one foot in front of the other and made my way to her bedside, sitting on the edge next to her. She took me by the shoulders and stared deeply into my eyes. I collected myself and took a breath.

"I'm an alcoholic," I said, and burst into tears once again.

She smiled and pulled me close and cradled me in her arms, rocking me back and forth, pushing the melting snowflakes from my brow and wiping the endless stream of tears from my eyes.

"I know, baby. I know."

14. Bullies and Heroes

On my last night of being twelve years old, I dreamt that there were spiders, thousands of them, crawling all over the floor of my room and I was trapped in my bed. The dream was so real that when I woke on the morning of my thirteenth birthday, I wasn't sure if it had happened or not. The floor was clear, no sign of arachnids, but I was afraid to venture out. Afraid of being thirteen. The day was here.

Beginning years before, I had been warned by my father, with increasing regularity, that if I didn't "change" by the time I was thirteen, I would be in great trouble. I think he saw thirteen as the transition from boy to man—the time to relinquish forgivable childhood eccentricities before it was too late. He never specified what it was I should change or what trouble I would be in. However, without giving it a name like chicken pox or the measles, I knew that I carried an unspoken affliction, which I'd been reminded of at every turn, in sometimes overt but more often in subtle, nonspecific ways. It had been left for me to figure out and fix. Today I knew for sure. If I wasn't a normal, red-blooded American boy who liked normal, red-blooded American things, including normal, red-blooded American girls, all would be lost. It appeared all was lost.

I pulled back the blue corduroy bedspread that had protected me in my twin bed during the night and gingerly lowered a toe to the green shag carpeting, then scampered across it, knowing the spider nightmare was just that, but hedging my bets just the same. I ran to the single tiny bathroom, shared by the entire family. The pale blue tile floor was covered with a damp bath mat, and multiple, variously colored towels were hung over the sliding glass shower doors, providing the only privacy. The policy in our house was come-and-go-as-you-please save for my mother, who was the only one of us allowed to lock the door. One of her Carol Brady blond-streaked shag wigs sat on a Styrofoam head atop the toilet tank. I turned its pocked face toward the wall and removed my pajamas and stood before the mirror, naked, to give myself a careful and thorough inspection. Thirteen.

I wondered if I'd physically changed. Slightly doughy and pasty pale, but with muscular legs, broad shoulders, a strong jawline, and fantastic hair, currently bed-headed, but typically parted in the middle and feathered on the sides, I wasn't horrible. But that was just the outside. Inside it was scary. As I stared at my reflection, I wondered if the pounding of my heart and the fear in my soul was visible.

Then I ran back to my room and dressed in cutoffs and a Mickey Mouse T-shirt.

I had flag girl practice and I didn't want to be late.

Deana was the sinewy-muscled, tree-climbing leader of the girls' gang on our street and she hated me. I wanted the neighborhood kids to play "town," in which we each had a pretend business and we rode around on our bikes to the "bank" and the "restaurant" and the "nightclub," which was my establishment of choice, where I served Kool-Aid and performed my act. Deana wanted to play football or skin-a-squirrel or track-a-possum, I don't remember. She actually had a wild skunk as a pet, trained for battle.

Deana sent a message to me through one of her eleven-year-old lackeys that I had better stop encouraging this "stupid queer town game." My father saw this as an opportunity for me to step up my manhood, and convinced me to send back a message for her to meet me in my front yard to settle this. "Settle this," to me, meant talk it out—find a compromise. I was much more articulate and would have the upper hand. To Deana, "settle this" meant blood would be spilled.

Deana arrived, skidding to a stop on her rusty, sun-faded blue Huffy. The girl's bar had been removed so that her balls wouldn't get injured. Her long, ever-tanned arms and legs flexed in a tank top and cutoffs, which only made me look pastier and puffier in comparison. All of the kids surrounded us to see who would win the neighborhood crown.

Then Deana proceeded to beat the shit out of me.

She punched and kicked and spat and scratched. I didn't have time to play out the convincing speech about neighborly fraternity I had rehearsed only minutes before. I was terrified. This was uncivilized. We weren't little kids anymore. I had hair growing under my arms for Christ's sake. But Deana had more.

She grabbed me firmly by my moppy hair and swung me around so hard I was lifted off the ground in a circle like in a Popeye cartoon. Which would give way first, Deana's super-human powers or my hair? Finally, she let go and I missiled into a crumpled pile of exhausted flesh under a thorny bush. I pulled myself up from the dirt, dizzy and discombobulated. The crowd cheered and jeered. Deana kicked me in the stomach and I was down again, for the last time.

I looked up and saw my parents watching through the window: my mother's face registered panic and it was clear that my father had probably tied her to a chair to prevent her from rescuing me. His eyes pleaded for me to get up and try again. Did he really want me to hit a *girl*? Even if I could? Was he too humiliated to stop the fisticuffs and rescue his sissy son? One way or another, he was going to let me fight my own fight. Even if I might not live to see morning.

That night I soaked in a hot tub while Deana was off somewhere, I was sure, ripping open a live rabbit with her teeth and smearing the blood all over her body in some kind of victory ritual. My muscles were tender and bruised. My hair hurt. But I knew that I was lucky it was the beginning of summer and I had three months for this to be forgotten before the gossip of the school year began. Deana was clearly the champion, but I took refuge in the thought that she would probably get fat, be a grandmother in her thirties, and sell army surplus. And I would be a star.

Jerry was a massive, lumbering, redheaded, freckled bully whose head was vastly disproportionately larger than the rest of his body. Like one of those effigies people burn at political rallies. In eighth-grade English class, when we were discussing electives for next term, our teacher asked what we'd be taking, and Jerry muttered, "Drugs." Everyone in earshot snickered except me. I thought he was an idiot and I was sure he knew it from the eye roll I couldn't stifle. He hated me.

At the end of class, he cornered me at the door and told me to meet him after school at 3:30 because he was going to beat me up. Why anyone would make an appointment to get the shit knocked out of him was beyond me. I should have told him I had a previous engagement, a rehearsal, a late luncheon. Instead, I reported that 3:30 worked for my schedule and I agreed to meet outside by the basketball court. I didn't tell anyone about my appointment for assault and I was hoping Jerry didn't either. If I was going to get beaten up, I preferred that it be a private pummeling.

I was punctual as usual, and after waiting ten terrifying minutes for Jerry to arrive and rip me to shreds, I decided that if he couldn't be on time, it was his loss. I started around the corner of the adjacent brick building and there he was. Alone. His head seemed even bigger and bloatier than it had earlier in the day, teetering on his shoulders. His cheeks were red with freckly rage.

"Going somewhere, Sissy Boy?" he scoffed, with a curled lip and a cruel smile.

He clenched his fists and stepped toward me and my breath fluttered quick and shallow in a race with the speed of my thoughts. I had no idea what to do. I certainly wasn't going to fight him. I prepared for my fate and hoped he wouldn't disfigure my face, because I was going to be in show business and I was not really a character type. As he took another step closer, I blurted out, "I thought your joke about taking drugs next term was hysterical."

My comment literally jolted him off balance as his giant head rolled to one side and his dilated pupils registered confusion. I had thrown the first punch, albeit verbally, and it had landed—Pow!

Round one—Sissy Boy!

Before he could recover, I said, "You should be in the talent show. Everyone thinks you're so funny."

I thought his head was actually going to roll off his body. Muhammad Ali could not have stung more effectively.

Round two—Sissy Boy takes it again!

"You could be a professional comedian," I continued with growing confidence.

Finally, he spoke. "Are you serious?"

"Dead," I replied. "You're like George Carlin."

A lost, inquisitive blankness came over him.

"I mean Cheechen Chong," I added, hoping to score.

"Which one?"

I realized that Cheech *and* Chong must be two separate people.

"Both!" I said. "*That's* how funny you are!"

And he lit up like a Christmas tree—with only half its bulbs working.

Knockout! Ding ding. Fight over!

Jerry invited me to come over to his house and hang out. We ate Hostess Ding Dongs and talked about school. He was thinking of dropping out. I said I thought that was a good idea and encouraged him to pursue comedy. He smoked weed and nodded a lot. He warned me that at school, or anywhere in public, he could never acknowledge me, but he knew we had a secret bond.

I knew, of course, that we had nothing in common other than the fact that we were both carbon-based life-forms sucking the same humid Oklahoma air.

It suddenly occurred to me that if there had been a public fight, things would be very different. I would already be dead. Jerry would have had no choice but to kill me, it was that simple. So I would be happy to keep our "bond" under wraps and play along with an occasional covert smile. Because I was alive and it was Jerry who was already dead.

• • •

Michelle dyed her hair a distinguishing shade of Julie Andrews cantaloupe, which framed her enormous, penetrating blue eyes, further accentuated by eyelashes that were so long they looked false. Michelle was outgoing and funny-funny, dry and sardonic, and possessed a wicked laugh that revealed a soul beyond her years. Finally, I'd found a kindred spirit. The closest thing to another me. Another who rode the social teeter-totter, managing to placate the popular and embrace the disenfranchised—but not really a part of either.

Michelle was an extraordinarily gifted actress who had created an entertaining, if not completely believable, fantasy life. She'd claimed her father was a famous radio announcer and often quoted her clever and doting mother. They supposedly vacationed abroad and were the closest of friends with all the society mavens of Tulsa, who constantly lavished gifts upon her.

As Michelle and I spent more and more time together, her masquerade slowly melted away and I gained scarce entry to the truth. Michelle's family was poor. Not the kind of poor that insisted on simplicity but didn't compromise pride. This was the poor of resentment and delusion. There was not a blade of grass behind the rusty, lopsided chain-link fence overgrown with suffocating morning glories that separated her house from other impoverished neighbors, where snot-crusted toddlers meandered in soiled cloth diapers, barefoot and unsupervised, sipping mixtures of beer and milk to keep them quiet.

The house was gray, inside and out. The tattered furniture was gray. The soiled carpet was gray. The light was gray. Michelle's father was, indeed, a radio announcer, with a euphonious voice and a masterful economy of language that betrayed his station. And he was crazy as a bag of hammers. He was a drug addict and a pathologically adroit liar who could talk anyone into anything, including giving him a position as an unqualified, uneducated psychotherapist at a home for troubled boys. He also considered himself psychic and read tarot cards for extra money, but didn't require cash to drop into a trance at any given moment.

Michelle's mother was short and round and ruddy and wore cat's-eye glasses and the tight, black polyester knit pants and mannish white button-down shirt required of all employees who worked at Bowden's Quick Stop Gas Station, where she managed the night shift. At home, she slept until midafternoon and spent her waking hours curled up on an unsheeted mattress—dragged daily to the middle of the tiny living room floor—on which she read paperback romance novels with erotically illustrated covers and ate fried SPAM sandwiches while she smoked Newports in swift succession.

I practically lived at Michelle's house, slipping into their grayness as if to claim it as my own, and we happily took charge of everything: We laundered and cleaned and helped her brother and sister with homework. We dragged the mattress and fried the SPAM sandwiches. We cooked dinner every night—mock chicken fried steak and mock apple pie made with Ritz crackers. We played mock house. We mock made out. And we genuinely laughed all the time.

As a little girl, Michelle had found a way to alter her reality and create a world in which she could survive—better than the circumstances, better than the truth. I joined her, and it helped me survive too. We acted as if, and so it was.

She was my mock girlfriend and I loved her.

Joe Allen Restaurant was Danny's and my hangout in New York. It was everybody's hangout in New York. At least the everybodys we hung out with. On any given night, at least a dozen familiar Broadway-ites and enough tourists to garnish an actor's ego could be found hobnobbing there. It was more like a speakeasy than an eatery. The club room for the club.

When I first moved to New York, I'd called to make a reservation under "Harris," and the maître d' had glibly asked, "Julie, Rosemary, or Sam?" I already belonged and it was safe.

I had recently ended my stint in *The Life* on Broadway to complete my latest album, and on the day of its release, Danny and I were ready to celebrate at our favorite home away from home. We were welcomed at the door and shouted bubbly hellos to friends as we made our way down the brick-walled, bar-flanked corridor to our regular table in the back corner. The waiter brought my minipitcher of white wine without my asking and had already placed my order for the La Scala Salad and Danny's cheeseburger. There was comfort in our predictability.

We toasted to the CD's success. It was the end of a long, drama-laden undertaking, which had centered on a producer who'd answer his door in a pair of dingy, pee-stained boxer shorts and a tattered wifebeater, and who had attempted to destroy the actual recording tapes until Liza's man Friday, an ex-bodyguard to some Saudi king, went to the studio in a perfectly pressed suit and tie and politely threatened to kill him. Still the record had turned out well. Some of my best singing ever. We had a lot to celebrate.

Five men sat at the next table an elbow away. They were loud and happy and drunk. Really loud and really happy and really drunk. They took turns commenting on the Broadway shows currently on the boards, assassinating this one and lacerating that one. Stars of the shows, some of whom were in the restaurant and in earshot, were not spared.

Our waiter brought our food and apologetically rolled his

eyes. He asked if we wanted to move to another table. We declined. This was *my* table and surely these guys would leave or pass out sooner than later.

The hit men continued their witty massacre and finally, annoyed to my limit, I turned in their direction and testily shushed them. Their table quieted for a brief moment. Then the apparent leader of the pack said, for all to hear, "Ooooohh. I've been shushed by a pathetic *Star Search* winner!"

At Joe Allen. My club.

In a single second I was back in the halls of Charles Page High School, someone had just called me "faggot," and I was an outsider. The man was facing away from me, so, thankfully, there was no direct visual confrontation. I played deaf and buried my red face in a hunk of buttered bread and stuffed it into my mouth, followed by an ample swash of wine. I attempted to resume lighthearted conversation with Danny but he wasn't listening.

"A *Star Search* winner has spoken!" the man further proclaimed to the room. "Ssshhhh! We should all be quiet!"

Danny slowly rose from our table and steadily walked the two feet between us and the culprit. "May I see you outside?" he said, with threatening diplomacy.

"I don't think so!" the man slurred. "I'm eating my dinner!"

And then Danny grabbed the little brute around the throat in a headlock, hoisted him from his chair, and dragged him down the corridor past frozen faces at crowded tables. Roscoe Lee Browne sat perched in his regular spot at the end of the teeming bar. I loved Roscoe. He was an African-American classical actor and a master of cerebral eloquence who, in response to criticism that he sounded too white, had famously responded, "I'm sorry. I once had a white maid." As Danny passed him with the kicking man in tow, Roscoe's rich, sable voice interrupted the stupefied silence: "New dancing partner, Danny?" And they were out the door.

Waiters swarmed to my table in celebration.

"That was amazing!"

"I can't believe he did that!"

"Someone finally put Michael Riedel in his place!"

MICHAEL RIEDEL?! The *New York Post* theater reporter and critic who, often single-handedly, decided which Broadway shows made it and which didn't? The guy who had enough pen power to make or break a Tony? THAT MICHAEL RIEDEL?

I was so fucked.

Danny had defended my honor. It was the kindest, most loving and heroic thing anyone had ever done for me. The only thing missing was a white horse. But now we would have to move from New York to the Midwest, where I would direct community theater productions of *Pippin*.

The police came but no arrests were made, though both Danny and Riedel were guilty of assault. Danny remained outside to smoke and cool off, but Riedel returned and shuffled directly toward me, pulling up a chair and plopping down with his elbows on the table and his head in his hands.

"I'm sorry," he said with a casual impishness. "I'm with my friends. We're *all* journalists. And we were just having fun. Now, I know you and Patti LuPone are friends and I heard . . ."

I couldn't believe my ears. He'd been dragged by force from the Broadway bistro of all Broadway bistros and had returned looking for a scoop. No one could say he wasn't dedicated. I politely declined to provide the dish he sought and he left the restaurant with his friends, none of whom had so much as batted an eye during the entire ordeal.

When Danny reentered the place, he was greeted with

applause. Our meal was comped and we were told we wouldn't have to pay for anything for a long time. Danny was a hero. My hero.

When we got back to our apartment, the answering machine message light flickered furiously and a touch of the play button was followed by "You have thirty-six new messages." In the last hour, friends from both coasts had heard about the incident and were calling to offer their enthusiasm and condolences. My publicist, Judy Jacksina, was among them. "Darling!! It's *everywhere*," she shrieked in her thick Long Island–ese. "*Everyone* knows. It's going to be in the *Post* tomorrow. This is *not* good. I'm dehydrated from the news and I had to put on *another* coat of moisturizer. *This is not good.*"

The next morning I threw on a pair of shorts, walked the two blocks to the corner bodega, and leafed through the *Post* to Page Six. I scanned the bold-faced names in the gossip column and found nothing, breathing a sigh of relief. And then I saw it. The skirmish had merited its own separate feature:

B'WAY FIGHT NIGHT AT JOE ALLEN!

The story recounted the conflict, pointing out that Riedel was overtaken by "Harris's burly companion."

Danny is five-eight and 165 pounds. Burly.

The story ended with:

"I'm sure lots of people on Broadway have wanted to punch me in the nose, and I have to admire those people who actually try it," says Riedel, who has nothing against Harris and has written favorably of him over the years. "Besides," he says, "Harris's pal was clearly defending his honor against an insult. There are no hard feelings."

If Danny had gone to school with me, things might have been a lot different. I might have had a boyfriend and a protector. On the other hand, if Michael Riedel had gone to school with me, we probably would have been best friends. He'd been thirteen once and most likely had his own version of the spider dream.

We were both misfits, besotted with Broadway, and we were just trying to fit.

15. As Good as It Gets

Opryland USA was a theme park in Nashville devoted to musical shows. There were a few roller coasters and carousels, but it billed itself as "the Home of American Music" and it was a magnet for young talent. At sixteen, I was cast in a show called *I Hear America Singing* and was finally in a glamorous, hour-long singing-and-dancing extravaganza featuring music from the 1920s to the 1970s, multiple costume changes, and a live, eighteen-piece orchestra.

Jason, who had been my strip-poker buddy when we were both newsboys in the Tulsa Little Theatre production of *Gypsy*, was cast in another show at the park. We'd kept in touch, and he invited me to share an apartment with him and two other guys from Cincinnati Conservatory of Music, who'd been hired as well: Jay was a bookish prodigy pianist who could turn a simple tune, say "Jingle Bells," into a lavish concerto. And then there was Scott.

Scott Pierce looked like Cary Grant. He was tall and dark and lean with spellbinding brown eyes framed by thick, broad eyebrows and a permanent five o'clock shadow. I was bewitched. And we were cast in the same show.

The first day of rehearsal was exhilarating and intimidating. The cast assembled in a giant wood-slat-floored dance room with one wall completely mirrored and the opposite wall affixed with ballet barres. Ballet barres! This was a whole 'nother league. And for the first time I was in the company of equally ambitious, dangerously driven performers, each of whom was dedicated to being the best.

We were fed vast amounts of material at breakneck speed—medleys, chorus parts, backup parts. Vocal solos were assigned and we were each taken to a private room to learn them, then immediately deposited back into the main rehearsal room to present them. Once again, I was the youngest, but I'd come to count on my voice as a social entrée. So when I sang "Stormy Weather" for the cast, it was as much an audition for friendships as it was a rehearsal. I belted my guts out, picturing myself in a trench coat and fedora, languidly leaning against a lamppost as if I were waiting for glamour photographer George Hurrell to show up. Ironically, I was told that's how the number would be costumed and staged. At last, fantasy and reality were becoming one.

Opryland was not unionized and we worked twelve hours a day with breaks spent at costume fittings and coachings. We danced until our feet blistered, and kept dancing when the blisters burst and bled. Every day I had a *dancer's lunch:* a cherry ICEE and a Salem Menthol long.

It was all horribly grueling and terribly romantic.

The entire cast was absurdly gifted—except for Scott. He had a pleasant baritone voice and could dance okay, but he was clearly hired for his height and beauty. I didn't care. As the weeks progressed Scott and I became inseparable. We lived and worked and shopped and cooked and ate together. We laughed together. I got high for the first time with him and we took pictures of our toes surrounding a dill pickle. We were playful and smart, and equally contented in silence. At times I would lose myself, time gone, at the wonder of his plump lower lip, or the tanned nape of his neck, or the angle of his scruffy chin— and my body would startle me with a sudden gasp, reminding me to breathe. This feeling was something new and I could not name it. Some mishmash of peril and promise.

The cast was filled with guys of questionable sexuality, but only one was what you'd call "out." He was self-deprecating and vulgar in that *Boys in the Band* way in which gay men used to define themselves. While the entire cast rolled our eyes at his flamboyance, his freedom was admirable, as the rest of us had no sexual identity at all.

Hidden away was a budding romance between Scott and me that inched forward in baby steps, usually after drinking too much or having the occasional joint. Knees would brush. Hands might linger. Eyes would lock. Boundaries were blurred but never crossed, and were always reestablished, industrial strength and infrangible.

After a few weeks, with the show up and going strong, Scott and I and another cast mate named Katie decided to go to nearby Cincinnati's Kings Island theme park on a rarely scheduled two days off. Katie's four-foot-eight frame belied a belt that lived somewhere between Ethel Merman and Shirley Bassey. She was sturdy and gutsy and wild. After a full day of singing in the car and careless fun at the park, we got a single motel room and a case of beer.

Katie brought pot and we smoked and drank and crowed with laughter, and before we knew it, she had mischievously initiated a ménage à trois. We piled upon one another, nervously giggling at first, all the attention on Katie, two guys, one girl. My heart raced. If I could not be with Scott, at least I was in the same bed, in the same deed, using the same lips and tongues but absent of contact—like making love through glass.

Then suddenly, slowly, Scott's hand found mine and we scrutinized every digit, softly, thoroughly, in covert union. My fingers moved up his forearm, tracking a fluttering muscle that led to a sharp collarbone spiking against his taut skin. He found the curve of my back and I moved in closer, my legs still wrapped around Katie's. She was oblivious to the love story that was playing out over and around her.

When all three of our faces were inches apart, Katie tilted her head back and out of view, and Scott and I let our gaze meet. His dark eyes were full and tender and the air hung still between us. We were alone.

And finally, we kissed.

His mouth was hot and sweet and his taste spread through me like a shot of sloe gin. Though the sexual tension between us had been sizzling anxiously in the wings for weeks, the kiss was unexpectedly gentle. Quiet. Compassionate. Examined. As if we were on a private moonlit beach in Saint-Tropez and not leaning over a naked girl in a cheap motel in Cincinnati.

Until now, our connection had been unable to blossom in even the smallest, most natural way of any other "normal" couple. It was clumsy and inexpert. But in this moment, we were transported to a place immune to judgment or permission or approval. There was only now. I cupped his bristly face in my palm and our gentle kiss erupted as if it were starved. He shifted closer to offer himself and took me in his hot hand. We were alive and charged and the world around us disappeared.

So did Katie.

At first she tried to keep up, insinuating herself into the insuppressible pulse that was steadily mounting. But there was only Scott, and I climbed over her and onto him to eliminate any space or air between us, pressing, strained, drinking him in. I wanted every part of myself to be connected with him. To be *of* him. Katie eventually gave up and accepted her role as drunken matchmaker. She even laughed and shrugged with a crooked smile. And then she did the damnedest thing. She got up, dressed, and, with a kind of wry grace, said, "Glad I could give you boys a kick start. I'm gonna go out for some smokes." And she left us alone to consummate the undeniable.

Our sex was, at once, delicate and raw, innocent and eager and sweet and sweaty and thirsty; the joyous deliverance from repression, and a pureness of heart that was surely love as true as any that had come before it.

We returned to Nashville the next day and there was no mention of our liaison—not even between Scott and me. There was no significant difference in our interaction. We didn't hold hands. We didn't exchange knowing looks. We didn't smile confidentially. We were back in the mode. But I was changed. And I knew I could never return to what it was. Not completely. I would play by the rules, but I would test them.

As soon as my three roommates were out of the apartment, I moved Jay's things out of Scott's room and moved mine in. I didn't ask. And once again, it was never mentioned. Apparently the veil worked both ways. Even Jay, whose belongings I had packed and moved and unpacked, walked into his old bedroom, noticed his things were missing, and then walked into the other bedroom and accepted his new digs without question. It was like a universal secret code of protection that couldn't even be discussed in private.

I knew in my heart that there was no shame in what I was feeling for Scott. It was pure and it was good.

When he discovered I'd switched the rooms, Scott threw his head back and laughed out loud, and when his eyes returned to mine, his smile was like the sun. It was the first acknowledgment of what was to be and there was relief in the knowing. Finally, we were able to explore our relationship. We were in love. And like all love affairs mired in taboo—Romeo and Juliet, Tristan and Isolde, Lancelot and Guinevere—there were strict mandates if we were to carry on. But as the summer progressed, Scott and I were able to define our separate life together, not only at work but even within the confines of our apartment with two roommates ten feet away. After a night of intimacy we returned to our separate twin beds. Like Ricky and Lucy.

And even if that was the way it was to be forever, it was fine with me.

The summer ended much too quickly and I returned to Sand Springs a different person. Everything seemed less alive. Less colorful. Less acute. Less. I didn't know how I would endure without Scott, not to mention the daily validation of performing in the company of the real deal. Long-distance phone calls were costly and forbidden, so communication with Scott was limited to coded letters, like we were espionage agents or thieves. I hoped we would return to Opryland the following summer, but who knew if we'd both be asked back or if Scott would accept. He was in college and had a bigger life than mine.

Worse than not being able to see him was that, back in Sand Springs, it was impossible for me to talk about him, share my happiness or even acknowledge it. If I was misunderstood and burdened with secrets before, the fact that I had tasted truth, only to leave it behind without so much as an acknowledgment, magnified my disparity all the more. I was worse for knowing love. And now the stakes were even higher. My fear of being found out was overshadowed by the fear that, if revealed, my relationship with Scott would be denounced. That we would be rendered nothing.

I nearly told my friend Teri. I nearly told my friend Michelle. It never occurred to me to tell the voiceless clan of suspected brothers who would have been freed by my induction, and who would have freed me in return. In the end, it was not worth the risk, and there was no one.

My summer of Scott became for me a symbol of what never could be. I'd known it would be impossible to have a real life in Oklahoma, but I'd learned that even away, in an environment with others like me, there was still a suffocating shroud of secrecy. It seemed that I would never have an honest life with anyone and my destiny was to be lonely and unfulfilled. Sex would be something that was scored, clandestinely, elusively, illegally, in cryptic places and in camouflage. But a real relationship with someone I loved, with whom I could have a proud and ample future, was unimaginable.

When the school year began, so resumed the anonymous "queer" yelled from across the parking lot and the "faggot" roughly whispered from a crowded classroom doorway, unowned and unacknowledged, like a voice in my head. A photo of me in my Opryland finale costume was published in the school newspaper, in which I wore a white polyester one-piece jumper with a black puffy-sleeved shirt and a matching white bowler with a black sequined band, cocked Fosse-ly style over one eye. It was me at my most showbiz resplendent. But as I walked down the hall to my locker, a group of large, senior football lunks were waiting. "There he is," I pretended not to hear. "Hey, pretty boy, love the picture!" was harder to ignore. Especially when they mimicked my *Chorus Line* pose and gave me a girly wink.

"Thanks. It was a great summer," I said in passing, as I aborted the stop at my locker and made my way down the hall as fast as I could without seeming to run.

The old Sam mask I'd mastered wasn't sticking. I couldn't convince or delude myself any longer. I became severely depressed. I only participated in required school activities and took to sitting alone in my bedroom, listening to the 45 single of Anne Murray's "You Needed Me" over and over and over again. The sad, rich voice of Anne praising the one who saved her from the depths of despair. It was, perhaps, the first time during any event of significance that I was not outside of myself looking in. I was in crisis and I was *in* crisis. The hopelessness was authentic and the escape tools I'd previously employed were useless. There was no fade-up on me, curled up in my chair. No key light. No crane shot, sweeping in close with the single tear running down my cheek. There was no "remember this feeling so you can use it onstage later." There was no later.

As the weeks went on, my sadness only deepened, hovering, loitering, spreading, until I had neither the want nor the energy to get out from beneath it; to duct tape myself together another morning in a charade I was no longer able to pull off. The jig was up.

I sought out my friend Craig, a trombone player, and whispered for him to meet me in the back corner of the band room by the instrument storage shelving. Making sure no one was within earshot, I asked if he could get some speed and downers. Craig had been offering to get me speed since the seventh grade and I'd declined, but now I had a different story. I lied to him, saying I'd been speeding all during the summer and I wanted to buy a lot to get a good price. I didn't tell him I had no use for the amphetamines, but I had to justify the downers as a balance for the uppers in order to score them for another purpose. A couple of days later I got my order—black beauties and Seconals—and I hoped it would be enough.

On a Friday afternoon, I wrote a letter to my parents on a sheet of blue-lined paper from a spiral notebook. I said I loved them but knew they would not want me to be miserable and that this was the best way. For everyone. The only answer. I asked them to forgive me but to be happy that I was out of pain. There were no details and no admissions.

My parents had plans that night. Memo was staying with us, which I thought would be good for my mother after I was gone. At about eight thirty, my eleven-year-old brother, Matt, and my grandmother were downstairs watching TV and I told them I was going to hit the hay early. I went upstairs and gently tore the letter from the notebook, carefully removing the frayed edges so that it was clean. I folded it neatly, put it in an unmarked envelope, and placed it on my bedroom desk. I pulled the sandwich baggie of Seconals out from under the carpet slit where I'd hidden cigarettes and a magazine photo of a bronzed man in a loincloth, and walked to my parents' bathroom and stared at myself in their mirror.

I was hollow but calm, decided. I took all of the Seconals with a giant glass of water and stared some more. I don't know why I went to my parents' bathroom to commit the act. There was no malice in my action or need to punish them. More than anything there was a sense of solution. A sense of relief. And there was something in me that wanted a connection to my mother and father, or perhaps not to feel alone, as I made the most important and last decision of my life.

I walked to my bedroom and removed my clothes, replacing them with a long white T-shirt and fresh white underwear. I carefully pulled back the covers with silent procession, in an ordered ritual of self-respect. I lay down, not in my regular side-stomach-one-foot-over-the-edge position but on my back, with my hands on my chest, like the pictures of Lenin lying in state I'd seen in the history books.

It was how I would be found. Not messy and disheveled, among rumpled sheets and doubts, but in purposeful and contemplative peace.

I waited for the pills to take effect. Was it three minutes? Five? Thirty? I was growing groggy. Suddenly, a bloodcurdling scream ripped through my silence. It was Matt, and something horrible had happened. I vaulted from my bed and ran downstairs as quickly as I could. Memo was holding my brother in her arms and there was blood all over the carpet. He had stepped on her darning needle and it had broken off in his foot. Memo, typically strong and in charge, seemed useless. Not knowing if I should call an ambulance, I first phoned Sandra Hanner, our best family friend, and she said she would be over in five minutes.

I held my brother and rocked him back and forth, calming him and wiping away his tears. The stub of the needle was barely visible. I promised him everything would be all right. Suddenly, I felt a little woozy and remembered that I had taken thirty Seconals. Shit. My brother needed help. It wasn't my night. I handed him over to my grandmother and raced upstairs to the bathroom and stuck my index finger down my throat and threw up the gelatinous capsules that were dissolving in my stomach by the minute, desperately trying to squelch any gagging noises that would reveal me. I ran to the refrigerator and sloppily downed milk from the container so that I could throw up again and again to rid myself of any remains.

Moments later, Sandra rang the doorbell and I swished and spit mouthwash before running to the door to meet her. She examined my brother's foot and cautiously plucked the darning needle out with pliers and then sanitized and bandaged the wound. My brother was calmer now and Sandra looked at me oddly and asked if I was okay. She said I seemed a little wobbly. I told her I was fine, just shaken. Sandra left us and I put my brother to bed, with my grandmother following soon after.

I sat alone in the crowded space of my thoughts. My brother's blood stained my white T-shirt like a Rorschach. I was afraid to sleep. I made coffee and stayed up for my parents' return to tell them what had happened to my brother. But I knew I wouldn't tell them what had happened to me. That I'd tried to commit suicide and that a darning needle mishap had saved my life.

That holding my brother and promising him that everything would be all right, in the way I was so desperate to be comforted, gave me enough sense of value to keep me holding on a little longer.

Wayne McDowell was my high school psychology teacher. He was highly intelligent and clever and challenged his students to explore concepts beyond what we knew—or thought we knew. His class was the one hour of the day that provided a respite from my gloom and self-obsession.

McDowell encouraged and inspired us to dig for answers and, being a research freak, I decided to investigate my malady on my own, in secret. I went to the Sand Springs Public Library and scoured the small psychology section. There were no books expressly about homosexuality, and I would not have checked them out had there been. A record of my interest would surely have given me away as soon as the librarian stamped the check-out card inside their covers. Alarms might sound. Steel doors might slam down. Baptists in robes might appear through

Sam Harris

secret panels behind bookcases and carry me off to a pot of boiling red-eye gravy. I stuck to books that dabbled in homosexuality but weren't devoted to it. A bit like myself. My criteria for checking out a book was simple: I flipped to the index of likely candidates and if the word "homosexuality" was listed, it was mine.

At night, after everyone was asleep, I would study for hours. I removed the pages from the oversize binding of an *Encyclopedia Britannica* volume ("Light" through "Metabolism") and hid whatever book I was reading inside its cover so that if I were caught, I would appear scholarly. I made endless notes on a legal pad, drawn from experts on the subject: Havelock Ellis. Sigmund Freud. Alfred Kinsey. William Masters and Virginia Johnson. All of the books were fairly consistent in their assessment that homosexuality was a mental disorder. Pathological. Perverted. Possibly genetic, but probably environmental. Some cited sexual trauma as the cause and others reported that an absent father and strong mother were the lethal combination.

If that was the case, I thought, all of the kids I grew up with should be gay.

Masters and Johnson said it might be reversible. I conjured up electroshock treatments or being strapped to a chair with subliminal pictures of female genitalia flashing on a giant screen. Alfred Kinsey claimed that ten percent of the population was gay. That seemed like a lot. Clearly fewer in Sand Springs, which, looking at the national average, helped explain San Francisco.

Mr. McDowell was a lighthouse in a very foggy world. Beyond his ability to make psychology fascinating through exercises and examples that shattered the pretaught constraints of his students, he had an unerring radar for the psychology of the individual. In spite of my attempt to be undetected as someone on the very brink, McDowell saw in me what no one else had.

256

Not even my parents. He knew I was in trouble. Perhaps he had seen it before. Perhaps he had been a troubled teenager himself. Whatever it was, he had a gift.

It began one day with a friendly tap on the shoulder as I exited his class. He asked how I was. I responded with a broad, phony grin and a litany of distracting activities. A few days later he heard me asking around for a ride after school and offered to drive me home. We got in his truck and he asked about my summer away. Nothing deeply inquisitive. Small talk. Very big small talk. He said, "It must have been quite a transition for you to leave Sand Springs."

"Not so much as coming back," I replied.

"People experience a lot of discoveries and changes when they go to a new environment. There is a freedom."

In the days that followed, after-class exchanges continued and several more rides were offered and gratefully taken. I mentioned Scott, as my best friend, and that I missed him. Mc-Dowell gave me his home phone number and told me if I ever needed to talk about anything to let him know.

The days slogged by, always ending with me in my room, knees to chest in my gold-flocked upholstered rocking chair playing "You Needed Me" continuously on the stereo. Anne Murray would finish her song and the familiar sad, scratchy dead space followed as the needle leap-frogged over the remaining bands of the 45. The stereo arm lifted in a shocking jerk and mechanically moved up and out and down again to begin the same sad scratchy sound before the ballad played for the thirtieth time in a row. I'd Scotch-taped a penny, then two, and then a nickel to the top of the arm so that the needle could dig farther into the worn grooves of the vinyl without skipping. It was only a record, but poor Anne Murray should have been suffering from chronic laryngitis by then.

My wallet safely guarded the folded scrap of paper on which McDowell had scribbled his number. It tempted me. One night, in a momentary gust of courage, I cracked open my bedroom door and peered into the hallway to see if the coast was clear. My brother was asleep and my parents were downstairs. I dialed the number and shook as I waited for an answer, nearly hanging up after the first ring. Second ring. Third ring. Finally his wife picked up. I introduced myself and asked for Mr. McDowell, and he promptly came to the phone.

"Hey, Sam, what's going on?" he said with a friendly, care-free tone as if I called every day and this was nothing unusual.

"I'm sorry to bother you at home."

"Not a bother. That's why I gave you the number."

"I think I would like to talk to you about something," I continued, keeping my voice down. "Privately. But if you don't have time, it's not that important."

I was trembling, plunging into the most terrifying territory I could imagine: a pledge to confess.

"Great," he said. "Why don't we meet before school starts tomorrow. Can you come in early? I can get there by seven o'clock."

"Yes. I'll be there . . . Thank you."

"I look forward to it, Sam. I'm glad you called."

I hung up and couldn't decide if I was more relieved or frightened. I knew that I could not sustain much longer the slow, sinking sorrow that had so overtaken me. My thoughts of suicide were keeping me alive like a trusted friend who would be there, patiently waiting, in case no one else showed up. I didn't want to die. And McDowell might be the one who showed up. He seemed smarter than the others. He didn't accept the norm as the norm. He seemed safe. I knew he liked me, but it was an enormous risk. What if he reported me? What if he called my parents? What if . . .

I didn't sleep.

I rose early and collected the notes I'd taken from various books as if I were going for a test, or to share my findings with a research colleague. Maybe that's how it was supposed to go, more academic than personal. I tucked the yellow sheets into my notebook and headed to school.

I arrived at McDowell's locked classroom door fifteen minutes early. Seven o'clock came. McDowell didn't. Time thickened like wet cement. He'd probably forgotten or decided it wasn't important enough to get to school so early. I decided that when I saw him later at class time I wouldn't mention it.

What seemed like hours was only a few minutes before the glass door on the side of the building burst open and McDowell hurried in, wearing his regular brown tweed jacket with elbow patches, wrinkled khakis, which draped sloppily over his scuffed saddle oxfords, and an ill-fitting duck-hunting hat. He carried his well-worn brown leather case in one hand and juggled a Styrofoam coffee container in the other as he fumbled through a key chain so overloaded it could have belonged to a slumlord.

"Sorry I'm late."

"I just got here," I lied.

He unlocked the door and opened it for me, slowing his pace to assume a casual, no-big-deal demeanor. He threw his things on his desk and pulled up two student chair-desks to face each other. He sat down and took a swig from his coffee and just looked at me with a sort of patient strength that didn't suggest the least bit of gravity. My heart pounded and my face grew hot, my hands as cold as clay. I smiled. I paused. I assembled strength.

"I'm different," I began, slowly.

"Well, thank God for that," he said with an easy laugh.

I took a deep breath and sat silent another full minute. He waited. And then I summoned the words. "I'm gay."

I told him everything. I told him that I'd known I was different since my earliest memories. Long before it had a name that specified shame. I told him about falling in love with Scott. I told him about the Seconal. I waited for shock to register but it never came. I told him I was afraid. And he listened. He listened with a kind of active intensity most people have only when talking. And when I had exhausted myself, he gently spoke.

"There is nothing wrong with you."

I stared at him, fixed, trying to digest the words I had wanted someone, anyone—my father, my mother, a friend, Scott, a doctor, a preacher, a politician, Walter Cronkite, a newspaper editor, a character in a book or on television or in a movie, anyone—to say.

There is nothing wrong with you.

It couldn't be that simple. The years of anguish justified proof. I began to argue the opposing side and took out my notes—scientific verification and expert opinions. I even resorted to the tactics of the Bible-thumpers, quoting Leviticus and Corinthians for corroboration. They were the only scriptures I knew by heart.

McDowell slid out from his student chair-desk and easily located an American Psychiatric Association book and showed me that in 1973, only five years prior, homosexuality had been declassified as a mental disorder. It said that clinical studies demonstrated that same-sex attractions, feelings, and behaviors are normal and positive variations of human sexuality.

What? How could this be? The books I'd been reading were completely out of date. If only the Sand Springs Public Library had modernized its inventory. But then, if Sand Springs had modernized at all, I might not have this dilemma. I'd been desperately looking for any evidence of normalcy and even sanity and was, once again, stuck in a time warp. If I'd been looking for medical advice, the local library probably would have suggested literature on bloodletting or lobotomies. Still, even the research McDowell revealed to me was very new and had not reached or been accepted by the general public. Especially not my general public.

"Okay, so *you* know this," I said. "What about everybody else? What about everyone in this town and everywhere else?"

"They're wrong," he stated bluntly. "They're just wrong."

McDowell said that few people are completely straight or completely gay. That most of us fall somewhere in the gray, with the majority of our sexual orientation leaning to one side or the other. He said that most males bristle in fear at the part of them, no matter how small, that has been attracted to other males or has, God forbid, even experimented on some beerful summer night. Manhood is in jeopardy. And anger and even violence is the first choice for the uneducated because when we accept anything as absolute without personal investigation, our flimsy foundation is threatened by the smallest chink in the armor.

"Also," he said, "some people are assholes."

I genuinely laughed for the first time in weeks.

And then he talked about my contribution to the world, which he said came from the amalgam of *all* of me, and that if I took away any part of the amalgam, I wouldn't be the singular person that I am.

"Where do you think your particular talent comes from?" he asked. "And your drive and your humor and your compassion? You can't pick and choose and snatch away pieces of who you are and expect to be the same person. It's all one thing. Either you accept and like yourself as a complete picture or you don't. If I were you, I wouldn't trade the person you are or any of what got you here. What a loss that would be."

He asked me to promise that if I ever again decided to kill myself, I would call him first.

I promised.

"I would be very, very sad and very, very angry if you didn't call me."

A stillness fell. And then I suddenly declared, "I want to be happy."

"Then be happy," he said. "It's not easy. People who have the most to give are very often the people who have the most to overcome. You're not an accident, Sam. You have a purpose. And part of that purpose is to be happy. Just be a good person. And live your life. Live *your* life."

I might have wept in his arms, but he didn't offer them. Instead, he looked resolutely into my eyes and, in doing so, was the first adult to acknowledge my true self.

The bell rang and it was time for school.

The next two hours were unaccounted for as I showed up in body only for my first classes. I entered McDowell's classroom for third period. He gave me a nod that acknowledged I hadn't imagined our talk.

After roll was called, McDowell told us to put away our books. He was leaving the planned curriculum and was going to talk about something else. He took to the floor like Clarence Darrow and lectured on prejudice and hate. He spoke of America's perception of blacks and how it has too slowly evolved through education and legislature. He talked about the treatment of American Indians and the unfair stereotypes we'd placed on them. He talked about Hitler and anti-Semitism. He talked about using religion as a platform for judgment.

I didn't raise my hand or participate. It was a demonstration that I knew was for my benefit, and perhaps the kindest thing anyone had ever done for me. Then, in the last fifteen minutes of class, McDowell strode to the blackboard and wrote in enormous block letters, clicking and clacking: BLACK, INDIAN, JEW, HOMOSEXUAL.

"Which one of these people would you *least* want to live next door to?"

There was one black student and a couple of "Indians" in class who were surely startled by the brazen question. McDowell pointed to the person sitting in the front far left row of desks.

"You start."

"I don't know . . . a homosexual, I guess."

"Why?"

"Because it's against God."

McDowell pointed to the person at the next desk.

"A homosexual."

And the next.

"A gay."

"Homosexual."

"A Jew."

"Why?"

"Because you can't always identify them and they're sneaky."

"A fag."

"A queer."

"A homosexual."

"I don't care who lives next door to me."

"Queer."

"Queer."

"Why?"

"Because they're not real men or real women."

"Because they're evil."

"They molest children."

"Because God hates them."

But for the single Nazi and abstainer, it was a landslide.

McDowell then asked, "Do you know any gay people, personally?"

"Well, no."

"Not that I know of."

"Ooooh, gross."

"Then how do you know what you're talking about?" he asked. "Did you know that ten percent of the population is gay? That means ten percent of your friends, your neighbors, your families. That means three people in *this* classroom."

Everyone looked around suspiciously. I did the same, feigning bewilderment and secretly wondering who the other two might be.

"And none of you have been adversely affected or threatened by a gay person, am I right?" he continued.

The class fell silent for a moment and then McDowell resumed the exercise. The responses remained the same.

"A homosexual. Sorry. It's weird."

"Queer . . . It ain't natural. I don't need to know one to know it ain't right."

I wanted the black kid and the Indians to leave the room so at least I had a fair shake. My desk was situated fourth row in, halfway up the aisle. As McDowell continued to question, desk by desk, row by row, I grew more and more afraid. What did he want me to do? Choose another minority to live next door to? Be honest? Say I knew gay people? Say I was one? Was all of his empathy and goodness just a trick meant to set me up and destroy me, publicly, like some kind of witch hunt? Or was it part of his plan for me to disclose my true identity while he was present in order to protect me from the angry mob?

"A homosexual."

"I'd keep a close eye and a cocked gun."

As the questioning etched its way to my seat, I knew I didn't need to be polled—the sweat pouring down my pekid face was enough evidence to convict me. My eyes darted to the clock every few seconds. Class was almost over, but there were only two people ahead of me. I imagined a fuse spitting like a Fourth of July sparkler, making its way to a cluster of dynamite named Sam.

"If I have to choose . . . I guess a gay person."

"Queer."

I was next up. McDowell began talking. Something about ignorance. Something about responsibility. Something about unqualified hate. But I couldn't concentrate on what he was saying because I was trying to figure out what I was going to say myself. And then the bell rang. His timing was planned. A bit torturous, but planned. As the class poured out into the hallway, I held back for a private exchange to understand his purpose.

"I told you," he said. "Ignorance. Fear. Also, some people are assholes."

A few weeks later, I got the call from Opryland. In addition to the season at the park, they wanted to shoot a television special and take the company to Hawaii for a corporate performance. Rehearsal would begin in a couple of months. I asked if Scott had been asked. Yes.

My parents had known that I would more than likely go away again for the summer, but this offer would mean quitting high school and leaving Sand Springs and them forever. They knew there was little choice.

I moved back to Nashville and received my high school diploma through correspondence courses. Scott and I shared a one-bedroom apartment and a life together. We kept the Lucy and Ricky beds for show, but unless we had guests, they remained pushed together, joined, like we were.

We may not have held hands in public or even acknowledged our relationship openly among friends, but if this was as good as it would get, it was okay with me.

16. Better

It wasn't that I'd come to terms with a childless existence. It was just that when I was growing up, fatherhood was simply never part of the possible picture.

Ten years into my relationship with Danny, the parental horizon had completely changed and I was sober. The United States and I had both evolved. All of my natural fatherhood desires that had been sequestered to an out-of-the-way corner of my heart were suddenly ignited and unleashed.

Every Saturday morning, Danny and I went to our neighborhood farmers' market where vendors from all over California set up tented stands on a narrow street, bookended by a latte café and a bicycle shop, to sell organic produce and artisanal goat cheese and herbs and honey and hummus and flowers. Behind the stands is a grassy square with family-packed picnic tables on one side and a Spanish tiled fountain on the other. A punked-out haberdasher is perched within splashing distance. "Old Eddie Dred" sits on a foldout stool behind a worn blanket, spread and strewn with miniature percussion instruments for the kids, and plays the conga while he sings homespun songs about "sunny days at the marketplace" in his scraggy, chapped voice. The smell of fresh pupusas and mango salsa is strong enough to taste. Neighbors shop and congregate, and kids' stained faces tattle of pilfered blueberries.

The place is Eden with a nose ring.

My recurring Saturday-morning fantasy was that Danny and I would take our brand-new baby to that market in a Bugaboo stroller and parade down the single aisle as a part of our family weekend ritual. I would be wearing checkered Bermuda shorts, leather sandals, and aviator sunglasses, and a porkpie hat would conceal my morning bed-head hair, adding to my funky-hipster-tattooed-dad look. We would attempt to shop, but it would be difficult because everyone we encountered would interrupt us to ogle our darling child and remark on the momentous occasion of our exceptional family. We would nod in gratitude, radiating pride, and manage, somehow, to settle on pluots and Casablanca lilies before onlookers began to tread too heavily on our privacy.

Like many couples, straight or gay, Danny and I didn't arrive at the idea of expanding our family at the same time. My desire for a child had grown into a tender ache, to the degree that being around our friends' children became punishing. Danny was concerned about what we would have to give up—our time, our travels, our privilege to spend money on what we wanted, when we wanted. Basically, our free, spontaneous, and fabulous life. Fancy dinner parties and junkets to St. Barts might be replaced by Chuck E. Cheese's and Disney cruises.

"We're happy now," he argued. "It's all so perfect, why would we want to change it up?" But that was exactly the reason I wanted a child, not because a baby would fill a void or save our marriage or make our lives whole. If our life together was already so big, why not make it bigger? It was like God was knocking on my heart and saying, "You think you know love? You think you know happiness? I am going to give you love and happiness beyond your imagination. Beyond your wildest dreams. Beyond what you know as possible."

So, what, am I gonna say to God, "Hmm, I'm not sure . . . let me think"?

Danny pointed out that we were in our forties and twenty years older than our parents had been when they started families. I asserted that, while they may have possessed the endless energy of youth, we would bring an economy of energy and sense of maturity and priority that younger parents just don't have.

Like my father before me, my twenties and thirties had been about me—my career, my identity, my drama, my impatience. So had Danny's. If not then, when? But at this point in our lives, I was ready to make it about someone else.

"There is no perfect time," parents told us. "The perfect time is when you say yes."

That would be one of the phrases Danny hated.

My simpatico friend, the actress Bridget Moynahan, asked me to be her birth partner after a tumultuous and highly publicized tabloid drama, which took the father, Tom Brady, out of the immediate picture. I said yes before she finished the request. We studied and planned and bonded and doulaed. We watched 1970s videos of au naturel water births with giant, hairy vaginas. We had to bow out of a very serious couples yoga class because we were cracking up silently as we formed heart-shaped tableau stretches, and then fully busted out when our Zen-monotone instructor urged us to "fe-e-el the love flo-o-o-owing between Mo-o-o-mmy and Da-a-a-dy and Ba-a-a-by."

To maintain her anonymity, when we were in public, I was to call Bridget by her given name, Kathryn. A couple of months before her due date, we went shopping for a crib and a changing table at a particularly pissy baby store, and I mistakenly called her Bridget. For the sake of the saleslady, she asked, "Who's Bridget?" adding a hint of suspicion to her tone.

I took her cue and we both dove in to play out the scene.

"No one," I said, with guilty innocence.

"So you just can't remember my name?"

"I'm sorry, Kathryn," I said.

Suddenly emotional, she shouted, "I hope you can remember the baby's name!"

"Please don't get upset. I'm just tired."

"*You're* tired?! I'm the one lugging this thing around. This is all your fault," she cried, touching her belly. "I can't believe you did this to me!"

And then she turned on the tears and I comforted her as we headed out, making excuses to the saleslady, and we barely hit the door before exploding in laughter.

When the big day arrived, I experienced the entire momentous birthing process with Bridget from timing contractions through a difficult labor and delivery. It was the most primal, fulfilling, otherworldly happening of my life.

And it only magnified my desire to have my own.

But it takes two. At least it does when you're in a relationship. Danny was suffering for his reticence. Everybody knew he was born to be a father. He had long been known as "the child whisperer," with kids drawn to him like a *Toy Story* sequel, and the pressure on him was pythonic. I prompted and planted the subject at every opportunity. Comedienne Rosie O'Donnell, who had been advocating that we have kids for about ten years (and who has sixteen or seventeen children of her own), cornered Danny with the question "Do you not see yourself as a dad? Afraid you don't have what it takes?"

Danny sputtered, "No, it's not that, I just—"

"Well, that's the only question," she lasered in. "If you don't think you're parent material, you don't like kids, you don't think you've got what it takes, you're missing the dad gene, then that's the end of the conversation. But if you do, well, everything else just works out."

That was another one of the phrases that Danny hated.

When he would voice his concerns, every parent we knew said, over and over, "You just have faith and it works out. *It just works out . . . it just works out . . .*"

This was followed quickly by "It changes your life—for the better." Blah blah blah . . .

Or worse: "God doesn't give you what you can't handle," which is the same phrase people use after a death or fire or cancer. It didn't help.

At one point, Danny was convinced that all parents were members of a secret society with required, join-the-club phrases meant to scam others into parenthood so they would not be alone in their wretched misery. Parents would stare at us with a vacant twinkle and say, "It just works out," as if they'd been universally prepped at a murder trial. It didn't seem reality-based to Danny. He wanted someone to say, "Run for your life, schmuck!" But no one did. I supposed anyone who might have said that had already run.

Danny needed time, and not on my oddly ticking biological clock. Not technically, anyway. I didn't want to bully or threaten him, so we sought therapy to get the advice of an outside, non-partisan, unbiased, completely and thoroughly objective couples expert who would tell Danny he was wrong.

I knew I was making headway when baby room possibilities began to sprinkle into our conversation. The obvious choice was to convert my home office, a large room with a lot of light and a walk-in closet. This meant Danny would have to share his office with me. As an alternative, he suggested we convert the small bathroom to a baby room.

"We can build a bed over the tub and the toilet is so convenient!"

He also suggested we utilize the garage, which was separate and on a different level from the rest of the house with no interior entrance, and was unheated and un-air-conditioned. I imagined the jarring, mechanical grind of the garage door opening for late-night feedings, with our child's crib set against a wall between a chain saw and a bike rack. Danny was grasping at straws, but at least he was imagining the prospect. I begged him not to tell anyone about his baby room ideas.

We hadn't even begun the process and Child Protective Services would already be at our door.

I was confident that, beneath his angst, Danny wanted to be a father. He'd said as much many times, so I knew this wasn't just a Sam thing. Though he'd been the spontaneous life-embracer when we'd first met, our roles seemed to reverse around anything that spelled big change or ongoing obligation. Bull running or cave diving sounded great, but buying a houseplant was paralyzing. It had been the same when we first moved in together on the road, then moved to New York, then got a dog, two dogs, moved to Los Angeles, bought a car, two cars, a house. He was a foot dragger. But once he was in, that was it. Forever. I once said to him, "I've had to pull you into everything in your life that you treasure most!"

Translation: *I know more about you than you do.* Not really a welcome opinion in a relationship . . . even if I was right.

But he was being justifiably cautious. Becoming a parent is scary stuff—Big—the single most important decision we would ever make. Most straight people grow up presuming they will have children, so not all of them look at the gravity of the decision. If there is a decision at all. Gay people really have to map it out. We don't get knocked up, try as we might.

On September 17, 2007, at 7:32 p.m., Danny told me he was ready. I said, "Are you sure? For real? This is what you want?" He said he was sure, for real, scared but sure.

And so it began.

The next morning at nine o'clock on the dot, I called David Radis, an adoption attorney, whose number I had already programmed into my phone to save the four seconds it would take to manually enter it. His name had come up repeatedly as *the* guy in town. Another actress friend, JoBeth Williams, had hired him nearly twenty years earlier when she adopted her two boys, and she said that David "matches souls." I dug the idea of soul matching. It sounded metaphysical, spiritual, and organized, like socks, all at the same time.

We met with Radis the next day. His offices were in one of the very intimidating, monstrous buildings in Century City on Avenue of the Stars, which is as pretentious as it sounds. Thankfully, David Radis wasn't. He was warm and direct and looked just like Robert DeNiro, with the same uneven grin and arched eyebrow and even the distinguishing mole. With the vast DeNiro film catalog flashing through my mind, I somehow landed on *The Deer Hunter* and it made me like him even more. I sensed he would see us through this undertaking heroically, even as we felt we were playing Russian roulette just like in the movie.

We sat at a formal conference table and Radis performed a few card tricks to ease the tension. A little showbiz is always a good opener. He asked if we'd considered surrogacy and we explained that since the child couldn't biologically be both of ours, and there were so many kids in need of a loving home, we'd chosen to adopt. Danny admitted his concern about potentially not knowing the medical history of the birth parents. I reminded him that between our two families, our own pedigrees included various cancers, diabetes, heart disease, high blood pressure, osteoporosis, diverticulitis, fibromyalgia, rheumatoid arthritis, chronic alcoholism, drug addiction, acid reflux, acne, and restless legs syndrome. Plus everyone in both our families was basically crazy.

Danny and I agreed that the genes of almost anyone else would give the kid a better shot.

Radis explained that it could take as long as two years to find a match but felt that we'd have a child much sooner because we'd been together for thirteen years and we had a good parental profile for the "book of our life" we would prepare.

I presumed he meant we were photogenic.

He asked if we had a gender preference. Danny *really* wanted a boy. Or rather, he was afraid that his athletic, high-energy, rough-and-tumble nature would fall flat on a girl unless she turned out to be a tennis pro or a lesbian or both. He is not the princess-and-tea-party type. I knew he'd be a great dad no matter the gender and I didn't want to limit our opportunities, so we agreed that if the birth mother knew it was a boy, great. If she knew it was a girl, we'd hold off. But if she didn't know the sex, we were up for that possibility.

There was an absurd amount of information to absorb and tasks to complete, which included interviews, physicals, fingerprint scans, criminal background checks, endless paperwork, agency meetings, house inspections, classes, written essays, and money flying out of our hands at every turn. We didn't mind. We were proving our qualifications to be parents and it was a constant psychological reminder of the mammoth role we were asking to take on. In the middle of it all, I felt that even biological parents should have to jump through the same hoops. There'd be a lot fewer lousy parents out there, and a lot fewer screwed-up kids.

On the other hand, my mother and father might not have passed the bar, and that would have been a shame. At least to me.

Our "book of our life" was a meticulously prepared pictorial scrapbook, created as a sort of audition for potential birth mothers. We assembled a retrospective that dated to our meeting and included photos of our house, our dogs, our world travels, our humor—and every word toiled over like a final thesis for a parental doctorate at the University of Hallmark.

> *Your baby will have two loving daddies.*
> *We have been together for 13 years*
> *of extraordinary love, adventure, and joy.*
> *We share an enthusiastic zest for life.*
> *It is time for us to pass on*
> *all of this love to one special child.*

All of it was true.

We announced to our family and closest friends that we were "in the process." Everyone was thrilled beyond expectation, except for Danny's born-again brother and his wife, who said, "We feel sorry for the child to have gay parents." We tried to feel sorry for *them* and particularly for their children. They asked if we would be "raising the child as a homosexual."

"Most definitely," we confirmed. "Just like our parents did. All gay people we know were raised as homosexuals by their straight parents."

Seriously?

In my first year with Danny, my introduction to this

particular brother was his refusal to attend Thanksgiving if we were coming. Danny's mom wisely said, "All my children are invited. If you choose not to come, that's your prerogative." They didn't come.

I'd always been a take-the-high-road-and-love-will-always-win kind of guy, and we exhibited the kind of character most would deem "Christian," continuing to turn the other cheek. The years brought a sense of slow progress and everyone began to attend family gatherings; however, a kind of contempt, carefully tucked behind a mass of scrambled Jesus and counterfeit grins, continued to be scattered like drops of acid.

Danny and I had grown up in a generation that had encouraged us to accept bigotry as beliefs and we blamed their insolence on everything but them: culture, ignorance, religious dogma. I even convinced myself that part of their behavior was due to an overabundance of dip.

Every single time we saw them, they only ate dip.

Taco dip, crab dip, spinach dip, BLT dip, buffalo-chicken dip, seven-layer dip, artichoke dip, Reuben dip, hoagie dip, shrimp dip, corn dip, and, for adults only—beer dip and margarita dip. Technically, all the food groups and accompanying beverages were represented, but I still believed lack of chewable food could have significant mental, dental, and spiritual repercussions.

However, this newest slur changed me. It changed us. Or rather, it woke us up. You can only turn the other cheek so many times before both sides are equally raw and bloody and require reconstructive surgery.

"Love the sinner, hate the sin," was their credo.

"Love the hypocrite, hate the hypocrisy," had been ours.

Though not yet fathers, our new motto was "You can fuck with me, but don't fuck with my child."

For the sake of the family, we chose space and caution over

confrontation, but finally, their very public plea to collect signatures for legislation against marriage equality was the last indignity. The pack of straw was backbreaking and the camel was dead. And we could no longer assemble the patience or empathy for a malevolence we'd previously excused as merely ignorant or dippy.

I'd never understood "gay pride." How could I be proud of something I had no part in, like having brown hair or green eyes? Pride came from accomplishment, I'd thought. But now I got it. While we were sadly forced to acknowledge that love doesn't always triumph, we were unflinchingly proud to have emerged from the brainwashing of our adolescence, resolute in knowing that bigotry under the guise of beliefs was no longer unacceptable. Ever. From anyone. And *that* was an accomplishment.

Thankfully, the born-agains were the exception. Throughout the entire adoption affair, their sad comment was the only dollop of prejudice we encountered. Soon we were telling everyone: all of our friends, acquaintances, and, finally, strangers—usually people with strollers or pregnant women.

"We're having a baby too!"

"When?"

"We don't know."

"Well then . . . congratulations."

Everyone was happy for us.

Adoption does, however, invite some strange encounters.

"My friends adopted a boy," someone we barely knew shared with us. "And then a year later they had a *real* boy."

Danny and I stared in shock. Then, to break the silence, I said, "Did they name him Pinocchio?"

"What did they do with the fake one?" Danny added.

Only a month after our first meeting with the attorney, we got a call from a birth mother carrying twins who was deciding between us and another, older, straighter couple. Twins! I trembled at the thought. Optimistically, I reasoned that though the first years would be a living, breathing nightmare, they'd have each other to play with . . . and to gang up on us. We took a deep breath and proceeded. The birth mother sent a picture. She was tiny and round and blond. Adorable. She loved to sing. Fantastic.

The only slight drawback was that she couldn't leave Wisconsin because she was under house arrest with an ankle bracelet alarm and transmitter.

She'd been convicted for laundering money. Ever the liver-loving optimist, I found the bright side to her being a federal criminal: "It's white-collar crime! She's smart! This is great!"

I spoke with her almost daily for a few weeks and we scheduled the trip to meet her in person. When I called Radis to tell him of our plans, he informed me that she'd already chosen the other couple. Apparently, she hadn't wanted to give up the attention we were pouring on her: the calls, the care, the packages of prenatal vitamins and chocolates and belly cream. It was a mind-blowing, gut-crushing hurt. That hollow, absent aching place like when a death happens.

We told ourselves that our baby would come to us when our baby was ready.

Three months after the first meeting with Radis, we got another call from a potential birth mother. Danny was out of town, so I spoke to her by myself. She was due in six weeks. She also lived out of state but didn't have an arrest record and was free to travel unescorted by a G-man. She asked if we were sure we wanted a child and I told her, "Yes, more than anything in the world. This child will be the most important thing in our lives, above all else, forever." She told me no one had said that before.

I FedExed the "book of our life" with a personal letter. Radis faxed over a photo she'd included in her profile. She was beautiful. Dazzling, in fact: high, round cheekbones, dark, expressive eyes and a crooked, dimpled smile that I hoped was inheritable. Danny and I had told ourselves that looks didn't matter. That anyone who chose us and was properly vetted would be the woman who "grew our child." We hoped only for health and intelligence and a sense of humor—the vital elements that make for a good life. But the fact that she was beautiful was a plus and we admitted it. Pretty never hurts.

The next morning I was at my publicist's office talking about *me me me* and my phone rang. I had already put this woman's number in my iPhone and recognized it. I nervously ran into a private office and after a trepidatious "Hello," I heard the words: "I choose you and Danny to be the parents of this baby."

And so it really began.

The adoption agency and the adoption attorney told us about the legal aspects. They recommended rules and boundaries. They told a few horror stories and a few sob stories, but most of the stories had happy endings. Still, no one could possibly have prepared us for the most intense, emotional, trusting, mistrusting, thrilling, terrifying, volatile, roller-coaster relationship of our lives. Strangers one day, forever tied the next, we entered into an alliance more profound than we'd ever known. Would she betray us? Did she make the right choice for herself? Would she keep the child after all, or decide that an aunt or grandmother might do a better job?

She left everything familiar and traveled to Los Angeles in the care of two nervous daddy-wannabe outsiders and was put in a hotel. They say teeth are the window to overall health and I found myself sneaking glimpses at her incisors and molars as if she were a filly. The next day, we escorted her to a series of meetings with our attorney and social worker, who grilled and prodded to ferret out lies and inconsistencies and red flags, albeit with respect and etiquette. It was like waterboarding with fine linen and Pellegrino. They pried into her personal life about her sexual conduct, her drug history, her personal habits, her philosophies, her religion, her family. She answered each question with an easy honesty that belied her age.

At the next stop, our obstetrician examined her, also with worthy respect. Her tummy was jellied and the sonogram wand was rolled gently across her. Danny and I gaped at the monitor, glued to each other as we saw, for the first time, the tiny living being, shmushed and somehow levitating—all in vivid black and white.

Our child. It had long fingers and ample lips and a nose and everything.

"Looks perfect and healthy," our OB reported. He turned to our birth mother and asked, "Would you like to know the sex or should I tell Sam and Danny privately?"

"I can know," she murmured.

Danny grabbed my hand. We held our breath and waited in an interminable pause reminiscent of key moments on reality shows. I could feel the camera cut from me to Danny to me to Danny to the doctor to me to Danny to her to me to the doctor to Danny. I heard anticipatory underscoring and feared we would go to commercial. Then the doctor looked to Danny and me and said, "Gentlemen, you're having a boy."

And so it really, *really* began.

We wanted our birth mother to come to Los Angeles for the remainder of the pregnancy so we could care for her and bond with her. Also, statistics showed that women who left their homes were more likely to follow through with their decision.

She asked if she could bring her family with her.

We put them in a house near our own, and for the next six weeks, our single purpose was to keep this woman healthy and happy. We broke nearly every rule and crossed nearly every line in the process. We said yes to anything and everything she wanted or needed and tried to pick up on clues to furnish her with whatever whim, gift, surprise, or treat she might crave. If she tugged at her blouse, we went shopping for new maternity wear. If she glanced at a Pizza Hut from the car window, we turned around and got takeout. I made mountains of mac 'n' cheese and baked brownies and gave foot massages and rubbed belly butter on her swollen tummy.

I will admit that some of our indulgence was out of fear that she would change her mind or sneak away in the middle of the night. But mostly it was out of gratitude. During one of our weaker moments near the end, when the hoops were getting drastically higher and we were frayed and drained and scared and complaining of the emotional slavery of our situation, a friend pointed out, "This is your labor." It became our mantra.

Our son was due the second week of April. At the beginning of the month, the phone rang in the early evening. "This is it!" she said. "I'm having really painful contractions and we need to go now!"

We had rehearsed this moment a dozen times, which involved neighbors and multiple cars and family and friends to call and suitcases to grab and lists to bring. We arrived at her house in less than three minutes. We burst in the door but she was nowhere to be seen. The TV was blaring from the next room and we rushed in, calling out her name. She was lying back comfortably on the bed, noshing from a bag of chips and slurping a milk shake, grinning from ear to ear, dimples dimped.

"April Fool's!" she screamed, and the jumble of her upswept hair danced with her naughty laugh.

The depth of my patience and the ability to stuff my feelings suddenly reached a new magnitude.

I tasted blood in my mouth and realized I'd bitten the inside of my cheek and was still clenching. Danny and I glanced at each other, smiling through the impact. My heart pounded and I knew I was going to cry. Instead, I offered a toothy, blood-stained grin, fought to regulate my breath, and said, "Ohhhh, that's good. You really got us! Ha! You are *so* funny!"

This is your labor. This is your labor. This is your freaking-fucking labor . . .

As the next days ticked away, psychobiology kicked in and I found myself waking every three hours at night, subconsciously preparing for a feeding schedule. I reorganized drawers and scrubbed floors at two o'clock in the morning. I sanitized every surface of every thing at every time. UPS and FedEx were daily visitors, bearing uncountable gifts, like Christmas for a prince. I decorated the border of the nursery with hand-dabbed stencils of jungle animals caravanning in an endless parade. Hand-painted monkeys hung from trees on an archway that framed his crib area. Martha Stewart would have been proud—envious in fact. I got a P-touch labeler and labeled everything: places for diapers, bibs, onesies, pants, socks, crib sheets, binkies, pack 'n' play sheets, baby wipes, changing table covers . . . Everything has a place, and that place was going to have a goddamn label on it.

Danny and I were more in love than ever. Like soldiers lost in the deepest forest, with only each other to rely upon, steadying ourselves for the unpredictable, and we began to honor each other in a new way. We really listened. Egos were put aside.

Competition was not an option. Our child came first. *Our child.*
The words alone changed us. And we fought. God, how we
fought. If there was shit to work out, this was the time. Just like
the cabinet door that needed repairing and the car that needed
to be replaced.

People still asked stupid questions:

"Is it Chinese?" (The concept of a gay couple adopting an
American child seemed impossible and even wrong to some.)

"What is she?" (Translation: Is the birth mother white?)

"Is she healthy?" (Translation: Is she a crack whore?)

"What's the biological father like? I only ask because I saw
a movie where the father came back four years later and took
the child." (Translation: Tell me every sordid detail you know
about the situation.)

We found two good answers when anything personal about
the birth parents was asked—no matter how *concerned* people
claimed to be:

"And why do you need to know?" and "That is our son's
story. He will know everything about his biological history, and
when he chooses to tell is up to him."

But the worst thing people would say left me angry and
dumbfounded:

"You wonder how could a woman give up her child?"

I had never felt anything more clearly than the realization
that when a woman comes to the understanding that she cannot
keep her baby without severely compromising and even damag-
ing the life, health, and future of that baby as well as that of any
already existing children, the choice to place the child through
adoption is the single most noble act I could possibly imagine.

She could have terminated the pregnancy. She could have
remained in her own city and delivered at a county hospital,
leaving the state to deal with it and putting the infant in care

of the system. She could have secretly popped him out at home and dropped him at a fire station or in an alleyway dumpster. But this woman chose another path that would require strength and selflessness beyond measure.

In addition to the ongoing physical and psychological drama of being a young pregnant woman, moody and hormonal, hot and cold and uncomfortable, stripped of her surroundings, friends, everything familiar, emotionally in turmoil, and in the care of strangers, at the end of it all, she was going to hand her baby to someone else—a family of *her* choice—in the hope that the baby would have a better life than she could provide. It would be the last and most important decision she could make for this child's welfare. Mother's love at its zenith. She was a heroine and I resented any implication that she or women like her were anything otherwise.

We had all decided in advance that Danny and I would be in the delivery room and cut the umbilical cord.

On April 7, 2008, we stood by her side as she pushed, focused and present, throughout the delivery. When our son was lifted into the air, covered in vernix and blood, screaming and gasping his way into this strange new world, our entire relationship with our birth mother had culminated in, and was defined by, this single instant of polar opposites. At the exact same moment that we wanted to jump through the roof in celebration, she stared silently at the ceiling in mourning. Our greatest gift was her greatest loss. In the same room. At the same time. Respect was paid to both. That is what the entire six weeks had been—a balance of respect.

She had requested that the baby be placed on her chest so that she could have a private moment with him. We left the room and stood in the hallway. It was cold and white and a thousand miles away. I asked Danny how long we should wait before going back in. Every second in which mother and child could potentially bond was an eternity. Danny took my hands and wisely said, "We will have our son forever and we should give her as much time as she needs."

A minute or so later, a faint "okay" came from inside and we walked back into the room. She was holding our son. Her son. Our son. Gazing at him as a mother does.

Then she took a deep breath and looked up and out, at nothing in particular. Her jaw clenched as we watched her attempt to disengage. Her dark eyes darted to mine for a split second and I knew that it was time. Danny and I walked to her bedside and she lifted our little baby boy ever so slightly to meet my arms, her stare remaining fixed ahead. I cradled his tiny, swaddled body against my chest, and Danny and I backed out of the room, facing our birth mother, whispering "Thank you, thank you, thank you."

A single tear tracked down her cheek as we left the room.

Danny and I and Cooper Atticus Harris-Jacobsen spent our first night together at the hospital. The Atticus was for Atticus Finch, my favorite literary character—our attempt to imbue him with a sense of moral obligation. But the four-name name sounded more like a law firm. Some of our closest friends came to welcome him, and Cooper's godfather, Bruce, swears that upon meeting him, Cooper actually lifted his face, all puffy and puckered like a wet knuckle, and spoke the words "Uncle Brew-w-w." It might have happened. Miracles abounded everywhere.

Our birth mother was moved to a nonmaternity floor so that she would not hear the cries of newborn babies.

The next morning, she and her family boarded a plane.

• • •

In the following days and weeks, everyone in our families, except the born-again dip lovers, visited to welcome our son.

My parents were more joyous than I'd ever seen them. And there was a bond between us that hadn't, couldn't have existed heretofore. One late night, when Cooper was sleeping between feedings and the house was uncommonly quiet, I found my father on the balcony, weeping.

"Are you okay?" I asked.

He said, "I never knew."

"Never knew what?"

"I watch you and Danny and the way you look at Cooper and the way you are with him. Feeding him and changing him and being up all night. The way you hold him. And I know what's coming and how fast it goes . . . and I missed it. I wasn't there for you or your brother or your mother. I'm sorry. I just wasn't there. You're a good person. A good man. And you're going to be a good father. A better father than I was."

I held him close, as if, for a moment, I was the father and he was the son. Then he took my face in his hands and kissed me on the forehead long and hard. I remembered a conversation I'd had with my friend Frank Langella, who'd said that so many of us who are wildly driven to succeed in approval-based professions were victims of "the first kiss syndrome."

"It's when our fathers gave us one kiss when we were very young," Frank said. "One crumb of clear encouragement without qualification"—he took an all-too-personal sigh—"and we spend the rest of our lives trying to get the second kiss. From our fathers, then friends, lovers, audiences . . ."

My father was now a different man than I'd known growing up. The man whose ever-evident disapproval and disappointment had both crippled me and driven me to dance harder—the man who never played catch, or taught me to shave, or tie a tie, who believed his role as a father was to provide hoops of expectation to be jumped through, who couldn't spare a compliment without a camouflaged insult to obliterate it, who told me life was a "bowl-a shit" when I was five years old—was gone. Before me stood a man, human and good, with a loving and heavy heart; a man who had struggled so hard. So. Hard. Whose unforeseen circumstances had made him a boat against the current of his time, his culture, everything he thought he knew, to find peace with himself, with me, at last. If I had spent my life looking for the next kisses, I was being smothered in them now.

And I had changed too.

I accepted them.

A month later, when the last visitors had departed and the last baby gifts had been received and Danny and I were attempting to settle into our new life, Cooper was given the pediatric thumbs-up to go into public places. It was time to make my fantasy a memory. With an excitement that exceeded any preshow buzz I'd ever known, I dressed in my Bermuda shorts, porkpie hat, sandals, and aviator sunglasses, rolled up my sleeves enough to certify tattoos, and our brand-new threesome headed to the neighborhood farmers' market.

The summer sky was blue and uncomplicated. The air spoke of recently plucked rosemary and the clean, yeasty scent of freshly baked brioche. I shifted the diaper bag on my shoulder as we entered the thoroughfare, pushing Cooper in his hybrid stroller, but leaving his face completely visible so awestruck onlookers wouldn't have to rubberneck. As usual, underscoring accompanied the event in my head. This time it was the majestic theme from *To Kill a Mockingbird*. We strutted slowly and deliberately as I feigned casual, but I nearly bestowed a royal wave when the strings entered.

Only no one gave us a second look. Not a single glance.

My great fantasy was shattered in an instant.

But in the next, I realized that what was actually happening was much more breathtaking and historical than any fantasy.

Two dads pushing their child in a stroller at a market on a Saturday morning was simply no big deal.

And so it really, really, *really* began.

Acknowledgments

First and foremost, I must thank the godfather of this manuscript, Frank Langella, who told me to write write write, without result in mind. His mentorship, encouragement, and constant friendship were the birth of this effort. Thank you to David Elzer, who planted the seed years before I put fingers to keys. Also to the friends who read and listened to stories and ideas: Joel Brooks, Karen Newberg, Todd Schroeder, David Kaufman, Diann Duthie, Matt Harris, Nancy Berglass, and Bridget Moynahan. And to those who loyally read again and again: Michelle Zabel, Laura Brugnoni, and especially Sarah Rutan, who was my insightful touchstone throughout the entire process. I am most grateful to Bruce Newberg, who could not be a more stalwart, inspiring, and gifted friend, who asks the right questions and always, always makes me be better. Thanks to Ed Razzano for the business of songs. Thanks to Michael Agostino for his web magic and tireless inventive dedication. Thanks to Liza Minnelli, who also encouraged me to write write write and gave her blessing to put forth my truth in stories which included personal accounts of our long friendship. I owe thanks to the citizens of Sand Springs, who did not always understand me, but ultimately embraced me nonetheless. To my parents, who were endlessly asked to rattle their memories for odd facts and time lines, and who trusted and supported my perspective without question. Thanks to David Forrer, whose contribution to this effort surpassed that of any agent: he is an editor, advisor, challenger, enthusiast, and friend. To Mitchell Ivers at Gallery Books, my dream editor, who shepherded, nurtured, and waved a banner for *Ham* before it was fully cooked—and then supplied spices and cut fat and brought it to the table. To Louise Burke and Jen Bergstrom for their unparalleled enthusiasm, intelligence, and rare sense of joy, and the fiercely dedicated angels at Gallery Books/Simon & Schuster, especially Mary McCue, Ellen Chen, Liz Psaltis, John Paul Jones, Natalie Ebel, and Natasha Simons. To Sandi Mendelson, Judy Hilsinger, and Cathy Gruhn for the ballyhoo. And finally, to my husband, Danny Jacobsen—my mainstay, and the very essence of partnership, who inspires and colors my days. I'd thank our son, Cooper, but he doesn't yet read and has the attention span of a gnat and interrupted my writing every ten minutes for the length of the project. And yet, he is somehow the inspiration for . . . everything.

Author's Note

The stories in this book are true accounts as I remember them. In certain instances, I've left out people who may have been present, but weren't active in the drive of the story. Details of the timeline have also occasionally been omitted when they were not pertinent to the larger picture and would have bogged down the through line. Lastly, I've changed a few names, left off some surnames and avoided a few names completely—mostly those of people whom I feared might beat me up.